Saving Languages

Language endangerment has been the focus of much attention over the past few decades, and as a result a wide range of people are now working to revitalize and maintain local languages. This book serves as a general reference guide to language revitalization, written not only for linguists and anthropologists, but also for language activists and community members who believe they should ensure the future use of their languages, despite their predicted loss. Drawing extensively on case studies, it sets out the necessary background and highlights central issues such as literacy, policy decisions, and allocation of resources. Its primary goal is to provide the essential tools for a successful language revitalization program, such as setting and achieving realistic goals, and anticipating and resolving common obstacles. Clearly written and informative, *Saving Languages* will be an invaluable resource for all those interested in the fate of small language communities around the globe.

LENORE A. GRENOBLE is Professor of Russian and Linguistics at Dartmouth College, Hanover. Her research has focused on issues of language contact, language endangerment, and discourse analysis, and she has carried out fieldwork on the Tungusic languages of Siberia, extending more recently to other languages spoken in the North. She has previously published, with Lindsay Whaley, *Endangered Languages* (Cambridge University Press, 1998).

LINDSAY J. WHALEY is Associate Professor of Classics and Linguistics at Dartmouth College, Hanover, where he also serves as Chair of Linguistics and Cognitive Science. For the past ten years he has researched Tungusic languages in northern China and Siberia. His research interests include typology, Bantu and Tungusic linguistics, syntactic theory, language endangerment, and language revitalization. He has previously pubished with Lenore A. Grenoble, *Endangered Languages* (Cambridge University Press, 1998).

Saving Languages

An Introduction to Language Revitalization

Lenore A. Grenoble

Dartmouth College, Hanover

and

Lindsay J. Whaley

Dartmouth College, Hanover

CAMBRIDGE
UNIVERSITY PRESS

CAMBRIDGE UNIVERSITY PRESS
Cambridge, New York, Melbourne, Madrid, Cape Town, Singapore, São Paulo

Cambridge University Press
The Edinburgh Building, Cambridge CB2 2RU, UK

Published in the United States of America by Cambridge University Press, New York

www.cambridge.org
Information on this title: www.cambridge.org/9780521816212

First published 2006

A catalogue record for this publication is available from the British Library

ISBN-13 978-0-521-81621-2 hardback
ISBN-10 0-521-81621-1 hardback

ISBN-13 978-0-521-01652-0 paperback
ISBN-10 0-521-01652-5 paperback

Transferred to digital printing 2007

Contents

Preface

This book is designed for readers of various backgrounds who are interested in the fate of small language communities around the globe: linguists, anthropologists, and academics in other disciplines; language activists, missionaries, humanitarian workers, policy makers, and educators; journalists and researchers; students; and visionaries who believe that it is possible to hear their language spoken for many centuries to come in the face of many who claim otherwise. With this diversity of readers in mind, our goal was to write a book that would serve as a general reference guide to language revitalization, providing the necessary background, highlighting the central issues, indicating common obstacles, and pointing to sources of further information.

Our own experiences with language revitalization efforts have come primarily through fieldwork in east Asia on several Tungusic languages (all of which are undergoing rapid loss in the number of native speakers), and secondarily through long-term relationships and professional collaborations with fieldworkers and activists in Africa, South America, and North America, particularly the United States. This background has sensitized us to several important facts. First, although many similarities can be found in the causes of language loss around the world, this does not mean that similar approaches to language revitalization can be taken. There are simply too many differences in the political, social, and economic situations facing, say, a community in northern China versus one in southern Africa to make blanket statements about how revitalization should be carried out. Second, an honest evaluation of most language revitalization efforts to date will show that they have failed. There have been enough success stories to warrant optimism about the possibilities of taking a moribund (or extinct) language and moving it to a more vital state, but this is atypical. Creating an orthography or producing a television program for children in a local language is a major accomplishment in its own right, but it will not revitalize a language. A longer-term, multifaceted program, one which requires a range of resources and much personal dedication, is needed. Third, government policies affecting language use in public (or even private) realms are one of the two most basic forces that hinder (or help) language revitalization, the other being the connection that people make between language use and economic well-being for their family. Finally, where successes do occur in language revitalization, they result, perhaps without exception, from the efforts of people who want to speak a local language, and want their friends and neighbors to as well. Even with the best of intentions, an outsider entering into an endangered language situation with the goal of "saving it" will fail. This is not to say that outsiders do not have something important to contribute, such as linguistic expertise, connections to funding sources, moral support, and so on. They do, and their contributions are often vital to a program. But, that said, it is the members of the community where the revitalization is going on who need to be highly invested in the outcome. They need to control decision making; they need to take ownership of the effort and construct the revitalization program which suits their ambitions, needs, and resources.

The lessons from our own experience have greatly influenced the content and tone of this book. We have tried to present practical recommendations without giving the sense that there are guaranteed methods to language revitalization. We have tried to underscore the complexity of factors that must be addressed in expanding the domains where a local language is spoken without overwhelming the reader. And we have tried to keep in mind the balance between thoughtful planning in revitalization and the urgency facing speech communities where fewer and fewer people speak a language that used to be widely employed.

The chapters are designed to be read in succession or individually. The first two chapters of the book outline the conceptual framework in which we understand language endangerment and revitalization. Chapter 3 discusses different models for language revitalization, and Chapter 4 provides information coming from individual case studies as a way to connect the abstractions from the beginning chapters to actual practice. Chapters 5 and 6 address two major issues in language revitalization: literacy and orthography development. We have devoted two entire chapters to these issues because so many linguists and activists see literacy as a fundamental requirement for successful revitalization, yet the issues behind literacy and orthography development are so complicated that they are rarely discussed in depth in the literature on language endangerment. Chapter 7 provides a step-by-step account of how a community can assess its needs, commitment, resources, and goals, and then, based on these factors, how they can go about establishing the appropriate language program. We anticipate that some readers may want to begin the book with this chapter, skipping the background, and then go back to fill in the picture with the details of existing programs. The chapter is accordingly written to be read either following the background information of Chapters 1 to 6 or in anticipation of it.

The present work is by no means the only resource on language revitalization. There are many. Hinton and Hale's (2001) *The green book of language revitalization in practice* is perhaps the closest in spirit to our own work and contains a wealth of insights from people who have been deeply involved in designing language revitalization programs. Joshua Fishman, of course, has been instrumental in raising awareness about language endangerment and how communities can counteract the forces that lead to language shift. His 1991 book *Reversing language shift: Theoretical and empirical foundations of assistance to threatened languages* is already a classic and should be read by anyone with interests in the question of language revitalization. There are many collections of articles that explore the issues surrounding revitalization. Three of the more recent are Fishman (2001), Bradley and Bradley (2002), and Janse and Tol (2003). There are also a number of excellent books and articles dealing with language revitalization in specific regions of the world. Three that we have found highly instructive are: Amery (2000), King (2001), and Hinton et al. (2002).

We have worked with a number of people in preparing this book and would like to extend a special thanks to Scott Anderson, Chuinda Andicha, Oliver Bernstein, Nadezhda Bulatova, Er Dengguo, Kristen Foery, Elizabeth Gannes, He Qinghua, Manuel Hugo, José Juncosa, Kristina Kleutghen, Fengxiang Li, Denise McBeth, Tori Minor, Jauquin Najandey, Pablo Tsere, Laura Vacca, Rafael Vega Tsetsem, Luis Wamputsik Chinkias, and Tara Wharton. We are especially grateful to the many members of the Evenki, Oroqen, Solon, Hawaiian, Māori, Mohawk, and Shuar communities who have given so freely and willingly of their time and knowledge to help make this a better book. We would like to thank Andrew Winnard for his support for this project and for pushing us to finish the manuscript. Finally, we are indebted to Matthias Brenzinger for providing the photograph used on the front cover of the book.

1 Language revitalization as a global issue

1 Introduction

Over the past fifty years and with increasing frequency, innovative programs have appeared around the world with the aim of revitalizing languages that are at risk of disappearing due to declining numbers of native speakers. The nature of these initiatives varies as greatly as the languages that are their targets. In some instances, they are nearly national in scope, such as the efforts to preserve Irish, yet in other instances they involve small communities or even a handful of motivated individuals. Many of these programs are connected to claims of territorial sovereignty, though cultural sovereignty or a desire to maintain a unique ethnic identity is just as often the explicit goal. While in one context a revitalization effort may be centered around formal education, in another it may be focused on creating environments in which the language can be used on a regular basis.

Although tremendous variety characterizes the methods of and motives for reinvigorating languages, revitalization, as a general phenomenon, is growing and has become an issue of global proportion. There are now hundreds of endangered languages, and there are few regions of the world where one will not find at least nascent attempts at language revitalization. This comes as little surprise when considered in light of the confluence of several socio-historical factors. First, language death and moribundity (i.e. the cessation of children learning a language) are occurring at an exceptionally rapid rate. While the precise number of languages in the world is difficult to determine (see Crystal 2000:2–11 for a concise discussion), and predicting the total number of languages that will cease to be spoken is harder still (Whaley 2003), there is a general consensus that at least half of the world's 6,000–7,000 languages will disappear (or be on the verge of disappearing) in the next century. As Crystal (2000:19) points out, "To meet that time frame, at least one language must die, on average, every two weeks or so," a startling fact, to say the least.

Whereas the phenomenon of language death has been present in all epochs, the rate of decline in linguistic diversity is probably unique to

1

our time, perhaps only rivaled by the loss of linguistic diversity believed to have happened during the agricultural revolution 10,000 years ago (e.g. see Maffi 2001). Given this high rate of language death, we must recognize that a significant proportion of communities in the world today are confronted with the loss of a language that has traditionally been an integral feature of their identity. In many such instances, efforts are being made to halt the process of language shift and to promote the usage of a heritage language.

The sheer number of threatened languages cannot alone explain the ever-expanding number of language revitalization initiatives. To this we must add a second major socio-historical shift, the general trend towards recognizing the rights of minorities, both as individuals and as groups, within modern nation-states. Particularly since the end of the Cold War, there has been a collapse of hegemonic patterns in many portions of the world that had actively, and explicitly, worked to suppress cultural difference, and as a consequence in many places ethnic groups and minorities have increased flexibility in pursuing their own political agendas (Kymlicka 1995). In a very real sense minority communities have been emboldened to pursue territorial, political, and cultural rights. Though this has meant a burgeoning number of ethnic conflicts (Moynihan 1993), it has also meant rethinking human rights at a basic level to include the protection of such things as the choice of language. Consider, as just one example, language from Article 5 of UNESCO's Universal Declaration on Cultural Diversity, which states: "All persons should therefore be able to express themselves and to create and disseminate their work in the language of their choice, and particularly in their mother tongue; all persons should be entitled to quality education and training that fully respect their cultural identity." Similar statements can be found in declarations from many transnational organizations, such as the European Union, the Organization for American States, and the Organization for African Unity, as well as in recent legislation in a number of countries. Though the effectiveness of these proclamations and laws in ensuring cultural rights is a matter of some debate, there is little doubt that they have encouraged ethnic communities around the world to pursue activities that assert their cultural identities, and these activities often include programs to promote heritage language use.

A less understood factor that has had a role in the increased interest in language revitalization is "globalization." Very broadly defined, globalization is "a process of increasing international integration of economic life" (Whaley 2003:969); it is characteristically accompanied by the adoption of neoliberal political structures, at least to some degree. As the process has transformed or eliminated traditional political and economic barriers among nations, there has been a greatly enhanced ability for information, money, people, goods, and services to move between regions. Because of the political and economic might of the United States, it is hardly surprising that mass consumerism and American pop culture have now spread to most regions of the world.

Most discussions of globalization have concentrated on the modernizing and assimilatory effects that such forces have on communities, both big and small, as individuals in the communities are brought into the international economic system and are exposed with increasing regularity to languages of wider communication, the national culture of the state in which they are embedded and non-traditional economic habits. Much less examined is the fact that globalizing forces have triggered reacting forces as some people seek to assert, or better to reassert, their unique cultural identity. More often than not this effort to underscore uniqueness is represented by a "traditionalist" constituency within a community that finds itself interacting with a "modernizing" constituency which advocates greater integration with a regional, national, or international community. A great many language revitalization programs have emerged as a consequence of these dynamics. Since language is a visible and powerful indicator of group identity, it has accurately been recognized as an important way to maintain links with one's cultural past and to protect one's cultural uniqueness in the present.

This picture of broad social, historical, and economic trends that have prompted the appearance of numerous language revitalization programs is necessarily both simplified and incomplete, but it provides a general context for the implicit question underlying all portions of the book: How can language revitalization efforts be successful?

2   Assessing language vitality

Assessing and understanding language vitality is a complex enterprise, as a large number of intertwined factors enter into it, yet the degree of language vitality is the basic indicator used in determining the appropriate type of language revitalization program. A language spoken by several thousand individuals on a daily basis presents a much different set of options for revitalization than a language that has a dozen native speakers who rarely use it. Moreover, assessing changes in language vitality over time provides the easiest measure of success for attempts to revitalize a threatened language.

As interest among linguists in issues of language endangerment has increased over the last two decades or so, there have been a number of different studies focusing on how to assess language vitality. One of the most comprehensive comes from the collaboration of linguists in

UNESCO's Ad Hoc Group on Endangered Languages.[1] They have worked together to create a document entitled *Language vitality and endangerment* (UNESCO 2003), which lists nine factors in language vitality. The UNESCO Ad Hoc Group is very clear that the nine factors need to be considered in conjunction with one another, a point which we also would like to underscore here. As we discuss in Chapter 2, the particulars of each individual language situation will mean that some of the factors are more relevant than others.

Factor 1:   Intergenerational language transmission
Factor 2:   Absolute number of speakers
Factor 3:   Proportion of speakers within the total population
Factor 4:   Trends in existing language domains
Factor 5:   Response to new domains and media
Factor 6:   Materials for language education and literacy
Factor 7:   Governmental and institutional language policies, including official status and use
Factor 8:   Community members' attitudes toward their own language
Factor 9:   Amount and quality of documentation

As is clear from this list, the first three factors have to do with the numbers of speakers of a language, as well as their distribution across generations and throughout the population. Factors 4–7 identify how and where the language is used. Factor 8 addresses perceptions about the value of a language by its speakers. Factor 9 identifies the material that has been produced about a language.

Even under quick review, it becomes clear why one cannot separate the influences of these factors from one another. For example, the use of the language in both new and existing domains (Factors 4 and 5) is very much dependent upon community attitudes, as well as governmental policies. Factor 9 is somewhat of an oddity in this list since the existence of language documentation is not an evaluating factor *per se* in assessing language vitality; reasonably good documentation exists for some languages that are extinct, whereas there is poor documentation for highly vital languages. Rather, the level of vitality helps in assessing the urgency for new language

---

[1] The document was vetted and refined in a working symposium held in Kyoto, Japan in November 2002. The group members who contributed to the document are listed in Appendix 3 of the UNESCO guidelines (UNESCO 2003): Matthias Brenzinger, Arienne Dwyer, Tjeerd de Graaf, Colette Grinevald, Michael Krauss, Osahito Miyaoka, Nicholas Ostler, Osamu Sakiyama, Maira E. Villalón, Akira Y. Yamamoto, and Ofelia Zepeda. Some readers may object to what would appear to be a heavy reliance on UNESCO guidelines in this section. We have used these guidelines as the starting point for our discussion precisely because they have been endorsed by a relatively large group of linguists from around the world.

documentation and, in addition, may influence decisions about the viability of a language for revitalization. Simply put, a seriously endangered language should be documented as quickly and as thoroughly as possible.[2] The more extensive the documentation, the easier revitalization (or even reclamation) will be in the future should a community desire it. This is not to say that documentation must necessarily precede revitalization, but rather that revitalization efforts rely on dictionaries and descriptive grammars, recorded speech, and so on.

For assessment purposes, the fundamental question for vitality is the size and composition of the speaker population. Intuitively, it would seem that the larger number of native speakers of a language, the more likely it is to be maintained and be healthy (Factor 2). However, a large number of speakers does not guarantee vitality because speaker population must be considered in relation to other speech communities. For example, nearly 200,000 people speak Tujia, a Tibeto-Burman language in southern China, a number that would place it well within the "safe" range for some measures of language endangerment (e.g. Krauss 1992). However, in nearly every community where the language is spoken, Tujia speakers are outnumbered by speakers of another language (typically a dialect of Chinese) by a ratio of 10:1. Indeed, only 3 percent of ethnic Tujia are able to speak the language, and probably less than half that number use it regularly. Clearly, Tujia is endangered despite a speaker population that dwarves most in the world. Therefore, absolute speaker numbers, though an important demographic, are not a good diagnostic for determining the vitality of a language.

At least equally significant is the percentage of the total population which can speak the target language (Factor 3); language shift is indicated if a large percentage of the (ethnic) population speaks a different language instead of the local language, as in the case of Tujia just described. Note that this does not mean people speaking one or more languages in addition to the local language; multilingualism is a reality for much of the world. Instead, Factor 3 is concerned with the percentage of the community which does or does not know the local language. The higher the percentage for a particular region, the greater the vitality of the language in most cases.[3]

---

[2] We consider language documentation to be one of the primary roles of linguists (see also Newman 2003). We discuss the relationship between documentation and revitalization in Chapter 3, section 8, and the role of the linguist in Chapter 7, section 7.

[3] Though in general learning second (or third, or fourth) languages in addition to a local language does not serve as a good indicator of language shift, there are regions of the world where it does, particularly those where multilingualism is not the norm (e.g. the United States).

The intergenerational transmission of a language (Factor 1) is typically, and appropriately, used as a benchmark for whether a language will maintain its vitality into the indefinite future. In the broadest of terms, one finds three types of situations. In the first, all generations, including children, have fluent use of the language. In the second, the language is used by parents and grandparents but not the children, though children know the language; and in the third category, only the grandparent/elder generation would maintain knowledge of the language. This kind of characterization is helpful as a way to frame the issue of intergenerational transmission and to highlight the fundamental fact that only when children are acquiring a language does it stand much chance of long-term use. For a language to be vital, it must be actively used by children.

Intergenerational transmission, however, is not necessarily uniform across a speaker population. In one village children may regularly use a local language, but not in another. In one family children may be discouraged from using a local language, while next door it may be an expectation. In these ways, there may be a dwindling number of children overall who learn a language (not a good sign for long-term viability of the language), yet there are pockets of robust use (which may cause one to deem it vital). The dynamics of intergenerational transmission are perhaps more important to understand than any other relevant factor in assessing the need for language revitalization.

In light of this fact, we pause in our discussion of the UNESCO factors in assessing language vitality to present a more finely grained categorization system for intergenerational transmission. Krauss (1997) employs a helpful ten-way distinction.

a	the language is spoken by all generations, including all, or nearly all, of the children
a−	the language is learned by all or most children
b	the language is spoken by all adults, parental age and up, but learned by few or no children
b−	the language is spoken by adults in their thirties and older but not by younger parents
c	the language is spoken only by middle-aged adults and older, in their forties and up
c−	all speakers in their fifties and older
−d	all speakers in their sixties and older
d	all speakers in their seventies and older
d−	all speakers in their seventies and older, and fewer than 10 speakers
e	extinct, no speakers

Given the caveat that there may not be uniform patterns across a speaker population, a language is healthy and has high vitality if ranked (a), somewhat less so at (a−), and by level (b) is already endangered where revitalization is required if the language is to survive. As one goes down the scale, the language is increasingly endangered and closer to complete loss, making it more and more difficult to implement a revitalization effort.

Is such a detailed scale necessary in assessing language vitality for a particular situation? At some level perhaps the answer might be no, since it is quite clear that at stage (b) the language is already on a clear path towards moribundity. However, the scale (and others like it) have some important uses. First, it is helpful for indicating the comparative vitality of a language spoken in different places. For example, Inuit is robust and safe in Greenland, where nearly all children learn it (a), but varies in Canada from safe to endangered (a in the east, b in central, and c in the west of Canada), to Alaska (b–c), and in Russia, where Inuit is seriously endangered (d), with only a couple of remaining speakers (Krauss 1997:26). In some cases, such information can be employed to make decisions about where a language revitalization effort should be focused, or where fluent individuals are most likely to be found. Furthermore, the scale is a helpful guide in assessing the feasibility of different sorts of revitalization programs, a point we take up again in Chapter 7 and very important in determining the urgency for language documentation.

Returning to the factors in language vitality outlined by UNESCO, yet another diagnostic is the range of domains where the language is being used. Simply put, the "stronger" a language, the more domains in which it is found. Thus a healthy, vital language is used in a range of settings with a wide variety of functions, and the most healthy language would accordingly be a language used for all functions and purposes. Extinct languages are found at the opposite end of the spectrum, no longer spoken at all and used in no domains. (Note that there are some languages which are no longer utilized for conversational purposes, but are used in some domains, frequently religious. This suggests degrees of extinction, a matter we consider in section 3.) In between the two ends of the scale are a variety of intermediate stages, with languages used in limited settings. A prime example is provided in situations where individuals use one language primarily in the home and for casual social encounters, but another language as the primary means of communication at the workplace, at school, and in public and/or official settings.

Domains are often geographically determined, with one (local) language used in the local community, whether that be socially, in stores or service encounters, for educational purposes, and in forms of public address. A different language (one that is regionally or nationally dominant) is used outside of the community, and only this language is used for education, government and commerce outside of the local setting. It is common for this to be a situation of stable bilingualism that can occur over a long period of time, with the use of each language having clearly defined domains.

The UNESCO guidelines for assessment recognize six levels of usage in existing language domains: (1) universal use; (2) multilingual parity; (3) dwindling domains; (4) limited or formal domains; (5) highly limited domains; and (6) extinct. Universal use refers to the active use of the language in all domains. Regardless of whether speakers are multilingual or not, they feel comfortable using the local language in any setting. Multilingual parity indicates the use of one or more dominant[4] languages in official and public domains versus the use of non-dominant languages in private and more local domains. As was just noted, stable bilingualism often arises in this situation, and as a result it is not uncommon in many places in the world. It is somewhat misleading, however, to consider this multilingual *parity*, as the terms *dominant* and *non-dominant* suggest in and of themselves. The dominant language is generally favored by more people in absolute terms, while the non-dominant one almost always has a more restricted speaker base and in most cases is not learned as a second language by first-language speakers of the dominant language. Moreover, as UNESCO (2003) points out, the dominant language is often viewed as the language of social and economic opportunity. Therefore, there are pressures on speakers of the non-dominant language to shift to the dominant language, but not *vice versa*. Parity, then, must be understood to be a stable balance in domain use for individual speakers, and not as a descriptor of the more general relationship between the languages involved.

The next three levels represent incrementally decreasing use of the language, beginning with the category of dwindling domains. The local (i.e. non-dominant) language is used increasingly less, with the marked and significant shift occurring when parents cease to speak the language at home. This, of course, most often effectively ends intergenerational trans-mission, and children no longer learn the language. The next level is the use of the language in only limited or formal domains, such as religious ceremonies, rituals, and festivals. The domains included here often involve the elderly generation, and the UNESCO definition states that these limited domains may include use in the home where the elderly (grand-parent) generation is present. One diagnostic of this level is that, although people may continue to understand the language, they cannot speak it. The next step beyond this is very limited domains, where the language is

---

[4] The terms *dominant* and *non-dominant* are found in UNESCO (2003); see section 3 for our discussion of terminology.

used only on very restricted occasions, and only by particular community members (such as tribal or religious leaders, generally of the elderly generation). Here the use of the language is ritualized, although there may be people who have some memory of it. Finally, extinction occurs when the language is not used in any domains.

In cases of language attrition, a language has been moving along this scale, since it is used in fewer and fewer settings with fewer and fewer functions (and, usually, by fewer and fewer speakers). As this correctly suggests, the relationship between language and domains is a dynamic one for many local languages, and thus the trends of change are relevant. If a language is used in increasingly fewer domains, it is a sign of lessening vitality. Alternatively, if a language is used in an increasing number of domains, it shows signs of returning vitality and may even be gaining ground over other languages.

Related to the issue of current use in domains is the question of whether the language is used in new domains as they emerge (Factor 5; see section 1.2). If, for example, a store is established in an agrarian community for the first time, the relative vitality of a language is signaled in the choice of language use there. Is it the language used by the farmers with their families and in their work, or is it the language used when farmers leave the community and sell their produce at a market in a nearby town? The latter signals a greater stress on the local language; not only is a new language being brought into the daily experience of the community, but there is now present in the community a symbol that all spaces of economic exchange belong to the non-local language. As the actual number of domains increases, if use of the language does not expand into these new domains, that is a signal of declining vitality, for although the absolute number of domains in which it is used remains steady, the relative number has decreased.

New domains are often created in the modern world with the emergence of new technologies and media. Some local languages have been used in radio broadcasts around the world, far fewer in television broadcasts, and almost none in major films. As these media come to isolated regions, they become domains of usage that make quick inroads into a social space previously connected to local languages. For example, the advent of video rental trucks, which distribute videocassettes in Native American communities, has been cited as contributing to language attrition. These trucks have provided easier access to videotapes of major Hollywood productions to even relatively remote communities in the US, not only facilitating the spread of English but effectively creating yet another domain where the Native American language is not used. The internet offers another example of the emergence of a new domain which is accessible for some communities in the world, in particular in Europe and North America. While the internet might potentially supply a creative way to increase local language use (indeed, many revitalization efforts see it in just this way), the fact remains that the internet, at this point, is overwhelmingly dominated by a handful of languages. Therefore, it is a difficult matter to co-opt it as a domain for local languages. Even if some web sites arise which employ a local language, speakers of the local language will make greater use of the internet in a non-local language. Thus, the presence of a language in any given domain does not in and of itself guarantee vitality. The greater consideration is how much the language is used in that particular domain: thirty-minute weekly radio broadcasts, a website, or a page in a newspaper which is otherwise written in the national language may have powerful symbolic value, but they do not translate into signs of high vitality.

A critical domain for language usage is education. In regions where a nationally (or regionally) administered education system exists, the languages of education become a key determinant of language use in other domains. When mandatory schooling occurs exclusively in a national language, the use of local languages almost inevitably declines. When local languages are part of the formal educational process, they typically maintain a higher degree of vitality, though here again the amount a specific language is used plays into the equation. Many schools which purport to have local language education teach the language as a secondary subject, and the curriculum as a whole is taught in a language of wider communication, yet "Education *in* the language is essential for language vitality" (UNESCO 2003).

In most cases – anywhere where formal schooling takes place – this requires literacy in the local language, and so the extent of literacy is yet another marker of language vitality (Factor 6). Ideally, for sustaining vitality in a local language, all subject matter needs to be taught in the language, and pedagogical materials must be available to teachers and students. This in turn mandates the existence (or development) of discipline-specific materials, which in turn requires technical terminology in the lexicon of the language. In terms of ranking the correlation between the availability of such materials and language vitality, again there is an overall continuum with a fully developed literacy on the one end, with the language used in writing and reading in all domains, especially education and governmental and other official business. In addition, a wide range of written materials exist and are used, such as literature, religious texts, newspapers, textbooks, dictionaries, and so on. On the other end of the scale is a lack of literacy, no orthography, and no written language. Identifying the different levels in between these two end points is complicated. UNESCO recognizes four intermediary levels. These focus on the existence of written materials and the role of the schools in teaching literacy. In most basic terms, though, the fewer written materials, the less they are taught, the higher the level of endangerment.

There is, of course, a high degree of local variation in the development and use of literacy, as is clear in several case studies (Chapter 4) and is discussed in Chapter 5, where we focus on literacy. The existence of an orthography does not mean that the community has access to local language literacy, just as the existence of written materials does not ensure that they are being read. Some communities may have multiple orthographies, and multiple literacies. The picture is further complicated by the fact that in many cases of language attrition, part or even all community members may be literate in the language of wider communication but not in their own language; beliefs about the appropriateness of the local language for literacy may interfere with its development. At the same time, others may adapt their knowledge of literacy in the language of wider communication for use in the local language. In language attrition and endangerment, the potential and actual roles of different written languages need to be considered in assessing vitality and the role of literacy.

In addition to numbers of speakers, domains of use and degrees of literacy, attitudes toward a language are critical in assessing language vitality (Factor 8). We provide an overview of the possibilities here and discuss methods for obtaining data on language attitudes in Chapter 7. Language attitudes exist on multiple levels: at a national, governmental level; among the majority population (if there is one); and finally, at a local, community level. Governmental and institutional attitudes are often influenced by, and even determined by, the attitudes of the majority population. Moreover, these same attitudes can have an impact on how (minority) communities view themselves, their cultures, and their languages. The governmental attitudes are often reflected directly in language and education policies and in policies which determine the allocation of financial resources. They can be indirectly reflected in the media, which can manipulate perceptions of any given group and its language. Many nation-states see the value of a language in state building; the underlying idea is that a single language has a unifying effect and has great symbolic value. This stance has an impact on national policy, as it gives priority to only the national language. We consider such national-level variables in depth in Chapter 2, section 2.2. Here we outline UNESCO's framework for assessing the relationship between attitudes as articulated by governmental policy and language vitality.

UNESCO (2003) differentiates six levels of treatment of the local language vis-à-vis the national language: (1) equal support; (2) differentiated support; (3) passive assimilation; (4) active assimilation; (5) forced assimilation; and (6) prohibition. Equal support is defined as *all* languages of a country being treated as assets, with explicit policies in place to encourage the maintenance of these languages. Though conceivable, and therefore worth including on the list, this strikes us as an ideal which is rarely maintained with regard to local languages. Even in situations where equal support of languages is codified in legislation or a constitution, actual government practices belie a very different set of objectives. The second level on the list, differentiated support, is more common; here "non-dominant" languages are protected by governmental policies but are not used in all the domains where the "dominant" or official language(s) are found. Instead, the local languages are more often used in private domains, often with encouragement from the government. Canada, though imperfectly, serves to illustrate this type. English and French are equally supported by the Canadian government; local languages receive varying degrees of support. Bilingual education is mandated nationwide for English and French. The government, however, does not promote the use of First Nations languages in school, such as Cree or Ojibwe, which are not recognized as official languages of Canada. Even so, there is a greater level of support for them in the form of federal funding and legal protections than in many countries.

Both of these levels can be distinguished from passive assimilation, whereby there are no governmental policies to assimilate minority groups, but similarly there are no policies of support, and so a dominant language functions, by tradition and convenience, as the language of wider communication. As a consequence, local languages do not enjoy prestige in most domains, nor are they used in domains where the government plays a significant role. The final three levels – active assimilation, forced assimilation, and prohibition – differ in terms of degree of governmental intervention to coerce people to give up their local language in favor of the approved official language. In all four of these levels, one expects to find declining vitality in local languages barring some sort of language maintenance or revitalization effort.

The ways in which the government addresses issues of language policy can have an impact on a group's attitudes toward its own language. Local attitudes toward the local language are critical in language maintenance and revitalization; negative attitudes are often at least part of the motivation behind language shift (although governmental policies of any level of assimilation can play an active role as well, of course). For revitalization, ideally all members of the community will have a positive attitude toward their language and culture, but more often the attitudes will vary among different people. If most members have a negative attitude, it is difficult to imagine a successful revitalization program getting underway. Indeed, the negative attitudes of any core group of people, even a numerically small one, can prove to be a major impediment to revitalization and to overall vitality. For this reason, we encourage assessing language attitudes before starting a revitalization program (see Chapter 7).

As we have seen, assessment of language vitality needs to take into account a complex set of interrelated factors: size of speaker community, intergenerational transmission, domains of language use, and attitudes on a variety of levels. While it is difficult universally to rank the importance of these factors, as they affect one another and have different levels of import in different circumstances, the one factor that tends to rise above the others is intergenerational transmission: once the children stop learning a language, it is in a precarious state. In cases of rapid or accelerated language shift, disrupted transmission to children can move a vital language to near extinction in the course of a single generation. Where intergenerational transmission is strong and steady, local communities should consider maintenance programs to ensure the continued vitality of their language. Elsewhere, revitalization programs are necessary. As a general rule, the sooner they are implemented, the easier it is to reverse language shift.

3   Terminology

Though the majority of readers will be familiar with the phenomena of language endangerment and revitalization, and they will have a good handle on the terminology which has developed to discuss them, we briefly summarize the rationale for our choice of terms in this book.

As this discussion above implies, we draw a conceptual distinction between language revitalization, or what Fishman (1991) calls reversing language shift, and language maintenance, which supports a language that is truly vital. Whereas the goal of revitalization is to increase the relative number of speakers of a language and extend the domains where it is employed, maintenance serves to protect current levels and domains of use. Revitalization almost always requires changing community attitudes about a language, while maintenance seeks to protect against the imposition of outside attitudes. In theory the difference between the two is quite clear. However, in practical terms the distinction is often unimportant, as the dividing line between the need for maintenance and revitalization is inexact and, regardless, the programs involved in both can be very similar. Therefore, most of what is found in the following chapters is of equal relevance to both maintenance and revitalization situations, yet we continue to use the two terms distinctly.

The choice of labels for languages involved in endangerment situations varies greatly among authors, and so our particular choices require comment. Language endangerment typically involves two languages (and cultures) in contact, with one replacing the other. In the canonical case, then, Language A is being adopted by speakers of Language B, and Language A is replacing Language B in the sense that fewer people use or learn B. In the case of Language B, the language has been referred to variously as the *minority language, heritage language, mother tongue, dominated language, threatened language,* or *endangered language.* Alternatively, Language A has been referred to as the *majority language, mother tongue, dominant language, killer language,* or *matrix language.* We have opted to avoid most of these labels here for a number of reasons.

First, *minority* and *majority language* can be misleading, and in some cases, inaccurate. *Minority language* implies the language spoken by a minority within a larger population, but in fact the status of a language as minority or majority depends very much on the specific context of use. What was historically a majority language in a given region or among a given group of people can become redefined as a minority language as geopolitical boundaries are redrawn. Second, the term *minority* suggests that the absolute number of speakers (or of members of an ethnic group) is the single biggest factor in determining language vitality. As discussed in section 1, this is simply not the case. Finally, *minority* is used to refer to both immigrant and indigenous languages, such that Spanish, for example, is considered to be a *minority* language in the United States. It is not, however, by any means endangered. Though cognizant that many of the same issues are involved, we are concerned in the present with the endangerment and revitalization of indigenous languages as opposed to immigrant languages. Speakers of the latter may also be undergoing language shift, but immigrant languages typically have a speaker base outside of the immigrant territory. By *indigenous,* however, we refer to languages firmly planted in a particular geography before the age of European colonization, roughly by the beginning of the sixteenth century.

Mother tongue is also potentially confusing. The term is often meant in indicate the language learned first by an individual, or the one typically learned first in a community. In endangerment situations, people may be learning Language A as a first language in increasing numbers, though Language B is the first language for others. To use *mother tongue* as a label exclusive to just one of the two languages is problematic.

We have also avoided use of the term *heritage language* in reference to Language B. In North America, at least, the term often refers to the loss of any language spoken by one's parents or other ancestors regardless of how many generations have passed. Thus debates around use of the "heritage language" in the United States, for example, most often center around the use of Spanish or Mandarin in the schools for those of Hispanic and

Chinese descent. As important as debates about the presence of such languages in the school may be, there is a different set of issues and dynamics involved than those involved in endangerment and revitalization.

Our preferred term for Language B is *local language*. Here, too, there is some room for confusion because non-endangered languages can be the sole language of a particular location. This is true, for instance, in Hanover, New Hampshire, where both of the authors are based. The local language of the town would clearly be identified as English if one were to ask around. However, *local language* has the advantage of drawing attention to the fact that language revitalization is tied to a particular geography, and that the people involved in revitalization desire that the language be more widely used in this location. We also find the term advantageous in being relatively neutral. Our preferred term for Language A is *language of wider communication*. Because, in nearly all cases of endangerment, Language A is used more widely, both in terms of numbers of speakers and in terms of a broader range of domains, the term is nicely descriptive, as opposed to *matrix language*.[5] It again has the advantage of being fairly neutral, as opposed to *killer language*, which seems to us to give too much a sense of agency to the language of wider communication.

At times, however, we also refer to Language A as the *dominant language* when it is useful to draw out an asymmetry in power, use, or prestige between a local language and a language of wider communication. These asymmetries are, of course, the root cause of the endangerment of Language B, and it is appropriate to bring attention to that fact. Corresponding to the term *dominant language*, we use *non-dominant language*, *threatened language*, or *endangered language* for Language B, depending respectively on whether we intend to note the asymmetry (*non-dominant language*), the pressures on language vitality that result (*threatened language*), or the outcome of pressures (*endangered language*).

One final note on terminology is needed. There is a difficulty in deriving an adequate label for that group of people who speak (or spoke) an endangered language, as well as those who wish to revitalize a language. In some cases they form what might properly be called a speech community, i.e. a group of individuals who are united by regular interaction in a language. In other cases, however, speakers of an endangered language

---

[5] *Matrix language* is a term drawn from the Matrix Language Framework, a model associated with code-switching (Myers-Scotton 1993), where it has a clear definition and stands in opposition to the "embedded language." While code-switching does often arise in endangerment situations, it does not necessarily do so.

may not use the language with one another on a consistent basis, and in these cases there is not a real speech community, only a potential one. They may not even live in close proximity to one another or know each other well. Add to this the fact that there is not a one-to-one relationship between knowledge of a local language and the desire to speak it. It is not uncommon in language revitalization scenarios to find individuals who have an imperfect grasp of the language (or even no grasp at all) driving the revitalization forward. They want the chance to speak a language that their parents or grandparents did. On the other hand, some fluent speakers of the language may see no point in using the language and therefore make little effort to do so. Rather than create different terms for all these constituencies, we have opted to be vague in our terminology. Throughout the book, we make reference to the *local community*. By this term, we mean that group of people who have some claim on a local language, either because of historical-cultural connections to it, ethnic connections to it, or an ability to speak it. We have attempted at several points to include reminders that the "local community" is not a monolithic block, but, like any social unit, is filled with variety as well as commonality.

4   Levels of language endangerment and loss

In section 2, we discussed characteristics of languages and their speakers that interact to determine degrees of vitality. Implicit throughout that section was the idea that at some point, usually associated with cessation of intergenerational transmission, a language moves from a relatively vital state to one of endangerment. In this section, we clarify the notion of endangerment in two ways. First, we briefly discuss the different rates at which language endangerment occurs; then we provide a categorization scheme for languages in terms of their level of endangerment. In doing this, we provide additional vocabulary relevant to language revitalization. More important, we do this with an eye to developing a richer conceptual framework within which better to understand the sort of revitalization efforts that are best matched to particular situations.

Campbell and Muntzel (1989:183–6) provide a helpful taxonomy of language endangerment situations by considering the cause of attrition coupled with the relative rate at which it proceeds.[6] This categorization is relevant to revitalization programs in two critical respects. On the one hand, the underlying cause of attrition may make revitalization more or

---

[6] Campbell and Muntzel (1989) use the term *death* in their discussion, as was common practice at the time of their writing. We have substituted it with the term *attrition*, which is more current.

less realistic; on the other hand, the speed at which loss occurs is crucial in determining the feasibility of particular kinds of revitalization. Revitalization is much more difficult – if not impossible – in instances of sudden attrition, for example, than it is in gradual attrition, which at least has the potential of being arrested.

Sudden attrition occurs when a language is abruptly lost due to the sudden loss of its speakers as the result of disease, warfare, natural catastrophe, and so on. Though few cases of sudden attrition have been well documented, it is likely that it occurred with some frequency during colonization, when people groups are known to have been decimated due to disease. The presence of civil strife and ethnic clashes in the modern world continues to raise the possibility of sudden attrition, as does the spread of AIDS.

Radical attrition is similar to sudden attrition in that it comes from a set of political circumstances which lead to speakers ceasing to use their language due to repression and/or genocide. It is a means of self-defense: speakers wish not to be identified with their ethnic group so as to avoid persecution and, accordingly, rapidly cease speaking their heritage language. One consequence of radical attrition is the loss of the age-gradation proficiency continuum which is more typically found in cases of gradual and bottom-to-top attrition.

Gradual attrition refers to the relatively slow loss of a language due to language shift away from the local language to a language of wider communication, whether that be a regionally dominant language or a national lingua franca. Most reports of cases of gradual attrition cite some transitional bilingualism, as the speaker population is in the process of shift, and it is here that one finds clearest gradations in intergenerational transmission. Because the attrition is gradual, it is often not a cause for alarm until the point where revitalization becomes quite difficult.

Bottom-to-top attrition has also been called the latinate pattern, where the language is lost in the family setting and most other domains, yet is used widely in religious and/or ritual practices. This is an advanced stage of attrition where the language is retained in those areas where its use is deemed most critical, in particular where certain ritualized texts are memorized. Because of the highly restricted but prestigious domains of use, it is sometimes difficult to assess the actual vitality of the language. In mild instances of bottom-up attrition, the language is still used spontaneously in the settings to which it has been assigned by members of the local community. In extreme cases, the only remaining knowledge of a local language may be memorized portions of a ceremony.

With this taxonomy in mind, we can now turn to a ranking of language status in terms of relative vitality/endangerment. The scale we use here is adapted from Whaley (2003), but see also Kinkade (1991:160–3) and Wurm (1998:192). In our view, a six-way scheme is minimally required to categorize languages with respect to endangerment: Safe, At Risk, Disappearing, Moribund, Nearly Extinct, and Extinct.[7]

Safe: A language is considered safe when all generations use the language in all or nearly all domains. It has a large speaker base relative to others spoken in the same region and, therefore, typically functions as the language of government, education, and commerce. Many safe languages enjoy official status within nation-states, and as such tend to be held in higher prestige than other languages.

At Risk: A language is at risk when it is vital (being learned and used by people of all different age groups) without any observable pattern of a shrinking speaker base, but it lacks some of the properties of a safe language. For example, it is spoken in a limited number of domains or has a smaller number of speakers than other languages in the same region.

Disappearing: A language is disappearing when there is an observable shift towards another language in the communities where it is spoken. With an overall decreasing proportion of intergenerational transfer, the speaker base shrinks because it is not being replenished. Disappearing languages are consequently used in a more restricted set of domains, and a language of wider communication begins to replace it in a greater percentage of homes.

Moribund: A moribund language is one that is not transmitted to children.

Nearly Extinct: A language can be considered nearly extinct when only a handful of speakers of the oldest generation remains.

Extinct: An extinct language is one with no remaining speakers.

The final three types of languages – moribund, nearly extinct, and extinct languages – are all characterized by a lack of intergenerational transmission. The challenges facing the revitalization of these languages are particularly daunting. Not only is there an urgency to act before fluent speakers die (or, in the case of extinct languages, anyone with some experience with the language), but also many of the individuals involved in revitalization may be semi-speakers (Krauss 1997) with widely different degrees of fluency, from strong or nearly fluent speakers to reasonably fluent semi-speakers to weak semi-speakers who are even less fluent, to those with more restricted speaking competence to "rememberers," for those who only know a few words or phrases (see Campbell and Muntzel 1989:181).

Although these categories are intuitively correct, the boundaries between them are blurred. How much does one need to know to qualify

---

[7] The present scheme is very similar to the five-way system proposed in Kinkade (1991), but contains two important differences. Kinkade groups Disappearing and Moribund languages together (his label for the pair is *endangered languages*). Second, Kinkade's equivalent to our At Risk category is more narrow, only referring to languages spoken by a small, isolated population.

as a weak semi-speaker as opposed to a rememberer? Campbell and Muntzel cite one rememberer of Chipanec (in Chiapas, Mexico) as having memorized a religious text in its entirety without being able to understand it. Such memorized texts are very important in language revitalization efforts, but they are static and do not represent living language.

Alternatively, there are cases where once-fluent speakers may find themselves in situations where they have not spoken their languages for many years. This happens when the remaining speakers of a language live in isolation from one another and simply do not have anyone to talk to in their language, such as the last remaining speakers of Yaghan (Grenoble and Whaley 2002; Hitt 2004), who live in isolation from one another or for other reasons do not speak to one another.[8]

As implied, levels of extinction and degrees of fluency (especially among semi-speakers) are of great relevance to language reclamation efforts. Disappearing languages will have fluent speakers of many ages who can be enlisted in the work of revitalization. For moribund or nearly extinct languages, this becomes increasingly less likely, and the importance of semi-speakers to the ultimate success of the process grows considerably. An extinct language may still have rememberers who, although they have no active speaking ability, may know individual words or phrases, such as greetings. Amery (2000) describes the role of rememberers in the Kaurna reclamation project (Chapter 3, section 7), who were able to supply helpful cultural information. One of the surprising aspects of this project was the discovery of such rememberers; it took many several years to realize that something they had heard as children was relevant to Kaurna reclamation. So, even in cases of extinction, there may be a variety of levels of lingering knowledge.

5   Why revitalization?

In the course of this chapter, we have looked at language vitality and endangerment from a number of different angles in order to bring a picture of the basic issues into view. One, however, might legitimately ask questions which are logically prior to this discussion. Why should a community opt to revitalize its language in the first place? And why should anyone care about the fate of endangered languages?

There is an extensive and widely available literature which addresses these questions. Many have responded by noting the importance of linguistic diversity to scientific inquiry and the fact that languages are cultural

---

[8] Jess Tauber (p.c. April 2004) reports that there is now one remaining fluent speaker of the language.

treasures which far exceed artifacts in their value to humankind (e.g. Hale 1998; Hinton and Hale 2001); others note the significance of cultural diversity, which is fostered by language diversity, in stimulating innovative thinking, and encoding alternative ways of seeing the universe (Nettle and Romaine 2000); still others note the centrality of language in protecting and expanding minority rights (Skutnabb-Kangas 2000). We would note, however, that the revitalization that we envisage is community-driven, a bottom-up kind of movement. The overall success of any revitalization program depends on the motivation of the future speakers and the community which supports them, so we presuppose some self-interest on the part of the community before engaging in revitalization efforts. We recommend a serious assessment of community goals, needs, resources, and commitment before undertaking language revitalization; the results of this assessment will provide clear signals as to what is feasible and what is required to make it feasible. We have provided a detailed analysis of these, and ways to go about thinking about them, in Chapter 7.

2   Issues in language revitalization

1   Introduction

Language revitalization involves counter-balancing the forces which have caused or are causing language shift. At a general level a similar set of forces can be said to operate in most language loss situations, but every case is, in fact, distinct. There are unique historical, economic, societal, and political factors that have affected the manner in which language shift occurs. Therefore, a successful language revitalization program requires addressing a complex set of factors that leads individuals in a particular community to make the choices about language use that they do. It requires, to as great a degree as possible, an understanding of diverse issues such as how uniform attitudes about a local language are within a community, the contexts in which speakers of one language interact with speakers of other languages, the spiritual or cultural values that may be associated with a language, national and regional policies concerning language teaching, and so on.

There is an understandable temptation when confronted with the monumental task of revitalization to look for that one single program which holds the key to success for different language groups around the globe, a tested framework that can be replicated for each situation. This simply does not exist, nor can it exist, because for every individual community a specific combination of issues enters into the picture. Each situation is unique, although there is a commonality of factors shared by most communities. An important aspect of language revitalization, therefore, is identifying these issues, recognizing how they interrelate, and assessing how they will affect and be affected by an attempt to alter patterns of language use. This is not a simple process, to be sure, and at the outset it must be stressed that judgments made about the complicated interplay of variables influencing language use in a community are inevitably inexact. They will, therefore, need reassessment at all stages of implementing a language revitalization program. Moreover, the revitalization program itself can be expected to have an impact on some of these variables (such as language attitudes and patterns of language use),

21

necessitating reassessment and potential adjustment of programs. Revitalization is a long-term process; strategies must be continually assessed and adapted over its course.

This chapter offers a basic framework in which to consider the issues involved in evaluating endangered language situations. The issues are divided into two basic categories: macro-level and micro-level issues. In most cases, macro-level issues are the laws, circumstances, policies, etc. which pertain at a national level, or even a transnational level. These include such things as governmental support for a local language or lack thereof, national language planning and education goals, attitudes towards bilingualism, and so on. By and large these kinds of issues are beyond the control of any given local community, but their importance and potential impact need to be identified before the implementation of a revitalization program. Micro-level issues, in contrast, are those which involve the demographics, attitudes, cultural practices, and circumstances of a local speech community. Do members of the speech community live in close proximity to one another? What sorts of formal educational opportunities, if any, are available? Is the community relatively homogeneous in its linguistic, ethnic, and economic make-up? These are the sorts of questions that arise when considering micro-level issues.

It cannot be emphasized enough that there is a crucial distinction between features of an endangerment situation which are internal to the group speaking the local language, as opposed to those which exist externally to it (see Brenzinger, et al. 1991; Sasse 1992). Accordingly, it is important to distinguish properties of the individual speech community from properties of the larger context in which that community is located in order to design a revitalization program which may have long-term impact. For example, if macro-level variables such as federal educational policies and national beliefs and attitudes that promote monolingualism are aligned in such a way as to thwart local initiatives for, say, teaching a minority language in a school, then planning a revitalization effort will necessarily include a strategy for overcoming the effect of these factors, or for teaching the language outside of the schools. A very different approach would be necessary in a situation where the macro-issues appear favorable for the promotion of a local language, but there are tensions among ethnic groups in the community where language revitalization is being considered.

2   Macro-variables

Macro-variables encompass the forces external to a linguistic community which have an impact on language vitality and, accordingly, on revitalization programs. We have proposed elsewhere (Grenoble and Whaley 1998b) that these are attributable to different spheres of influence: *local*, *regional*, *national*, and *extra-national*.

2.1   The extra-national level

Certain extra-national variables are often overlooked, but they can be powerful forces in social change, which in turn has an impact on language use. The most obvious contemporary example is provided by globalization, a term used in a variety of ways. We understand globalization not simply to mean the spread of a single, global language (e.g. English), but rather to refer specifically to a growing integration of economic life worldwide. This increased integration requires greater economic cooperation and more efficient transportation networks between countries; it requires the removal of legal and political barriers to trade and the efficient movement of manufactured goods; and it requires communication that is quick and not costly. Thus the "globalization of English" is actually the result of economic integration.

Consequently, we see the rise of international access languages, that is, languages which serve as a *lingua franca* for those who participate in international finance, manufacturing, and commercial exchange. The list of such languages is very limited, but at this point in time includes at least English, Spanish, Mandarin Chinese, and perhaps Arabic, each of which exerts a trans-national influence in certain sectors of the globalizing world. Knowledge of such languages is widely perceived as a path to social mobility, as well as to more varied economic opportunities and wealth. National and regional governments around the world, therefore, promote their use, and individuals/families often make decisions about language use in the home, or choice of language in schools, based on the perceived value of these international access languages. Among these, of course, English must be singled out as having become a *global language*, a lingua franca with worldwide reach, or, as Crystal describes it, a language with "a special role that is recognized in every country" (1997:2).

The influence of international access languages on local languages is not uniform for a variety of reasons, not the least of which is the fact that globalization impacts nations, regions, and individuals differently. A relatively isolated community that is sustained primarily by subsistence agriculture, for instance, is likely to sit on the periphery of the globalizing world, and there may be little motivation (or opportunity) for members of the community to learn an international access language. At least in the short run, the influence of international access languages in such a situation would not need to be given nearly as much weight in shaping a language revitalization program as it would in other situations where promoting local language use might be viewed as being in competition with promoting the use of an international access language. At the same time, because the local language is competing with one or more national languages of wider communication, the impact of the added competition of an international access language may become tremendous. In situations where speakers see the need to know a minimum of two languages of wider communication – a regionally dominant one and an international access language – the motivation to use and maintain the local language can be seriously diminished.

To this point, we have highlighted the economic underpinnings of international access languages, but they are also avenues to a wealth of information and entertainment via the internet, as well as to popular culture. The significance of this fact is well known to those working for language revitalization in many places in the world where youth are increasingly eager to communicate in chat rooms with people around the globe, to download music from the internet, and to watch movies that feature actors of international renown. While such opportunities do not necessarily involve international access languages, the number and variety of opportunities increases exponentially for those who know them, especially English. In cases in which language revitalization encourages the increased usage of a local language among younger members of a community, there is often a lack of motivation, or even resentment, because the local language does not seem to offer any obvious rewards.

Globalization is just one of the more obvious examples of an extranational variable. Others include the influence that neighboring nation-states can have upon one another. In North America, for example, language laws in the United States are sometimes interpreted against the background of Canadian legislation. Where the laws of the two countries have different consequences for related languages and their speakers, the contrast can be striking; therefore communities in one country draw ideas and inspiration from communities in the other. For example, the Hawaiian immersion education programs were based in part on French immersion schools in Canada, and the Inupiaq of Alaska look to Nunavut in Canada as a source of potential models of self-governance and of control over language and culture.[1]

---

[1] For example, Chipewyan, Cree, Dogrib, English, French, Gwich, Inuktitut, and Slavey are all official languages of the Northwest Territories. The right to use an official language is regulated by the Official Languages Act. In Nunavut, for example, all government offices are required to serve the public in both Inuktitut and English, except for the offices in Cambridge Bay (Iqaluktuuttiaq) and Kugluktuk (Qurluqtuq), which are required to serve in English and Inuinnaqtun.

Moreover, the policies of one nation-state can greatly influence those of another, and this in turn can affect local languages spoken there. Estonian and Latvian provide a good example of this extra-national variable. Of course, neither Estonian nor Latvian are endangered; they are currently instances of "safe languages" in that they are official state languages with large numbers of speakers, long-standing written traditions, and are used in education and law. Yet their position relative to Russian, and extra-national variables that come into play in Estonia and Latvia, put them in a situation where this could very well change (Druviete 1997). Prior to their incorporation into the Soviet Union in 1940, Estonian and Latvian functioned as full-fledged national languages, with well-developed literacy used in all domains, and were used in education and government. The combined impact of relatively heavy Russian immigration into the regions and a Soviet language policy which promoted and favored the use of Russian left the two languages in a curious state at the time of their independence. Russian had been firmly established as the language of economic advancement and had a certain level of prestige, despite relatively strong anti-Russian sentiments among the local people.

Although at the fall of the Soviet Union both Estonian and Latvian were poised to supplant Russian in all spheres of life, the change has not occurred as quickly or as smoothly as might have been anticipated. Russian maintains high prestige, due in part to historical circumstances which established it as a lingua franca throughout the former Soviet empire and to its present position of dominance in the Russian Federation. As Skutnabb-Kangas (1994:178) puts it, "Russian is thus a majorized minority language (a minority language in terms of numbers, but with the power of a majority language), whereas the Baltic languages are minorized majority languages (majority languages, in need of protection usually necessary for the threatened minority languages)." The impact on local languages that fall within the reach of the former Soviet Union have been and continue to be influenced even more dramatically than Latvian and Estonian.

2.2   The national level

The national context is a geopolitical construct that yields a high degree of influence in most places in the world; it is at the national level that language policies most often operate, though in most countries policies that have an impact on local languages operate at the regional level as well. The difference in the national contexts, though subtle, is helpful in understanding how strategies for revitalization must be developed with macro-variables in mind. While any number of issues from the national level might be relevant to the development of language revitalization programs, we mention just a few of the more ubiquitous ones here: language policy; national attitudes towards multilingualism; educational policies; regional autonomy granted to minority groups; and federal support. Each of these involve complications too numerous to discuss in detail here; the goal of this section is not to examine them thoroughly but to bring their relevance to language revitalization to the fore.

2.2.1   Language policy

Language policies shape patterns of language use in a variety of social spheres: the courts, the schools, and the offices of government, to name but a few. Thus they have a direct impact on the vitality of local languages and their chances – or lack thereof – for revitalization and maintenance. The impact can be difficult to predict because policies established at the national and regional levels often are in conflict, and many states do not have a uniformly coherent language policy. This is because language is involved in so many different aspects of society that a policy not specifically designed with local languages in mind can have a major impact on their usage. For example, a local language may have support in the legal system but not in the educational system. Native American languages in the United States are in this position, as is clear when one compares the Native American Languages Act and the No Child Left Behind Act of 2001 (section 2.2.3); the Native American Languages Act guarantees the right to education and development of Native American languages, yet the No Child Left Behind Act requires standardized testing in English. The goals of the two acts are in obvious tension with one another.

At the national level, language policies can range from supportive of local languages to neglectful to detrimental. On one end of the continuum are language policies which outlaw use of a particular language or languages and make their use an illegal and punishable offense. Where such outlawed languages are local, indigenous languages, the direct and arguably explicit purpose of such legislation can be the extinction of these languages. The Kurdish language,[2] for example, has been actively suppressed in a number of different countries. A 1983 Turkish law banned its use in that country; although the law was lifted in 1991, restrictions which

---

[2] Technically there are a number of Kurdish languages. These are generally grouped together when outsiders to the community speak of Kurdish language or human rights. Of particular interest to us here are the Kurdish varieties spoken in Iraq, Iran, Syria, and Turkey. Kurdi is a Southern Kurdish language spoken in Iraq (2,785,000 speakers) and Iran (3,250,000 speakers); Kurmanji, a Northern Kurdish language, is spoken in Iran (200,000 speakers); Syria (938,000 speakers); and Turkey (3,950,000 speakers). Both are also spoken in other regions. Speaker data come from Grimes (2000).

are specifically intended to prevent or limit use of Kurdish continue to the present, as reported in the *Annual Reports of the Kurdish Human Rights Project* (2002). Similarly, in Syria use of Kurdish has been banned; Kurdish personal and place names have been replaced by Arabic names; and Kurdish education and publishing have been forbidden (Spolsky 2004). Obviously, such language policies are openly hostile to the use of the target language.

At the other end of the spectrum, language policies can actively support a given language and foster its use. In the extreme, these kinds of policies require equal use of the language in official and administrative situations, in education, and in public spheres. Where such legislation is enforced and the resources are provided to make it possible to meet its requirements, it can have a very positive effect on language use. A well-known example is the promotion of French in Canada. In 1969, the first Official Languages Act was adopted by the Parliament of Canada, recognizing both English and French as the official languages of Canada. In 1988 a new Official Languages Act was ratified; its basic goals are to guarantee the use and status of the two official languages within Canada. Of course neither English nor French is a local language as we have defined it here, but the Official Languages Act is an illustrative case of legislation which has effectively shaped language behavior in Canada. It is perhaps not surprising that the prime examples of such effective legislation involve national languages like French or English; the indigenous view of this kind of legislation in Canada is presented in the discussion of Mohawk revitalization, Chapter 4, section 3.

In reality most language policies lie between the two ends of this continuum. A language can be instated as an official language, but its use may not be required. (This is the case of Māori in New Zealand, or historically in the former Soviet Union, where "national" [e.g. local] languages were guaranteed equal rights but rarely actually received them.) Use of a language can be supported legally but without any financial resources, which can in some cases be a form of real support, while in others it can be a clandestine way to promote language shift and attrition.

A change from negative to more positive attitudes and policies at the national level can result in positive change to the vitality of local languages (Wurm 2002). Although official recognition does not in and of itself guarantee language vitality, the symbolic effect of such recognition can be very powerful. For example, the European Charter for Regional or Minority Languages, ratified on 5 November 1992, provides a framework for language policy throughout Europe. (The labels *regional* or *minority* are used in the Charter in much the way that we use the term *local* here, i.e. referring to indigenous, not immigrant languages, which are also not official languages of the State, or dialects of the official language[s].) Ratification of the Charter commits the party to adhering to the objectives and principles in Part II of the Charter, which include the recognition of the value of local languages, and agreement to promote their use, in speech and writing, in private and public.[3] Furthermore, Part II contains specific language about the rights of speakers of regional and minority languages to education in these languages, which is further detailed in Article 8 of Part III. The Charter is a potentially powerful tool for local communities who wish to maintain or revitalize their languages. It is not surprising that recognition of a language as meeting the definition of a regional or minority language, and therefore being eligible for the rights and benefits of such is a goal which many groups in Europe seek to attain. (See the discussion of Cornish in section 4.)

A language policy that is positively disposed towards the use of local languages does not in and of itself guarantee positive results for local languages. The policy must be enforced, and it must have provisions in it that allow the policy to move beyond a purely symbolic role. When the Native American Languages Act was instated by the US government in 1991, it was seen by many as a largely empty gesture, as there was no funding accompanying the Act to enable people to put it into action. Even today there is only an annual total of $2 million allocated to the Act, which does not go very far toward meeting its stated purpose. In a somewhat different vein, the policies which were purported to support and promote native languages in the Soviet Union had no weight to them; they were paper promises which the Soviet government could refer to in defense of its actions, but the government was never required to act on the policies instated by law, and was never held accountable for its failure to do so (Grenoble 2003b).

We cannot overemphasize that any policy, in the long term, is only as good as its enforcement, an adequate level of funding for it, and the administrative commitment it receives. Adoption of a language as an official state language often represents an important shift from policies that have repressed or ignored local languages, but the moniker "official language" alone has little impact on how a language is perceived and used. Language policy must also include incentives toward the use of local

---

[3] Ten years after the initial adoption of the Charter, only 16 of the Council of Europe's 44 member states have ratified the Charter themselves. These are, specifically, Armenia, Austria, Croatia, Denmark, Finland, Germany, Hungary, Liechtenstein, Netherlands, Norway, Slovakia, Slovenia, Spain, Sweden, Switzerland, and the United Kingdom. Another twelve states have signed but not ratified the Charter (Azerbaijan, Cyprus, Czech Republic, France, Iceland, Italy, Luxembourg, Malta, Romania, Russia, former Yugoslav Republic of Macedonia, and Ukraine).

languages. Consider South Africa. The constitution names eleven official languages[4] (Afrikaans, English, Ndebele, Xhosa, Zulu, Northern Sotho [or Sepedi], Sesotho, Setswana, Swati, Tshivenda, Xitsonga), but only two of these, Afrikaans and English, are used for official purposes. This is so much the case that, in July 2004, the African National Congress secretary-general, Kgalema Motlanthe, voiced concerns over the continuing domination of Afrikaans and English in the country. This situation exists in spite of the fact that they are not numerically the most spoken languages. Following the 2001 census, the most commonly spoken languages are Zulu (23.8 percent), Xhosa (17.6 percent), Afrikaans (13.3 percent), and Sotho (9.4 percent); English and Setswana are tied (each at 8.2 percent).[5] Moreover, the overall percentage of speakers using Afrikaans or English declined from 1996 to 2001. Druviete (1997) makes a similar claim regarding the status of the Baltic languages (Estonian, Latvian, and Lithuanian) in their respective countries, arguing that despite the fact that they are *official* state languages, the linguistic human rights of their speakers are infringed upon because of the continuing pervasive influence of Russian.

Language policies are also a significant variable in that their influence typically endures far after they are changed. During the Cultural Revolution in the People's Republic of China, persecution against minorities was widespread; this included official attempts to stifle local language use. For example, the government terminated publishing in the Xibe language (a Tungusic language spoken in the northwest of the country) and prohibited its instruction in elementary school. Although these bans were lifted in 1978, the result of almost two decades of prohibition was that an entire generation had effectively lost use of the language (Stary 2003:84–6).

The effects of national policies are far-reaching. This includes both deliberate language policies, as well as policies primarily aimed at other spheres of life, but with repercussions on language use. The latter category can encompass a wide range of acts, most obviously those which affect education, publishing, and the media. A community must be aware of the kinds of policies it lives with: on one extreme such policies may virtually obligate the State to help promote the local language, while on the other they may prohibit a community from creating literacy, any formal educational program, or even a revitalization program. In order to bring about

---

[4] Chapter 1, section 6 of the South African Constitution, which was adopted 8 May 1996 and amended 11 October 1996 by the Constitutional Assembly. See also Skutnabb-Kangas (2000:298) for a similar critique of the official language policy of the country.

[5] Data taken from Census 2001, Statistics South Africa 2003, available at http://www. statssa.gov.za/publications/publicationbrowse.asp?PublCat = 34ce6h0f7o%20-%20fefkb0j8 ed&CatSel = 1

change at the local level, most communities will find that they need to address regional and national level policies first.

2.2.2   Language attitudes

For a variety of historical, political, cultural, and economic reasons, nations differ dramatically in their stance towards multilingualism within their borders (Dorian 1998). The United States, for example, has traditionally dealt with the issue of language diversity by not developing any official language policy, yet has typically promoted the exclusive use of English in the educational system, at times rather aggressively. Even after the Bilingual Education Act was passed in 1968, which ostensibly indicated an openness to multilingualism in American schools, the pattern has been to use bilingualism as a mechanism towards the acquisition of English (see, e.g., Crawford 2000; Schmidt 2000). In addition, there is pervasive sentiment that multilingualism leads to divisiveness, breakdowns in communication and inequalities, as well as a sense that the financial impact of multilingualism – in terms of translation costs, developing school curricula in multiple languages, training bilingual teachers, providing multilingual legal services, and so on – outweighs the benefits to be gained. Language revitalization, in this context, is tolerated on a small scale, but it is commonly viewed with skepticism as to its value, and it is likely to be opposed by a variety of constituencies when it is perceived to hamper the achievement of fluency in English.

The attitudes of the larger, more dominant population are critical in language revitalization efforts. Historically a number of regions (e.g. the United States, Australia, Canada, and the Soviet Union/Russia) have held negative attitudes towards multilingualism and so maintained negative policies toward local languages. In the United States, where indigenous languages and languages of immigrant populations have traditionally had limited or no legal status, and there has been no sustained official stance on multilingualism, many communities involved in revitalization programs have had to confront a national attitude toward language which finds monolingualism preferable and bilingualism suspicious or even dangerous. In such cases the dominant language speakers tend to be monolingual and view monolingualism as the normal human state; they often regard bi- or multilingualism with suspicion and hostility. These attitudes translate not only into negative policies, but also into negative attitudes at the local level (Wurm 2002). Dorian (1998) takes this further, arguing that the attitudes in Europe and her colonies are hostile toward minority languages, "despising them to death." The existence of the English Only Movement in the United States is symptomatic of the pervasive fear of multilingualism in that country. This is not a new attitude: in the 1750s Benjamin Franklin opposed German settlers teaching their children German, not English, in

Pennsylvania, arguing the need for assimilation (Crawford 2000; Spolsky 2003). Such attitudes do much to contribute to language endangerment in the first place, and are difficult for local communities to combat, both externally and internally.

The People's Republic of China provides an interesting comparison. The PRC has codified in its national constitution the right for minorities to promote the use of their language (see Grenoble and Whaley 1999; Mackerras 1994). From this vantage point, one might expect to find a rather liberal attitude about groups of citizens advancing the usage of a local language in daily life, either alongside Mandarin Chinese – the national lingua franca – or in its stead. In fact, this is precisely what has occurred in certain places at certain times. However, lurking behind this fact is the reality that such efforts at promoting a local language have been more a matter of practicality than an official endorsement of multilingualism. Until relatively recently, many parts of China, particularly in the west and the north, remained isolated from the sociopolitical center of the country in the east. As greater numbers of the Han majority have moved into these areas and the communication networks of the nation have improved, these regions tend to have far less autonomy than in years past. Constitutional language notwithstanding, the political practice within the People's Republic of China has been to curtail the cultural practices of minority groups that deviate too far from the national norms and to incorporate all citizens, regardless of ethnicity, into a common vision for a modern state that competes economically and militarily on a global scale. Activities by local communities that are seen to be at odds with this vision, including the use of minority languages, are discouraged or even suppressed especially in more politically sensitive regions, such as Tibet and Xinjiang Province.

Unlike the resistance to multilingualism in the United States, which, when it is articulated at all, is most often couched in pragmatic terms – drains on financial resources, disruption of communication, barriers to educational achievement, and so on – the Chinese situation is better described as one of tolerance towards multilingualism that was born out of practical necessity and is now driven by political expediency. Minority populations will be at least nominally supported by the central government in an effort to maintain or revitalize a language, but only if this effort is not perceived as a political threat.

In contrast to both of these situations are regions of the world where multilingualism is a norm of daily life. The advantages of knowing multiple languages in order to move in and out of different locations and activities are appreciated, and so the expectation is for individuals to speak more than one language. Naturally, these situations occur most frequently in areas of high linguistic diversity, which poses its own set of issues for revitalization (see section 2.3.2), but the cultural acceptance of multilingualism is one variable that works in favor of communities striving to protect or extend the use of a local language.

2.2.3   Education policies

Education policies are of course shaped by language policy and language attitudes, and for many of the issues involved in language revitalization it is language education policies which have the most obvious relevance. However, other kinds of education policies can have an impact on the potential for revitalization. One example in the United States, mentioned briefly in section 2.2.1, is the recent No Child Left Behind Act of 2001, which was signed into law by President George W. Bush on 8 January 2002. The new law redefines the federal government's role in education from kindergarten through twelfth grade. Designed to help close the achievement gap between disadvantaged and minority students and their peers, the new law is intended to change the culture of America's schools so that their success is defined and assessed in terms of the achievement levels of every individual child. One of the four basic principles[6] of No Child Left Behind is "stronger accountability for results," which is meant to be achieved by regular testing using standardized tests nationally.

The policy makes several stipulations regarding the testing of English proficiency. Specifically, by the 2002–3 school year, all states were required to provide annual assessments of English language proficiency in each of their districts. Special provisions were made for the reporting of scores for students with "limited English proficiency," or LEP students, though states are still required to measure speaking, reading, and writing skills in English for LEP students when they who have lived in the United States for three consecutive school years.

The lack of provisions for Native American students is a striking omission in the language of the No Child Left Behind Act, which presupposes that LEP students are immigrants to the United States. The Department of Education's website for the State of Hawai'i, for example, provides the parent letter and fact sheets about No Child Left Behind in English or translated into thirteen different languages (Chinese, Chuukese, Ilokano, Japanese, Korean, Lao, Marshallese, Samoan, Spanish, Tagalog, Tongan, Vietnamese, and Visayan), but not Hawaiian.[7] Understandably, multiple

---

[6] The remaining three basic principles are "increased flexibility and local control, expanded options for parents, and an emphasis on teaching methods that have been proven to work" (taken from the US government's official website for the Act, http://www.ed.gov/nclb/).

[7] These translations of NCLB are available at http://sssb.k12.hi.us/esll/NCLBtranslations.htm.

Native American groups have responded to the new law with concern. The law fundamentally equates English language proficiency with successful education, a presupposition which creates a major disincentive to local language revitalization programs, especially those which include immersion education. Consequently, official groups such as the National Indian Education Association and the National Indian School Board Association have testified to the Senate Committee on Indian Affairs about the difficulties implementing No Child Left Behind for Native Americans because it makes no provisions for the specificities of their languages and cultures, and is formulated on assumption that all children, communities, and schools are the same throughout the US.

In response, on 30 April 2004, President Bush signed the American Indian and Alaska Native Education Order, which establishes an interagency group to work with the Secretary of Education to report to the President on the educational status and progress of Native American Indian and Alaska Native students on meeting the goals of No Child Left Behind (Bush 2004). The Working Group is to be made up of representatives from a variety of federal agencies,[8] yet apparently without representation from agencies such as the Bureau of Indian Affairs or the Office of Indian Education Programs. Part of their study is to include "assessment of the impact and role of native language and culture on the development of educational strategies to improve academic achievement." It is too early to determine whether efforts by Native American groups to protest No Child Left Behind will ultimately have an effect on the way in which the law will be applied to Native American children or Native American immersion schools. Regardless, the episode reflects the challenge facing local language revitalization efforts; rarely are national (or regional) education policies drafted with the special concerns of local language communities in mind.

2.2.4   Regional autonomy

We treat regional autonomy here as a national level variable, although it is relevant both as a macro- and a micro-issue, and can be determined at multiple levels, ranging from extra-nationally to locally. Degree of regional autonomy within a country is a function of historical processes, geography, core political principles, and economic factors, though in exceptional cases it may be determined by extra-national factors. A prime example is the

---

[8] Specifically, representatives shall be taken from the departments of Education; of the Interior; of Health and Human Services; of Agriculture; of Justice; of Labor; and "such other executive branch departments, agencies, or offices as the Co-Chairs of the Working Group may designate" (Bush 2004).

instruction of Russian in schools in all regions throughout the Soviet bloc, mandated by the USSR during the Soviet era.

Within a nation, more or less autonomy can be granted to individual regions over education, language, the development of infrastructure, the formulation or interpretation of laws, the regulation of the media, as well as over allocation of resources. In those states where all such policies and resources are centrally controlled, local communities may have no say in what languages are taught in their schools, used in their media, or whether they receive funding for language revitalization. They may have no voice in shaping the legal and political context which governs the affairs of every-day life. Such centralized control, in particular in totalitarian states, may well preclude language revitalization which includes any formal education, use of the media, or even creation of a written form of the local language.

In nations where a high degree of regional autonomy is granted, there is a much better chance that policies can be enacted which are favorable to the use of local languages. In Switzerland, for example, each individual canton has a fair amount of independence in terms of setting its own language and education policies. This has permitted the continued use of Romansch in the canton of Grisons, where its five varieties are taught in a number of schools and it enjoys a set of legal protections (Posner and Rogers 1993; Schäppi 1974). Given that the language is spoken by less than 1 percent of the Swiss population, its status as an official language and its use in Grisons is in large part due to the political autonomy granted to individual cantons.

In many countries, particular regions might best be described as semi-autonomous, such as in the United States. While each state is given some measure of control over policy making, such as constitutionally guaranteed authority over its educational policies, the federal government can exercise control by the allocation of financial resources (as in the No Child Left Behind Act of 2001; see section 2.2.3). Note that, in the United States, American Indian tribes are guaranteed the rights of tribal sovereignty and self-determination, potentially placing them in even greater positions of autonomy for educational policies. Unfortunately, the actual practice of this sovereignty is under constant negotiation and renegotiation with federal and state governments, so even in this case the autonomy of local communities is only a matter of degree.

Each community therefore needs to make an honest assessment of its own level of autonomy and the possibilities or limitations offered to it by its national structure.

2.2.5   Federal support
A key variable in assessing the possibilities for language revitalization is the existence or lack of governmental funding for language revitalization. Although in principle a community may have sufficient resources on its

own, or may have access to financial assistance from non-government sources, the more typical pattern is for local communities to find their revitalization efforts hampered by insufficient funds for programs. And, typically, regional or federal funding for their work represents the best option.

Quite obviously, the availability of federal resources for language revitalization can be a major motivator for creating such programs and can do much to improve their chances for success. A lack of support has the opposite effect, and limits the choices a community may have. Similarly, unfunded mandates and legislation not only fail to supply the necessary resources to make it possible for communities to satisfy their requirements, but can also have a detrimental effect on overall morale. The community will often see such acts as empty gestures which do not entail true commitment on the part of the majority community.

2.3   Regional variables

The regional level is defined geographically, though the geographic unit often corresponds to a political entity within a larger national domain. Examples would be the western portion of Ireland, the Autonomous Regions of the People's Republic of China, provinces of Canada, all of which supply a significantly influential context for local language use. Most of the macro-variables that operate at the national level have corresponding regional level variables. Therefore, we mention just two variables in this section which are of particular import to revitalization: the role of regionally dominant languages and that of language density.

2.3.1   Regional languages

In the modern world, local communities will find themselves in part of a tiered system of language choices, where the tiers represent spheres of influence and use. The local language is on one tier, a regionally prevalent language on another, the national language on a third, and, in some cases, a language of international access on a fourth. The domains of usage of these languages will vary in individual situations. Typically, the national language is the language of higher education, law, and the government, while a regional language is used in commerce and lower levels of education, and the local language is used for informal social interactions, as well as unique cultural practices (religious rites, ceremonies, traditional holidays, and so on). The domains of local language are limited, not only regionally, but also functionally. In some cases, it may be used only in the home. In others, it is additionally used at the level of the language of village communication; in others, for communication with different villages; and so on.

The actual number of tiers would be a minimum of two, and in many instances the global, national, and regional language will coincide. This is clearly the case for Native American languages in the United States, where the national language – English – is clearly a global language and functions as the regionally prominent language nearly everywhere in the country. In contrast, the number of tiers may be greater, as in parts of Siberia, where the local languages can be divided into those majority indigenous languages with some official status (such as Yakut or Buriat) versus other indigenous languages (such as Evenki or Chukchi). Thus, in some areas in Sakha, for example, Evenki is used at the level of the village; Yakut, at the regional/provincial level; Russian, at the national level; and English, at the global. To be able to function proficiently at each and every one of these levels, a speaker needs to know four languages. The regional level, therefore, adds a layer of complexity to the language situation. Decisions will be required about how the balance among languages can be altered in order to extend the domain of the local language. Indeed, it may be that the most imminent threat to a local language is a regional language rather than a national one. This is true, for example, in much of Africa.

2.3.2   Language density

Language density and multilingualism (or monolingualism) are closely related variables that can have a significant impact on language vitality and on language attitudes (section 3.1). They are not unambiguously positive or negative factors in language revitalization, yet are always important. The languages of the world are very unevenly distributed geographically. Of the 6,800 or so languages spoken in the world, only 15 percent are spoken in the Americas combined, and only 3 percent in Europe. In contrast, 30 percent of the world's languages are spoken in Africa, and 32 percent in the Pacific (Grimes 2000). Moreover, the languages are very unevenly distributed over these vast regions, so that language density can vary greatly. South Africa is listed in the *Ethnologue* as home to 31 living languages, for example, while Nigeria has 505. Similarly, 47 percent of the languages in the Americas are spoken in just two countries: Brazil and Mexico. Differences in language density are discussed in Nettle and Romaine (2000:32–3), who illustrate that the majority of the world's languages are spoken in tropical regions. They show that 60 percent of all languages are spoken across seventeen countries which can be mapped geographically into two major "belts." One of these extends from the West African Coast, through the Congo Basin, to East Africa, encompassing Nigeria, Cameroon, Zaire, Ivory Coast, Togo, Ghana, Benin, and Tanzania. The other belt extends from South India and peninsular

Southeast Asia across to Indonesia, New Guinea, and the Pacific, including India, Vietnam, Laos, the Philippines, Malaysia, Indonesia, Papua New Guinea, Vanuatu, and the Solomon Islands.

So the experience of individual communities in different parts of the world can be radically different with regard to language density and multilingualism. At a simplistic level, it is clear that in regions with high language density, people are more likely to be multilingual and are more likely to have positive attitudes toward multilingualism. In regions with low language density, monolingualism may be more heavily promoted as a national policy (with the United States serving as a prime example).

A deeper analysis shows that the issues of language density are very complex and not at all straightforward. Nigeria is a country with an exceptionally high number of languages, a total of 505 spoken by a population of 106,409,000 (Grimes 2000). If the population were evenly distributed across languages, each would have just over 21,000 speakers. But it is not. There are nine official or national languages in Nigeria (Edo, Efik, Fulfulde, Hausa, Idoma, Igbo, Yerwa Kanuri, Yoruba, and English), accounting for approximately 64 percent of the population, not including any first-language speakers of English. So a large number of Nigerian languages have a small number of speakers. The "Middle Belt" zone of Nigeria has arguably the greatest linguistic diversity, with between 250 and 400 languages, depending on how the region is defined and how the languages are counted (Blench 1998:187). Four major factors for language loss in the Middle Belt have been identified:

(a) assimilation to larger, more powerful groups nearby
(b) assimilation to smaller but culturally dominant groups
(c) assimilation to English, the national language
(d) demographic crises caused by labor migration/urbanism (Blench 1998:198)

While these are all related to well-known socioeconomic factors in language shift, all but (d) stem from the contact situation. Of course, the kinds of language attrition we are concerned with here primarily involve contact situations of some sort, as we are specifically interested in those cases where speakers of a given language shift their usage to another language; these are inherently contact situations. But factor (b) is particularly striking in this regard; it shows shift in Nigeria from one local language to another. (This is in fact more typical of an African pattern of language shift than elsewhere in the world.) Note also that the general failure of literacy in local languages in Nigeria is often attributed the layers of multilingualism in the country. People receive their education in a regional language, which is used as the language of education for a particular region, while English functions as a lingua franca at the national level. Ultimately this is a disincentive to developing local literacies, which have no foreseeable role at either the regional or national levels, and appear superfluous at the local level (Grenoble and Whaley 1998b:32–3).

It is not just the number of languages, but also which languages are spoken in a given area, that is relevant. The existence of related languages in a region can further bolster the sense of prestige. To return to the Siberian example, Evenki see themselves as closely aligned with other Tungus groups. This alignment translates into a sense of shared ethnolinguistic identity, a sense of affinity with Even, Nanai, Negidal, and so on. Moreover, this reflects the historical reality of identity. Before the Soviet government created "nationalities" along ethnolinguistic lines, the different Siberian groups tended to define themselves more in terms of clan than larger tribal affiliation.

Another key point about language density is the geographic distribution of local languages, in relation to one another and in relation to the language(s) of wider communication. Speakers of languages on the eastern side of Botswana, for example, are more likely to shift to Setswana than those on the western side, while some of these may be more likely to shift to Sekgalagadi (Batibo 1998:273).

3   Micro-variables: the local level

In this section we present micro-issues which come to the fore in language revitalization. We would like to emphasize certain key points. First, as micro-level variables, these are considered from the internal standpoint of the community. Each local community is situated within a larger regional or national context; some of the same variables come into play at the macro-level but they do so from an external standpoint. In this section, we are concerned specifically with the way in which these variables operate internal to a local community. Second, it must be noted that any division between national, regional, and local issues though expedient for building a conceptual framework, is somewhat artificial. All levels of variables are interrelated and interact in complex ways. Thus, for example, language attitudes at a local level are usually heavily influenced by attitudes at the regional and national level. Finally, the list of variables presented here is by no means exhaustive; instead we have chosen to highlight some of the most pervasive and important variables. Local situations vary greatly from one to another, and there may be factors not cited here which are of critical importance in language revitalization in some communities.

3.1   Language attitudes

We have introduced language attitudes as a factor at the national level (section 2.2.2), but they play a critical role at the local level as well.[9] While it is obvious that positive attitudes toward the local language help sustain language vitality and are critical for successful revitalization, most communities are not homogeneous in this regard, with a multitude of different attitudes being found. Consider the case of Resian (Steenwijk 2003). Resian is usually described as a dialect of Slovenian which, due to geographic isolation, has developed independently of other Slovenian dialects and so exhibits certain divergent and distinctive traits. Thus its ethnolinguistic situation and the attitudes of its speakers must be understood against the backdrop of their linguistic heritage and attitudes toward standard Slovenian, and the extent to which speakers identify themselves as solely Resian, or as Resian and Slovenian, or as Resian but not Slovenian.

The group of Resians is small; the population of the municipality of Resia was approximately 1,300 in 1998, although Steenwijk (2003:217) puts the total number of people with some knowledge of Resian at 3,000, a figure which includes both inhabitants of Resia and emigrants. Resians live in two Alpine valleys in the autonomous region of Friuli-Venezia Giulia near the border of Slovenia. Therefore, in addition to Slovenian speakers living to the south and west, they are flanked by Friulian and Italian speakers to the north and east. In fact, Slovenian is spoken only by older generation Resians, and only 8 percent speak it well. At the same time, all Resians receive their formal education in Italian. In addition, 77 percent of Resians understand Friulian well and 42 percent speak it well. Only 7 percent of the population is monolingual (in Italian), so that the area is essentially bilingual (Resian–Italian) or trilingual (Resian–Italian–Friulian).

In sum, four different languages (or varieties) come into contact in this region: Friulian, Italian, Resian, and Slovenian. For Resians living as part of this community, their attitudes toward these four languages interact and come into play in making local decisions. It is specially with regard to issues of literacy and orthography development that these attitudes collide. Slovenian in some sense is the most distant of the three languages which come into contact with Resian, because it is spoken only by older generation Resians. Nonetheless, it does provide a logical model for a written language and an orthography because it is so close to Resian linguistically. Adapting the written system of Slovenian to Resian would be a relatively

---

[9] We discuss how local attitudes can be assessed in Chapter 7, section 1.4.1.

simple task. But to choose a Slovenian-based orthography would mean to align oneself with Slovenian and lose the distinct Resian identity. The issue is further complicated by policies which have been made at a national and an extra-national level. Historically, Resian was classified as a Slavic dialect closest to Russian or Belorussian as part of a general policy to divide Slovenian groups for political purposes (Steenwijk 2003:220). Both Austria and Italy have maintained policies and attitudes that generally treat the Slavic groups in their territories as distinct from Slovenian, so these policies have had a divisive effect, separating Resians and Slovenians. At the same time, Slovenian intellectuals draw attention to the linguistic affinity of Resian to Slovenian, in part in an attempt to align the two groups. At present, it would seem that the larger national politics have superseded, as Resians do not have a sense of Slovenian identity.

Another factor which inhibits the use of a Slovenian-based orthography is the strong influence of written Italian; writing is learned in Italian and, as the national language, Italian is used in most written and official domains. Although a written form of Resian was developed in the 1970s, very few people actively use written Resian. The influence of written Italian is so pervasive that its orthographic system is seen as the model for orthographies by most Resians, even if other systems would be better suited: "every proposal that deviates from this model is frowned upon by a large portion of the population" (Steenwijk 2003:222).

This Resian case points to the intricate ways that cultural identity is shaped by multilingualism present in a local community. Language attitudes, however, can be just as heterogeneous in communities where linguistic abilities are uniform across the population or where they vary along generational lines. In most revitalization situations, there is a tension between a "modernist" faction and a "traditionalist" faction. The modernists, even though they may hold a local language in high esteem, worry that imperfect command of a language of wider communication will limit opportunities for jobs and education. In this way, they see the local language as personally limiting. In contrast, the traditionalists worry that a loss of local language will deplete their sense of identity and erode community ties. They see the local language as a source of cultural liberation.

In undertaking revitalization, it is important to see that both positions have some merit. It is frequently necessary to compromise so that the revitalization efforts do not become a catalyst for division within a community. One positive way to do this is not to impose models on all community members against their will. In the Mohawk revitalization program in Kahnawà:ke, for example, parents can choose whether to send their children to a Mohawk immersion school or to an English school, with approximately half of the parents opting for the one, and half for the other (see Chapter 4, section 3).

3.2   Human resources

By *human resources* we mean the number of people, and their skills, which can be brought to a language revitalization project. First and foremost we are concerned with the numbers of speakers of the local language, their relative knowledge of the language, and the distribution of the speakers across generations. Speakers are the most valuable resource for a language. Levels of these resources can be placed on a continuum, with absolutely no speakers of the language on one end of the continuum, and a relatively large number of fluent speakers across all generations at the other end. As we have seen, when there are no remaining speakers of a language, we are concerned with language resuscitation; when there is a healthy speaker base, we may be concerned with language maintenance as opposed to revitalization, although not always. A revitalization program must begin with an honest assessment of human resources. Speakers are not just an important sign of the language's vitality; they are critical for teaching the language and for helping create new domains for its use.

In addition to speakers, a revitalization program needs committed, energetic people to implement it and to support it for many years. Revitalization is a slow process requiring years of continuous work. With successful programs, community members are often able to name key individuals whose efforts have made the program possible. It cannot be overemphasized that this effort needs to come from within the community itself. External human resources, such as linguists, professional pedagogues, teacher-trainers, and language planners can be brought in to assist the community. In fact, depending on the levels of existing language resources, they may be essential, but these external sources cannot provide the core of support necessary to create and sustain a revitalization program.

3.3   Religion

Religion is commonly overlooked in discussions on language revitalization, an ironic fact in that religious ceremonies and cultural activities imbued with spiritual value are often the last domains for a local language which is disappearing. The role of religion within a community results from interacting features of the national, regional, and local levels. The existence of a national religion, for example, plays a role in shaping society and the society's priorities, as well as in government allocation of resources.

Especially in countries where there is no separation of religion and State, this can have a powerful impact on language attitudes and how decisions are made regarding language and other educational policies. Thus, quite obviously, the position of a local religion (and the language practices associated with it) can be more fragile against the backdrop of a strong national religion than the position of a local religion in a country with a high degree of tolerance for religious freedom.

In this section we focus on religion as a local level variable. It is a particularly important factor in both language endangerment and revitalization for many reasons. First, religion is a vehicle for language use; because much of religious language is sacred, in many endangerment situations religious texts (spoken and written) are the best-preserved aspects of the local language and its use. Many religious texts are ritual texts of one sort or another, and are memorized, possibly verbatim. Moreover, there is a correlation between communities which maintain their traditional religious beliefs and practices and those which maintain their language and culture. In Siberia, for example, those shamans who managed to escape persecution in the Soviet era and survive became strongholds for their communities, such that to this day those individual groups which still have a functioning shaman are more likely to use their language and to have first-language speakers. This is a widespread phenomenon which occurs at a highly localized level, within individual villages and with specific herding groups. In specific Evenki villages in Sakha and the Amur region, for example, language retention is higher among those groups which still have a practicing shaman than with those which do not.

At the same time, the arrival of new religions to a community can bring with them a new language and new cultural values. In fact, religion is one of the primary forces driving choices about language use, although the relationship is complex and should be understood in the context of economic, political, geographic, and demographic factors (see Ferguson 1982, who gives a more thorough discussion of these issues). As an example, there is a strong tie between religion of a community and the orthographic system used for its language (see also Chapter 6). The Qur'ān is written in Classical Arabic, and the expectation is that it will be studied in this same language, so the Arabic writing system has become a symbol of Islam. In contrast, the spread of Christianity is tied to a spread of the Roman alphabet, and the spread of Orthodoxy to Cyrillic. (A clear split is seen in the writing of Croatian in the Roman alphabet, a predominantly Catholic population, versus Serbian, written in Cyrillic, by a predominantly Orthodox population, despite the fact that the two varieties are more dialect-like than language-like. Distinctions are determined along religious and political lines, not ethnolinguistic ones, yet these differences are represented orthographically.) Judaism, and Jewish identity, is linked to the Hebrew alphabet, and so on. Orthographic systems in these cases can be representative of more large-scale cultural spread and language shift.

Though religion can be a vehicle for spreading language, local languages can also be used as a vehicle for spreading religion. Buddhists and Christians, in particular, have allowed or encouraged translations of their texts, although they too have historically had attachments to specific languages (Chinese and Latin). An ongoing reflection of this is that SIL International (formerly the Summer Institute of Linguistics), in conjunction with the Wycliffe Bible Translators, has spent considerable time and effort in translating portions of the Bible into hundreds of local languages. In the process, they have become one of the biggest advocates for local language use. Their efforts are not without controversy, however, as Grinevald (1998) describes.

The actual effect of imported religions on language use is very much dependent on the particular community into which they come. Gùrdùŋ speakers in Nigeria who shift their religious beliefs to Islam or Christianity also shift their language usage to Hausa (Haruna 2003). Alternatively, the Jaru and Kalaw Kawaw Ya languages of Australia have been better maintained, and are now being revitalized, due to connections with the Anglican and Roman Catholic Church (Lo Bianco and Rhydwen 2001).

In revitalization situations, it is important to determine the connections between a local language and religion, both traditional expressions of religion and imported religions such as Islam and Christianity. In some cases, churches or mosques may represent one of the best domains to promote language use, while in others they are associated with colonial languages and cultures. Language revitalization is greatly enhanced by connecting it to traditional spirituality in some communities, but in others this may create tensions with a community that will hamper the effort.

3.4   Literacy

Literacy is a sufficiently complex issue that Chapter 5 is devoted to it entirely, and Chapter 6 discusses orthography in depth. In this section we discuss the overall situation of literacy. In any specific community, there can be multiple literacies, a single literacy, or no literacy, i.e. the community may be preliterate. The position and nature of literacy in the community help shape people's attitudes about literacy and their expectations of what it can bring to the local language. One of the driving forces of language endangerment is competition with the language of wider communication; and where this is a national language, in particular an official state language, it brings with it literacy. Most often there is an expectation that citizens of any given country will achieve not only spoken fluency in the official language, or one of the official languages, but also that they will be literate in that language.

The expectations of literacy in the language of wider communication may be set at the regional or national level, but how a community reacts to these expectations, and how they play into potentials for local language literacy, are often determined internally to the community, at a local level. Community members may so strongly associate literacy with the language of wider communication that they perceive the local language to be completely unsuited for reading and writing. In such cases local literacy should not and cannot be part of a revitalization program, or the program leaders must begin the revitalization process by educating others to understand the benefits of local literacy. Alternatively, local literacy may be viewed as a positive benefit for community identity; it may be seen as a source of pride to be able to read and write the local language; or literacy in the local language may be seen as a way to better access literacy in a language of wider communication.

3.5   Financial resources

We consider financial resources as micro-variables in two respects. First is the overall economic welfare of the community, its own levels of well-being, which help determine whether community members are in a position to be engaged in language revitalization or spend their time trying to provide food and shelter for themselves and their families. A subsistence lifestyle, in times of poor harvest or weather conditions, leaves little time for language revitalization. The same can be said for groups facing major health issues, such as HIV infection. Second is the question of the kinds of financial resources a community has available to it for a language revitalization program. These may be resources held locally, within the community, or they may be provided by the government.

Language revitalization is in theory possible without financial resources, but it is certainly easier to begin a program if money is available for education and for producing and disseminating materials. We discuss different models of language revitalization in Chapter 3; even the most economical (the community-based programs and the Master-apprentice model) have a greater likelihood of success with some kind of financial support. More formal educational models require greater funding, to create materials, train and then pay teachers, to outfit schools, and so on. A lack of financial resources can limit the kinds of programs a community can realistically implement, and so an early-on evaluation of potential resources – both internal and external – is critical.

4   Case study: Cornish

We can illustrate the complex interaction of these variables at multiple levels (local, regional, national, and extra-national) through an examination of the case of Cornish, which is relatively well documented historically and in modern times. Cornish is a Celtic language, originally spoken throughout all of Cornwall in Britain. It is relatively clear that English, at the expense of Cornish, was spreading through Cornwall as early as the beginning of the eighth century, with Anglo-Saxon occupation of the region. By the time of the Norman invasion, Cornish had largely been replaced by English in East Cornwall, but was apparently still robust in West Cornwall, with both English and Cornish spoken there. Its survival is somewhat of a "geographical accident," as West Cornwall was more isolated from the Anglo-Saxons, who ruled from East Cornwall (Wakelin 1975:72–97). The overall decline of Cornish stems from many of the usual factors in language endangerment; these include religion, education, and economic opportunities. One clear source of English contact was the spread of fishing and tin-mining in the area, although the spread of English through religion has been argued to be the more primary cause (Durkacz 1983:214).

The spread of English into Cornwall was very much a part of political and socioeconomic change; it may well be that Cornish would have declined regardless of English policies. That said, specific policies have definitely had a negative impact of Cornish vitality. One of these was religious in nature, although it came from the central English government. The English kingdom was officially Catholic through the reign of Henry VIII, but when his son Edward VI assumed the throne, in 1547, one of his acts as supreme head of the Church in England was to make Protestantism the official state religion. Even prior to this, the Protestant Church had been advocating the use of the local (or vernacular) language in religion. Thus the Bible was translated into English and subsequently into Welsh, for example.

In 1549 in Cornwall, however, the institution of English religious services and use of the English Bible and prayer book resulted in protests and rebellions in Cornwall. It is important to note that, in refuting the use of English, the Cornish at this time were not seeking the use of the Cornish language but rather a return to texts and services in Latin, along with the kinds of (Catholic) religious practices that a Latin-based service represented. Historians debate whether the decision to use English in the churches of Cornwall was a deliberate act of linguistic oppression (Davies 2000) or not (Brennan 2001), but it is certainly clear that a governmental act which was intended to legislate religious practices throughout the monarchy had direct sociolinguistic impact.

Over the next two hundred years Cornish continued to decline. The last *monolingual* speaker of Cornish, Dolly Pentreath, died in 1777, but Cornish monolingualism was already considered unusual by the second half of the seventeenth century. Spoken Cornish continued to survive for at least another century; the last native speaker (John Davey of Zennor) died in 1891 (Shield 1984). A movement toward reviving Cornish began in the end of the seventeenth century, but it was not until the late nineteenth century that the Celtic languages were actually deemed worthy of study.

The publication of Henry Jenner's 1904 *Handbook of the Cornish Language* prompted a renewed interest in Cornish revival, but there were relatively few followers at this time, and the group concerned with learning Cornish was almost exclusively constituted by scholars. The lack of wider community involvement kept the interests of the academics from evolving into an actual revitalization effort.

Jenner was followed by Robert Morton Nance, who created an updated and unified writing system for what he called Unified Cornish (or *Kernewek Unyes*), as the variant introduced in the reclamation was to be called (Shield 1984; Williams 2000). In 1929, he published his reconstruction of Cornish (Nance 1929). The Cornish revival movement began in earnest in the 1950s in a general climate of national awareness. In 1967 the Cornish Language Board (*Kesva an Taves Kernewek*) was founded with the charge of fostering and promoting the Cornish language (http://www.cornish-language.org/english/kesvaabouteng.asp). Its responsibilities include providing information about Cornish language revitalization, as well as publishing pedagogical and reference materials, and scholarly editions of classical Cornish texts. The Cornish Language Board initially promoted Unified Cornish, as advocated by Nance.

The Cornish revitalization movement gained momentum in the 1980s, but many were dissatisfied with Unified Cornish, finding it stilted and archaic, and disagreeing with some of the decisions Nance had made with regard to the phonological system. In response, Ken George (1986) proposed a reform of both spelling and pronunciation; George's version came to be called Common Cornish. Richard Gendall advocated a more radically different system, which has been named *Modern Cornish* (Gendall 1991a, 1991b). Note that the unhappiness with Unified Cornish is not universal; Williams (2000), argues that, although Nance's version requires some revision, it should not be completely replaced, as it is "the most secure basis" for a standardized Cornish writing system. Rejecting Gendall's Modern Cornish, Williams advocates a revised form of Nance's original proposal, or Unified Cornish Revised.

This aspect of Cornish exemplifies some of the shortcomings of a lack of agreement about a standard as it is being created. Early work on Cornish was done more by scholars for scholars; in the early 1900s we cannot speak of a revitalization movement with a body of language learners and potential speakers who contributed to the reconstruction of spoken Cornish. Since that time, there have been individual proposals for revisions or differing systems, all of which have sparked debate among proponents of one orthography over another. It is unclear that these debates have led to any kind of consensus. Despite a general agreement that a single standard is desirable, the result of multiple reconstructions is three systems for one language with an estimated hundred fluent speakers (Morgan 2003).

Nonetheless, the revitalization program has made remarkable progress. Today, language policy has helped in part to support Cornish. In a letter dated 11 March 2003, the United Kingdom declared its recognition that Cornish meets the definition of a regional or minority language for the purposes of Part II of the European Charter for Regional or Minority Languages (section 2.2.1), in accordance with Article 2, paragraph 1, of the Charter.

At present, the Cornish revitalization program appears to have had great success. Cornish is currently taught in a number of schools; the Hayle Community School included Cornish instruction as part of the National Curriculum – a milestone, as it was the first school in the United Kingdom to do so (Morgan 2003). There are also evening classes, taught in universities and private homes, and a correspondence course was created in 1983 to help spread language instruction. The estimated total number of speakers is quite small, but there is a total of approximately 3,500 people with knowledge of Cornish; of this total number, some 100 are fluent speakers and 500 use it on a regular basis (Morgan 2003). This is a remarkable comeback for a language which had been completely lost as a spoken language.

The Cornish case illustrates a number of the different variables we have presented in this chapter. First is the issue of policy. Historically the change in religious policy, a decision which may not have been directly intended to have an impact on language use, unarguably facilitated the spread of English at the expense of Cornish. More recently, a positive change in policy, recognition of Cornish as a minority or regional language in accordance with the European Charter, has translated into a tremendous boost for morale and self-esteem for Cornish revitalization. It is unclear, however, if this change has meant an actual change in allocation of resources, or is more a recognition of the validity of Cornish, which is itself an achievement of what should be understood as a Cornish reclamation movement. On another level, some of the difficulties the movement itself faces stem from the fact that there are competing standard varieties, and both confusion and dissent over which to use. Whether this could have been avoided may be debatable, but the present situation at least in part results from a lack of widespread community engagement in, and commitment to, the development of any one of these varieties. That said, the accomplishments of the movement to date are remarkable, with increasing numbers of people involved.

5   Establishing appropriate goals

Before beginning a language revitalization program, we advocate a full assessment of needs and resources. A community must be realistic about what it wants to achieve and what it can achieve with language revitalization. Some of the current language programs are "successful" because the communities involved have identified appropriate goals for their programs. The Cornish language program is not, for example, trying to create a community of speakers who no longer speak any English, but rather aims to have some people speak a bit of Cornish; note that activists in this program regularly report how many people (roughly 3,500) *know some Cornish*, distinguishing between this group and those who *use* Cornish, and those who are *fluent* in Cornish. Part of the success has come from having realistic goals.

A critical piece of establishing appropriate goals is a clear articulation of what community members want to do with their language, along with an honest assessment of the attitudes, beliefs, and other obstacles that may prevent them from achieving their goals. This is what Dauenhauer and Dauenhauer (1998:62–3) call "prior ideological clarification." As they point out, the politically and emotionally correct answer to the question of whether people want to preserve or revitalize their language and culture is invariably yes, although unspoken but deep doubts, fears, and anxieties about traditional language and culture may actually mean that people are not willing to become personally involved. Instead, they may believe that others can "save" the language for them. Yet any revitalization program requires an ongoing personal commitment from at least a large percentage of community members.

Realistic goals can only be set by a frank assessment of the resources and possibilities of a community has, the obstacles it may face, and the amount of time and energy community members are willing and able to bring to language revitalization. Dauenhauer and Dauenhauer (1998) discuss many of the ways in which communities can underestimate potential problems and the levels of commitment needed to achieve their goals. These include unrealistic expectations; a passive attitude which (perhaps even subconsciously) finds revitalization to be a job for someone else, resting on the assumption that other people will take over the task; failure to accept responsibility for language use; and lack of recognition of the time and effort needed to learn or teach what has become a foreign language. Issues of ownership about a language are often central, and it is reasonable and even appropriate for communities to worry about misuse appropriation, and desecration of their linguistic and cultural heritage. Yet, as the Dauenhauers point out, "ownership is only half of the traditional equation; the other half is stewardship and transmission to the next generation and the grandchildren" (1998:91). Communities need to find a way for their traditions to survive in the modern world.

Language revitalization is hard work. Any success comes only with a long-term, sustained effort, involving many parties. Critically, it requires a dedicated sense of collaboration, a willingness to put aside disagreements (about goals, spelling, "correct" speech, appropriate domains for language use, etc.) so as to reach consensus and work toward achieving these goals.

3   Models for revitalization

1   Introduction

This chapter discusses common types of revitalization programs found world-wide, what these programs involve, and how they match (or fail to match) the language goals of a given community.[1] The choice of the best program for a particular community is primarily dependent upon these goals, but the resources available for the project are also critical. We limit our discussion in this chapter to the portions of programs that deal specifically with increasing local language knowledge and use. However, it must be kept in mind that the language portion of the program must be complemented by fund-raising, political lobbying, legal work, and/or community relations efforts.

Most communities involved in revitalization have chosen to focus at least some of their efforts in educational programs. This chapter uses this fact to organize the presentation of revitalization programs. Existing types range from full immersion programs, where all instruction is in the local language, such as the Hawaiian and Māori "language nests," to partial-immersion programs, where local language instruction is found in conjunction with instruction in a language of wider communication, to programs where use of the local language is very limited.

While many would argue that full-immersion programs are the surest route to language revitalization and maintenance, few communities have the resources necessary to see them through. Therefore, in many communities, the local language is taught only as a secondary subject (i.e. as a "foreign" language); other communities, usually those in which there is only a very restricted command of the language, have opted to emphasize the teaching of songs, culturally significant terms, and ceremonies in a local language. Though such education is not geared towards fluency, it reinforces highly symbolic uses of the language. Still other communities

---

[1] An excellent overview of different approaches to revitalization is provided in Hinton (2001a: 7–13).

have created adult education programs, to (re)create a middle generation of speakers, and to train future teachers. Programs can be further contrasted in terms of those which aim to create a body of speakers, as opposed to those (such as the Master-apprentice program in California) whose goals are to educate individual speakers.

Although many groups have considered organized educational programs to be the first line of defense against language loss, not all communities have undertaken them, and so a final type of program to be examined is that which exists outside of formal education. For example, the Choctaw (Mississippi Band) promote the use of their language in "private" spheres of social, ceremonial, and family life, and English in the more "public" spheres of tribal government, business, and education.

After surveying different approaches to language revitalization, we end the chapter by describing the special challenges facing communities where the local language is already extinct. In these cases, there is a total reliance on the records of language (usually in written form, though audio resources are sometimes available). Therefore, we also note the crucial role that language documentation plays in aiding language reclamation and revitalization.

2   Total-immersion programs

Most linguists and educators would agree that total-immersion programs are the best option for revitalizing a language. They are built on the commonsense premise that the best way to learn a language is to create an environment in which that language, and only that language, is used constantly. Implementing such programs is not always possible due to various considerations, however, and in such cases other models must be employed.

The creation of such programs requires certain key elements to be present in the local community. First, total-immersion programs are better suited to communities where there is still some speaker base to draw from in creating the immersion environment. Second, although we know of no case where such programs have had unanimous support within a community, they certainly need widespread advocacy and endorsement from the outset. They are almost certain to fail if there is overt disapproval from too large of too influential a group within the community. As we have seen, for a language to thrive it needs to have domains of usage, and so community members are not only needed to work to create a speaking environment but also to sustain it, which is difficult if there is significant resistance. Third, many total-immersion programs will succeed or fail on the basis of financial resources. In a community with formal schooling, a total-immersion program requires that all school instruction be conducted in the local language. This means that pedagogical materials are needed not only for language instruction, but also for all other subjects (mathematics, history, science, and so on). The creation of these materials requires not only financial support but also cooperation and input from adult speakers in the community.

There are a variety of different total-immersion models. The models presented here are based on the assumption that the school and some form of formal education will be the center of any total-immersion program. In section 5 of this chapter we explore models which place the burden of language learning and revitalization outside of a school setting and on other areas of community life. The choice of formal education versus a community-based program rests in part upon the role of formal education within the community prior to initiating revitalization. If an established system of mandatory education is already in place which employs a language of wider communication, then creating an alternative immersion program will almost always require external support from external administrative bodies. In order for a school-based program to succeed, the regional and national government agencies minimally should not interfere, and ideally should invest in the program, both financially and administratively. As is seen in our discussion of several case studies, immersion programs such as the Hawaiian Pūnana Leo have faced difficulties due to non-supportive or even hostile legislation at the state and federal levels (Chapter 4).

2.1   Te Kōhanga Reo, the language nest

The language nest model represents a particular type of total-immersion instruction. The successes and controversies of this particular model warrant separate discussion, as opposed to treating it as a subset of the larger discussion of total immersion programs as a whole. The revitalization of Māori is one of the best-documented programs, and so there is an ample literature documenting perspectives about its effectiveness. J. King (2001) provides a thorough discussion of the history and development of the situation.[2]

The Te Kōhanga Reo model was first developed in the late 1970s and early 1980s for the revitalization of the Māori language (Austronesian,

---

[2] Our assessment here relies heavily on Spolsky (2003), as well as our own interviews conducted in February 2004. For more details, see J. King (2001), as well as Benton (1991), Biggs (1968), Dixon (1991), and Karetu (1994).

New Zealand). It was later adopted for Hawaiian revitalization, which serves as a case study in Chapter 4 (section 4). Even so, this particular model may work better in certain kinds of situations as opposed to others, and so some review of the Māori particulars is worthwhile.[3]

Use of Māori was established in New Zealand in approximately AD 1000 through migrations when the Māori people arrived on what had been an uninhabited island, thereby establishing it as the only indigenous language of New Zealand. Contact with Europeans did not occur until 1642, with heavier contact beginning in the late 1700s. Until more recent immigrations which have established Samoan as the largest non-European ethnic group in New Zealand, Māori were in contact (and in conflict) with white English-speaking settlers. From the standpoint of language loss and revitalization, it is the opposition between English and Māori which is critical, and in particular the fact that they were the only two competing languages.

An orthography for Māori was established in 1818 by missionaries to New Zealand who took an active role in the development of Māori literacy. Their active involvement has led to two very different conclusions from the modern standpoint. First, the development of literacy education was highly successful, and it has, in fact, been argued that by 1830 literacy rates were proportionally higher for the Māori segment of the population than those of the English-speaking population (Biggs 1968:73). One result is that Māori people have had a wide range of written materials of a variety of types for centuries and in this respect can be seen as having established a literary history.[4] It has even been claimed to be the largest body of writing from an indigenous group from within one century of European contact (Orbell 1996). In consequence the Māori have access to the kinds of language materials which simply do not exist for many other local languages. Another significant aspect of this is that the notion of literacy is by no means new or foreign to Māori speakers, and that the introduction of a vigorous language revitalization program did not entail a major cultural shift with regard to literacy. At the same time, a second major impact of the early literacy movement led by missionaries to New Zealand was that the high literacy rates arguably facilitated the shift to English (Mühlhäusler 1990, 1996). During the first few decades of contact, Māori was decidedly at an advantage. The early mission schools conducted all education in Māori,

---

[3] For a discussion of Māori with regard to the general scheme of macro- and micro-variables proposed in this work, see Grenoble and Whaley (1998b:49–52).

[4] Such resources include the impressive electronic database of Māori newspapers, *Niupepa Maori*, which based on thirty-four separate periodicals dated 1842 to 1933. Fifty-five percent of the collection (some 17,000 pages of printed matter) is written solely in Māori, while another 43 percent is bilingual. Only 2 percent of the collection is in English. The database is available from LEARN http://www2.auckland.ac.nz/lbr.

and all correspondence between the English-speaking officials and the Māori people was in Māori. The situation changed very quickly. The 1867 Native Schools Act made English the sole language of instruction in the schools. Thus, within less than fifty years of active Māori literacy, it was banned from use in the schools. English replaced Māori in government and official spheres as well, and Māori use went into decline.

Ultimately by the 1970s Māori was a disappearing language.[5] Although there were still a relatively large number of speakers (some 70,000), they accounted for only 20 percent of the population or less, and almost all were over the age of 50 (Benton 1981:15). One of the primary problems for vitality of the language was that its use was essentially limited to two domains: the *marae* (the traditional Māori tribal meeting place) and the church. Recognizing the necessity of intergenerational transmission, language nests, Te Kōhanga Reo, were created in the 1980s to transmit language from the older generation to the youngest generations of children. The Kōhanga Reo language nests began by bringing fluent elders to the preschools to work with the young children and teach them to speak and live Māori. The schools can technically accept children anywhere from birth to age 6, although many leave at age 5 to attend regular schools. The success of the preschools created a need for alternate systems for primary and secondary schools. In 1985 the first Kura Kaupapa Māori, a total-immersion program, was established. Students in Kura Kaupapa Māori receive all instruction in Māori, and a principle underlying the schools is the commitment to teaching within a Māori philosophical framework, to "affirm Māori culture."

The Māori program has served as more than a model: it has been an inspiration to a number of different groups. The Hawaiian language nest program is the most obvious (Chapter 4, section 4) but others – such as the Blackfeet revitalization program – have been influenced as well (Kipp 2000). Their reputation is well-earned: the Māori are the only indigenous numerical minority in the world to have attained official status for their language at a national level (Skutnabb-Kangas 2000:603) as instituted by the Māori Language Act of 1987.

Although the "language nest" model is generally used to refer specifically to the cases of Māori and Hawaiian, similar programs have been instituted, quite independently, elsewhere. For example, the Mohawk revitalization program at Kahnawà:ke was built up incrementally, from the lower to upper grades, beginning with preschool children (Jacobs 1998). One basic component of all these initiatives is to start educating

---

[5] For a more comprehensive account of the history of the progressive attrition of Māori and the circumstances which contributed to it, see J. King (2001).

the youngest children in a total-immersion setting, and build a progressive system by following the lead class, developing the program as they move through it.

3   Partial-immersion or bilingual programs

Partial-immersion programs are bilingual programs, with some classes conducted in the local language, and some in the language of wider communication. The basic difficulty with partial immersion programs is that they often develop into, or simply are, transitional bilingual programs. In general the classes conducted in the local language are language-learning classes, or parts of classes, and the other subjects are taught in a language of wider communication. Thus the local language is taught as a foreign or second language.

This is not a model which we advocate, nor does it hold wide support. Yet it is arguably the most frequently encountered model, in particular in certain parts of the world, such as the Americas, the former Soviet Union, and elsewhere, and so merits discussion. Note that language activists advocate against partial-immersion programs, a point made by Darrell Kipp (co-founder of the Blackfeet immersion school):

We all speak English too well. Bilingual programs are designed to teach English, not your tribal language. We aren't against English, but we want to add our own language and give it equal status. We don't allow slang or shortcuts; we teach the heritage language forms. Our immersion school children speak high-standard, high-caliber Blackfeet. You can accomplish that through immersion only, not through bilingual education. Bilingual education typically teaches the language fifteen minutes a day. (Kipp 2000:3)

Such programs are appropriate if the community is unable or not truly willing to commit to the time, effort, and cost necessary to make the local language a primary language of communication. If the goal is for children to have at least some limited knowledge of the local language, then partial immersion can provide that. In many places in the world, federal regulations on education may also proscribe anything more than partial immersion.

Bilingual or partial immersion programs are of two basic kinds. In one, the children enter knowing a local language (or their heritage language, in the case of immigrants), but they may have an imperfect command of the language of wider communication. The program, then, sees developing fluency in the language of wider communication as a primary goal. That is to say, the programs are instances of transitional bilingual education, used as a bridge for the children until they know enough of the language of wider communication (e.g. English, Spanish) to function fully in it. The second type presupposes knowledge of the language of wider communication, and varying levels of knowledge of the target (local) language. In these programs the local language is most often taught as a second, foreign subject. The children receive some knowledge of the target language, and may even receive full instruction in the grammar. There may also be some effort to use the target language during the instruction of other subjects in the curriculum, and in this way it can be seen as partial immersion in the language. At least in the Americas, such programs are not very well developed for any but the world's languages of wider communication, and local languages tend to not be taught with very much thoroughness. Appropriate teaching materials rarely exist, nor do trained bilingual teachers who might maximize the effectiveness of partial immersion settings.

Another alternative in partial immersion is what has been called the *formulaic method*, which refers to the teaching of formulaic language (Amery 2000:209–12). In the first stage, individual words and one-word expressions are taught, to be used intermingled with the language of wider communication. These words should be easy to pronounce and to remember, and should carry a high functional load. Examples include not only such obvious words as 'yes' and 'no,' but also expletives and exclamations like 'terrific' or 'shame,' as well as greetings, interrogative words, and simple imperatives (e.g. 'come,' 'sit,' or 'go'). When these have been mastered, longer and longer expressions can be introduced (e.g. 'Let's go,' 'Where are we going?,' 'When are we going?,' or 'I'm going home'). Ultimately the student has a fairly large stock of formulaic expressions which can be used more or less flexibly, and the expectation is that they be used whenever possible. As this method introduces a limited number of words and expressions, it is well suited to language reclamation programs (section 7) for extinct or nearly extinct languages. Beyond the obvious goal of increasing the student's lexicon, this model provides a method for enabling students to become comfortable using the language and so has the benefit of helping to create a context for language use. In reclamation situations where there is no body of speakers and no opportunity to talk with fluent speakers, the gradual introduction of formulaic expressions has proved to be a useful method.

4   The local language as a second, "foreign" language

By definition endangered local languages are languages which have ceased to have a vital speaker base. While this may not mean that there are no younger-generation speakers, it often does. Thus when endangered local languages are introduced into a school setting, they are something of a "foreign" language. In some communities, including some Native American and Siberian communities, for example, pedagogical materials were developed at a time when children entering the school system spoke the local language fluently (and not the language of wider communication). These materials are no longer appropriate in an environment where the students have little or limited knowledge of the local language. Instead, the curriculum must be reworked to first teach students the local language, and then to provide instruction in the local language (if a total-immersion program is the goal).

Currently this approach is dominated by two very different lines of thinking. One is to begin the revitalization of the language with the current adult, i.e. middle, generation, relying on knowledge of the elders to provide content for the teaching. This is the approach favored by UNESCO (see in particular Chapter 5, section 2.4). This approach links local language knowledge to literacy programs. The rationale is that language knowledge is tied to basic economic development. In order for a community to advance economically and to participate in regional, national, or even global markets, the community adults in general, and community leaders in particular, need to be literate. Inherent in the UNESCO approach is the presupposition that they need to be literate in the language of wider communication, not just a local language, but an extension of this is simply the view that it is the responsibility of parents to teach language to children, and so the adult generation must be educated first. This view might alternatively be dubbed the "mother's knee approach," signaling that language is best learned and mastered in the home. It speaks to the desire in communities to return to the days when the local language was vital and the community had ownership and control of its language.

The advantages to teaching the adult generation first are multifold. First, it requires a critical mass of people within a community to take responsibility for learning the language, and it means that the adults are the ones who create domains for language usage. Thus when the children learn the local language, they will find the need to use it already built in. Another advantage to teaching the adults first is that they are then in the position of being the language teachers and can assume what may be perceived as the more traditional or natural role as instructors, teaching the language "naturally" to their children. This approach also helps alleviate the potential problem of creating a lost middle generation, a situation which occurs when the parent generation does not speak the local language but the elders (grandparents) and children do. (The revitalization program at Kahnawà:ke has created a "lost" generation, i.e. the parent generation, which cannot understand the Mohawk conversation of the elders [the grandparents] and of the children; see Chapter 4, section 3).

The disadvantage is that language learning is difficult for adults. Not only have adults passed the critical period for language learning, they also tend not to have sufficient time to invest in the learning process. They are working, cooking, cleaning, rearing children, and tending to aging relatives. More often than not, language learning takes a back seat to other responsibilities. These factors make it less likely that the adults will attain fluency.

The second approach is to begin creating a new speaking generation with the youngest ranks, often starting in preschool programs. We discuss these programs elsewhere, as this is an approach favored by many grassroots revitalization groups such as the program in Kahnawà:ke (Mohawk revitalization; Jacobs 1998 and Chapter 4) or the language nest programs, as seen in section 2.1. This requires a stepwise or tiered approach to language development programs. Many programs opt to start language instruction in preschool or in the very beginning of elementary school. By focusing on a single target class, the faculty and staff are able to prepare materials one year at a time. Thus curricular development and the creation of pedagogical materials can move forward as that initial class moves through the grades. If one begins by targeting an incoming kindergarten class, for that one year there is only one class of language instruction in the local language. As that class moves to the first grade, materials are developed, and in the second year of the program language immersion occurs at both the kindergarten and first-grade levels, and so on.

We have restated these programs here to highlight the fact that in many revitalization programs most of the children are indeed learning their local language as a foreign language. This requires textbooks and other teaching materials to be developed just as they would be for foreign language instruction, with an eye towards points of interference from a language of wider communication. The materials also need to be designed with graduated levels of complexity. Some communities involved in revitalization may have access to pedagogical materials that existed at a time when children were entering the schools with a solid competency in the local language (and perhaps had limited knowledge of the language of wider communication). While these teaching resources have their role in helping to create new curricula, it is important to stress that they are not likely to be effective in the classroom on their own, since they were developed with a different sort of student in mind.

5   Community-based programs

While the models we have discussed to this point are primarily based on a view of education centered around a classroom setting, different approaches to learning are inherent to many native cultures or desired by certain communities. Many communities around the world are known to use what are called *informal learning styles*, or *natural learning*, and the more institutionalized classroom approach may be antithetical to their views about how learning should take place. In Australia and Papua New Guinea, for example, indigenous people learn more by observation, imitation, and individual trial and error (Waters 1998, citing Harris 1977). In these communities people do not segment a task into component parts and learn each part sequentially; they also do not discuss each stage (or any stage, it seems) of the learning process. Some examples which Harris provides include learning a dance, where the young boys watch the men perform the dance, watching over and over again, until they feel comfortable performing it as a whole. They then join the line of accomplished dancers and imitate them, repeatedly, and when they have reached a level of some proficiency, they receive praise or laughter, depending on how well they have danced. In distinction to typical classroom styles of teaching and learning, they are not verbally instructed on how to perform the dance, and the more accomplished dancers do not single out any moves that they could improve, nor do they demonstrate parts of the dance with an eye toward teaching. Thus the dance is received as whole and practiced as whole, over and over again, until it is perfected.

This kind of learning style comes into conflict with revitalization programs designed around institutionalized education. The situation is further complicated in that, in many cases of language attrition, and in particular those outside of Africa, the local language is being replaced in favor of either an Indo-European language (e.g. English, Hindi, Spanish) or by a language and culture with well-established written traditions and formal education systems, such as Mandarin Chinese. Thus the languages and cultures are in conflict, with the dominant culture introducing, and perhaps imposing, new learning styles on the local one. Because the sense of language is so deeply tied to a sense of culture, there may be strong resistance within a community to using foreign education styles to learn the community language. Consequently, people may decide to proceed with a program which is more compatible with the local culture. One well-known program that is designed in this way is the Master-apprentice program, which merits separate attention (see section 6).

Community-based programs that are developed within the framework of local learning styles focus on a domain (or domains) of language use rather than language instruction *per se*. They select a community activity that is particularly well suited to informal learning styles and encourage participation. Then, by consciously infusing the activity with the local language, language instruction becomes part and parcel of learning the activity as a whole and participating in it. Many communities, even those which may use formal education as part of their revitalization effort, will experiment with this approach in the context of summer immersion camps or after-school activities.

The advantage of community-based programs is that they automatically address the problem of creating a domain for use of the local language. This is a difficulty which plagues even some of the most successful language revitalization programs that have focused most of their attention to the schools (e.g. Hawaiian and Māori). The decision of opting for a more or less formal learning system ultimately rests on attitudes within a community. Outsiders and educators need to be aware of the potential for culture clash, even if the community chooses to teach its language in a formal classroom, and must be sensitive to students who may have difficulties in a formal classroom because of the fundamental differences in teaching and learning styles.

6   Master-apprentice program

The Master-apprentice program was developed in 1992 in California as a means to address language vitality in the face of a particular set of variables found in the state of California.[6] Specifically, California is home to a large number of indigenous languages, estimated to have numbered approximately 100 in the eighteenth century. Due to a range of political and historical circumstances, their numbers diminished rapidly, so that by the beginning of this century only some 50 languages were remaining, and only 4 of the original 100 languages had more than 100 speakers. The numbers for the other languages are desperately low, with 12 languages having 10–60 speakers, 13 only 6–10, and 21 languages have fewer than 5 speakers. The speakers can all be characterized as elderly, so that all of these languages are in serious threat of extinction. Thus the California situation is characterized by a relatively large number of indigenous languages with very few speakers and no real language vitality. This linguistic landscape means that there is no single language which is an obvious candidate for revival (unlike Māori in New Zealand or Hawaiian in Hawai'i), and that speaker numbers are so low that one cannot turn to a community of speakers to engage in the effort.

The Master-apprentice language-learning program was initiated as a response to these very issues. The program is designed to pair language

---

[6] The program is thoroughly described in Hinton (1997); a good overview is provided in Hinton (2001b). Hinton et al. (2002) is a manual designed for those who wish to set up their own Master-apprentice program.

learners with "master" speakers, i.e. the elders who still speak the languages, so as to form a language-learning team. Five key principles underlie the structure of this program: (1) the use of English is not permitted in interactions between the master and apprentice; (2) the apprentice needs to be a full participant in determining the content of the program and in assuring use of the target language; (3) oral, not written, language use is always primary in learning and communicating; (4) learning occurs not in the classroom, but in real-life situations, engaging in real-life activities (e.g. cooking, gardening, etc.); and (5) comprehension will come to the beginning language learner through the activity, in conjunction with nonverbal communication. Adherence to these principles assures that language learning and instruction take place in an immersion setting that nearly replicates the "natural" language-learning environment of children (as opposed to artificial classroom settings, for example). Admission to the program is competitive as there is a (small) stipend attached to participation; this stipend not only provides some incentive to the team members to carry through with the program but may also free them up from other work obligations so as to be able to spend regular time each week devoted to language learning. Each member of team receives $3,000 (US dollars) for 360 hours of immersion work (Hinton 2001b:219). The program has been funded by gifts from a variety of foundations throughout its existence, pointing at once to the widespread support for this program as well as to its potential financial fragility. Teams may receive funding for up to three years through reapplication. While it is clearly recognized that longer training is desirable, financial constraints mean that the three-year limit enables new teams to receive support. The ultimate goal of the program is to produce apprentice-graduates who are conversationally proficient in the target language and are prepared to teach it to others. It is explicitly recognized that they will not be able to achieve the fluency level of the master speakers in the course of three years; the hope is that the master and apprentice will develop a lifelong relationship which may enable this to develop.

The Master-apprentice teams face certain potential difficulties due to the very nature of their situation, and so before teams begin their work they come together for weekend-long training sessions. First, it is important to bear in mind who the language masters are. They are often tribal elders who may have not actively used their language for many years, due to diminished speaker bases, geographic scattering, intermarriage – due to the very factors which have led to severe language attrition. So the masters spend some time in training sessions getting used to speaking their language again, in a sense reactivating it. Second, given that the masters are not trained language teachers, the training sessions devote time to introducing the principles of language immersion, building and practicing vocabulary, and enforcing the importance of repetition, review, and patience in language learning. An important component of the training involves getting the participants used to nonverbal communication. Some of the session is devoted to teaching apprentices how to use key expressions in the target language, such as "What is this?" or "Say that again" so that they will be equipped with some basic phrases to facilitate language immersion training. Introduction to these expressions also begins raising awareness of important cultural information, such as the fact that in many native cultures it is not polite to ask direct questions, so these must be rephrased. The training sessions are described in greater detail in Hinton (1997) and Hinton et al. (2002), but it is worth observing here that the nature of the California linguistic map is such that the teams represent a wide variety of different languages, so the teams spend much of the training session doing individualized work one-on-one, with the master and apprentice beginning their work together. Despite the many linguistic and cultural differences, there is a commonality of experience which makes it very useful for all teams, from beginning to advanced, to come together for this training.

The goals and expectations for each year of participation are defined by the organizers (Hinton et al. 2002). By the end of the first year, apprentices should be able to ask and answer simple questions about themselves, describe pictures, use some culture-specific language (prayers, stories, etc.), and recite a short speech which they have prepared with the help of the master. This basic repertoire is expanded in the second year, with the goals of being able to speak in simple grammatical sentences, carry on extended conversations, have increased comprehension, be able to converse about most topics, and be able to give short speeches. Finally, by the end of the third year of the program, the apprentices should be able to converse at length, use long (and presumably complicated) sentences and develop plans for teaching the language. These goals are at once realistic and ambitious: language learning is a slow process, and the apprentice meets with the teacher only for ten hours a week. In other words, this is roughly the equivalent of a college-level language course. The founders of this program point out that the results of the program will vary among individual students depending on a range of factors, such as the overall time commitment, how much the apprentice is truly immersed in the language, and so on. Other such factors, such as the nature of the target language and the apprentice's prior experience studying foreign languages, are not discussed but are clearly relevant as well.

One important aspect of the Master-apprentice program which deserves highlighting is the commitment to oral, not written, communication. This is perhaps interesting in the face of a widespread belief that a fundamental component of the success of any language program is literacy (see Chapter 5). Yet literacy runs against the core principle of the Master-apprentice program, namely, that language teaching and transmission must occur in natural, real-life situations and must be incorporated into these activities. Given the oral nature of all of the California indigenous linguistic communities, there is no natural setting for reading and writing these languages. This program has been very successful to date in doing what it was established to do: it provides a new kind of transmission mechanism for languages with very few remaining speakers. In training a new cadre of adult speakers, it has kept these languages from permanent oblivion. With rare exceptions, the adult apprentices in this program do not acquire native-level fluency, and so it is very different than language transmission of vital languages, where children acquire the language from birth. The program does not attempt to revitalize speaker bases and make the target language a fully used system of communication in all aspects. Instead, it is a realistic, practical approach in situations of severe language attrition where it is most probably impossible to build a new speaker community.

Finally, we should add that there are valuable lessons to be taken from this particular model which can be applied to other programs. Appendix B of Hinton et al. (2002) discusses how to apply the principles of the Master-apprentice program to the classroom. The appendix is written with graduates of the program in mind, with the thought that they may well go out and teach their newly acquired language in a different setting. Although the one-on-one principle of Master-apprentice work cannot be duplicated in the classroom, other aspects of the program can. These include the commitment to a total-immersion setting, teaching in full sentences, and learning through activities, which is in some ways analogous to the *total physical response* system for language learning (see Asher 2000, for example).

7   Language reclamation models

Language reclamation refers to the revival or reclamation of languages which are no longer spoken (Amery 2000:17). This process has been given a variety of names, such as reclamation, resuscitation, and awakening; we take the name *reclamation* from Amery (2000), similarly avoiding the perhaps more frequent term *resuscitation* because of the connotations of language death. (Note that such languages are often referred to as "sleeping" or "silent.") *Reclamation* has also been called *revival*, as defined by Nahir (1984) or Paulston et al. (1993), with the term used specifically for languages which are "dead" in the sense that they have no native speakers. Hebrew is cited by Paulston et al. (1993:276) as "the only true example of language revival." Language reclamation necessarily differs from language revitalization. For the latter, native speakers are still available to serve as consultants and teachers; for reclamation, one is forced to rely on whatever documentation of the language remains. (We take up the separate issue of documentation, and what kinds of documentation are appropriate and needed, in the next section.)

The most successful and widely cited case of language reclamation is Hebrew, which is now spoken as a first language by over five million speakers world-wide (Grimes 2000). But Hebrew presents a very special case, and it is unlikely that many languages will have the same advantages as Hebrew. Although it had been lost as a spoken language of daily use, Hebrew had maintained its use as a liturgical language and, as such, had an uninterrupted history of use among the educated religious Jewish population. It also had the advantage of a relatively large body of written texts. Thus it is in many ways inappropriate to speak of Hebrew reclamation, but rather a reinventing and revitalization took place. Liturgical Hebrew needed to be updated for a modern world, the vocabulary needed to be expanded, and a conversational language needed to be created. An analogous situation would be found if there were a resurgence of interest in Latin, which has continued to be taught as a written language and was widely used by the Catholic Church until 1962, when the Second Vatican Council permitted an increased use of national and local languages in the church service (Mullarney 1987: 357). This is quite different from a reclamation of a language which has ceased to be used entirely.

There are very few cases of actual language reclamation. The circumstances surrounding each lost language vary considerably, and so the reclamation efforts may vary greatly from case to case. The situation with the Kaurna language of Australia (Amery 2000) is more instructive than most, as Kaurna is more characteristic of the many local languages being lost today and remarkable progress has been made in its reclamation. Kaurna was spoken by people indigenous to the Adelaide plains of Australia and is not known to have been spoken by a community since the nineteenth century. The term *Kaurna* does not appear in the main records of the language (Teichelmann and Schürmann 1840; and Teichelmann 1857); instead these people were referred to as "the Adelaide tribe," among other names. Kaurna was completely lost (or was "sleeping"), not having been spoken for more than a century prior to its active revitalization. By the time the reclamation movement began, there were no speakers and no sound recordings. The only words unique to Kaurna which had survived were place names on maps; a few other words were also known to be shared by other languages in the region. Thus the community had to rely on written records, although the records of Kaurna that have been left are incomplete. Both the language and culture are only partially documented, and here by outsiders: missionaries and other interested parties, and government officials. Thus the Kaurna people do not have their own records of their cultural heritage, and much has been lost forever.

In order to proceed, some basic documentation is needed. The bare minimum requirement is at least a rudimentary grammar and some basic lexicon. Clearly, the greater the documentation, the more likely the reclamation is to have some chance of success. In some instances there will be audio recordings, transcribed texts, and in some cases more complete grammatical descriptions. The remaining traces of a lost language can be found in traditional oral texts, prayers, songs, proverbs, or poems, which are memorized and passed on from generation to generation. Thus the obvious first step in language reclamation is gathering all available materials and assessing them. Regardless of how complete these materials are, there will always be gaps, as no documentation can take the place of a native speaker. In most cases there will be considerable gaps; few lost languages can boast the kind of documentation which Hebrew and Latin have.[7] Many languages that have been lost to date do not have sound recordings or, if they do, the recordings are of poor quality, made at a time when technology was not well developed (Grenoble and Whaley 2002). And unless they have been carefully made by trained linguists, they do not give a full phonemic and phonetic inventory. Pronunciation often requires some reconstruction; the phonetic systems of any related languages still spoken can provide useful information, although they too will have undergone sound change and cannot be expected to lend an exact representation of the sound system of the target language. There will be a fundamental difference in the reclamation process between those languages which have been spoken until fairly recently, and those which have not been spoken for at least a century.

In addition, even when the documented lexicon is fairly complete, it will have been frozen in time and new terminology will need to be created. (See Chapter 7, section 3 for specific information on constructing new terminology.) It is desirable to rely on both language-internal material and information from the sister languages wherever possible. Use of the comparative method can be helpful to reconstruct parts of the lost language which were not documented. Similarly, if one or more sister languages is still spoken, the sound system of the lost language may be reconstructed.

---

[7] Despite extensive documentation, even Hebrew could not be used in its classic form without any changes as a language for modern communication. First and foremost, the lexicon needed to be updated and expanded (see Alloni-Fainberg 1974; Fellman 1973; Kutscher 1982; Saulson 1979).

And related languages can serve as a source for missing vocabulary and syntax. If the only surviving documentation is a lexicon without any grammatical description, reclamation cannot proceed in the same manner. (Amery 2000 in fact does not consider this reclamation, since such a fundamental part of the language has been lost.) One alternative is to reconstruct some sort of grammatical structure based on the syntax of related languages. This is of course possible only if there are known related languages which have been documented. Another alternative is to use the local lexicon with the syntax of the language of wider communication. Neither solution is ideal, but there may be no other choices. Clearly, the language that is constructed following either of these methods will not be the language that was lost.

A critical aspect of language reclamation is having realistic expectations. Without native speakers to teach the language and to provide invaluable linguistic insight, one cannot possibly hope to reclaim the language in exactly the same form as it was spoken by the last generation of speakers. Second, language reclamation requires tremendous commitment and collaboration. In the case of Kaurna, the success of its revival cannot be based on whether it ever replaces English, or whether it becomes a language of daily communication. To the extent that it has become a language used in certain rituals and formal situations, the reclamation has already been successful. Thus when we speak of Kaurna as a remarkable success, we have in mind that the Kaurna community has moved from no knowledge and no use of the language to some limited but active use. Kaurna songs are very important in the community; it is the Songwriters Workshop held in 1990 that is seen as the beginning of Kaurna reclamation. The songs are used to introduce Kaurna to preschool and elementary children, and adults learn them readily. The number of Kaurna songs sung in public has increased dramatically, from just one in 1992 to twenty-five in 1997 (Amery 2000:189, 203). In addition to native Kaurna songs, popular mainstream nursery rhymes and songs ("Twinkle Twinkle Little Star," "Hickory Dickory Dock") have been translated from English into Kaurna. This is a decision which some communities will embrace and others reject. It involves transposing part of the culture of the colonizer onto the lost language, and so may cause concern, yet it has the advantage of taking something familiar and reworking it in a way to introduce the target language. But in general, the introduction of local songs to help introduce a domain for language use is a workable strategy. Songs are self-contained, they can be learned and memorized, they can be translated, and they are portable. The same text can be performed repeatedly. They can be used in a variety of settings and multiple parties can participate in their singing.

In addition to songs, Kaurna is used in public speeches. Beginning in 1991, community members started delivering what Amery calls "extended oral language delivery" (2000:185–8). These are primarily relatively short speeches, welcoming speeches, and introductions, used at a range of events, varying from larger public festivals to smaller and more closed events, with a total of fourteen such public speeches occurring in 1997, up from just one in 1991, and none prior to that. The total number of speeches may seem small, but it is important to keep in mind that they represent just one of many venues for the use of Kaurna. Another such venue, which at first may appear to be primarily symbolic, is the use of Kaurna names. As mentioned above, Kaurna place names represent the only continuous use of the language since colonization. By 1990, a number of place names were still in use, although some had been replaced (as seen on earlier maps). The last several decades have seen an increasing interest in using Kaurna names in the public sphere. In 1980, the naming of the Warriappendi Alternative School is cited as the first use of a Kaurna name in the modern period for a public institution. In 1991 the state government instituted a Dual Naming policy (Geographical Names Act, Section 8, Subsection 5), which allows local people to propose names in the local language to be used along with the names which already exist. Results are mixed. While there is a general trend toward using Kaurna names for Aboriginal organizations and for some educational institutions in Adelaide, at the same time some councils have rejected proposed names on the grounds that they are "too difficult to pronounce" (Amery 2000:182). Kaurna is now used on some signs, albeit in very limited places (such as the Kaurna Plains School or the Faculty of Aboriginal Islander Studies at the Underdale Campus of the University of South Australia), or on a postcard produced at the Kaurna Plains School.

At the same time, use of Kaurna at the conversational level is fairly minimal. People do use greetings, some expressions, kinship terms, and so on; these are all fixed phrases and do not require that the speakers have full knowledge of Kaurna in the creative and expansive sense of language use. In other words, to know and use a language entails creating and also interpreting new sentences and phrases that have not been used before; this is not currently happening in Kaurna conversation. Thus Kaurna has not become a language used in all domains and to hope that it would might seem unrealistic, although there are people in the community who do (Amery 2000:206–7). But the very practical expectation of reinstating the language in some key ways has proven attainable. One of the most striking things about the Kaurna reclamation program is the creative energy and effort that has gone into reconstructing the language, to make it usable as a modern spoken language, and into creating contexts for its usage.

8   Documentation as revitalization?

While it is inaccurate to consider documentation a model for language revival, we have included it here because many revitalization efforts begin, for the linguist at least, with language documentation. Linguists enter communities to document the languages spoken there; in fact, this is commonly seen to be the primary function of the field linguist (see Newman 2003). Significantly, in *The green book of language revitalization*, Leanne Hinton argues that "perhaps the most important thing to do when a language is down to a few speakers is to document the knowledge of those speakers as thoroughly as possible" (Hinton and Hale 2001:413). Given the critical role of documentation for future reclamation and revitalization efforts, it is important that fieldworkers collect a wide range of information, including pragmatic and paralinguistic, to give future generations an idea of how the local language was actually used.

Dictionaries, though often not a high priority for the field linguist, are an important part of language documentation; they can also play a role in local language learning, both in the classroom and outside of it (Corris et al. 2002; McKay 1983:58–9). Local language dictionaries are almost always bilingual, documenting the local language and defining it in terms of the language of wider communication (of the fieldworker or linguist). Such dictionaries have traditionally been compiled with the outsider in mind, the literate scholar for whom the linguistic data may be important. Yet, as we have seen in the preceding discussion of language reclamation (section 7), dictionaries are at times the only source of information about a lost language. They inevitably play a role in revitalization where literacy is an objective. Thus, in creating new dictionaries of local languages, it is critical to bear in mind the uses which they may come to serve.

4   Case studies

In effect, a language revitalization program is designed to change the social context in which people make choices about language use. Therefore, recognizing the particular set of variables, at both the macro-level and micro-level, that has led a language into an endangered state is pivotal in implementing a revitalization effort that has a chance of succeeding. The first three chapters each contributed to outlining a conceptual framework for understanding such variables. In order to illustrate how these variables come into play in revitalization programs, we present in this chapter four case studies. These particular cases have been chosen for a balance of geographic distribution, historical-political situation, speaker numbers and language density, type of revitalization program and the program's relative success.

First we discuss the case of Siberian native languages and the impact of the national level language policies of the Soviet Union and now of the Russian Federation. Beyond the impact of Russian, the national level language, this study also highlights the effects of multilingualism and heavy language contact at a more local level. In our analysis of Siberia we mention many different local languages, but the focus is on the Evenki language and its revitalization movement. Next we examine the Shuar language in Ecuador, which provides a very different view of language revitalization due to a different set of local and national level factors. Here the language of wider communication is Spanish; other local languages have played only a minor role, and the revitalization efforts emerged from an existing maintenance program. Of particular note in the Shuar case is the innovative use of radio broadcasts and the subordination of language maintenance/revitalization to other political goals. We then move to an examination of Mohawk revitalization in Canada, arguably one of the most successful language revitalization programs of the past forty years. Among other instructive features of this case, the Mohawk live in a country with two official state languages, French and English, which requires them to cope with multilingualism in a somewhat different way than the Shuar, for example. Finally we discuss the Hawaiian revitalization program, which was established on the language nest model of Māori in New Zealand. (see Chapter 3, section 2.1). The Hawaiian case differs from the other three in this chapter in that non-native speakers of the language were responsible for getting the program started and seeing it evolve. It also highlights the demands put on language revitalization efforts to confront legal and political obstacles.

1   Languages of the North: Siberian native languages and Soviet policy

We begin our case studies with a look at Siberia as an example of a region subjected to deliberate and careful language planning at the national level during the Soviet era.[1] Siberia is a region where a complex interplay of national, regional, and local factors have entered into language vitality and revitalization in an unusually clear way. The local languages of Siberia, for a number of additional reasons, present an interesting case study in the context of the present work. First, the development of local languages in Siberia initially came about as part of a mandate from the central government. In the early Soviet years, linguists were sent from Moscow and Leningrad with the directive of creating written forms for many of the local languages with the ultimate intent of full-immersion education programs in them, at least in theory. (This, of course, represents a very top-down approach to language planning and development and is in fact the opposite of the bottom-up, community-centric approach we have advocated for language revitalization.) This event, which was in full force in the 1920s, set the stage for language shift in the North, and any language or other indigenous movement today is to a very great extent a response to actions taken early in the Soviet era. In fact, it could be argued that the relatively passive approach to language revitalization generally found in Siberia stems from the lack of input local people have had, then and now, to the development (or destruction) of their languages and cultures.

Second, central to the Bolshevik campaign in the North was a component of what can loosely be called ethnic development, in the sense of the creation of a sense of ethnic identity where there had been none. Prior to this time, many of the different peoples of the North lacked ethnonyms and

---

[1] For more detailed discussions of Soviet language policy throughout its history, see Grenoble (2003b) and Lewis (1973), or Alpatov (1997) (in Russian). Kreindler (1985) includes articles which focus on the impact of Soviet policy in different regions of the USSR; Vakhtin (2001) concentrates on the languages of the North (in Russian).

saw themselves as more closely related to clans, or tribes, than to larger ethnicities, or "nationalities" in the Soviet sense of the term.

A third issue of interest is the ethnolinguistic map of Siberia. This vast territory is home to a number of local languages. Whether we can speak of high language density is another matter; the mere size of the region means that speakers may live in relative isolation of one another. Yet, prior to Soviet intervention, many of the local groups were still nomadic, and so came into occasional but sporadic contact with other groups, some speaking the same language, others speaking different languages. This meant that high levels of multilingualism developed among Siberian groups; even today one finds elders who speak three local languages, in addition to Russian (the language of wider communication), to varying degrees. We have argued elsewhere that as a result of the patterns of contact some of these languages, e.g. those of the Northwest branch of Tungusic, are better seen as part of a dialect continuum (Whaley et al. 1999) than as distinct languages, a point commonly made for the Turkic languages as well. This meant that at the time of Soviet "ethnic development" there were groups of people who did not have a strong sense of ethnolinguistic identity, were multilingual, and spoke one or more languages better described more as being part of a language/dialect continuum than discrete languages.

Added to this picture is the fact that there are significant differences in population size among the groups. The Soviet classification system, which bifurcated the newly defined ethnic groups into "large" people (i.e. populations of more than 40,000) and "small" people (less than 40,000) only exacerbated the differences. In addition to population size, there were other traits which distinguished various groups, including prestige and power, and the fact that the "large" languages had established written languages and, perhaps more critically, histories of formal education. In most cases, both literacy and education can be dated to the nineteenth century, and so in the Soviet sense these large languages were more "developed" than the small languages. At present there are approximately twenty-five (small) local languages spoken in Siberia, in addition to the national language, Russian, and several (large) languages which have well-developed written languages and official or semi-official status in their respective regions.[2] The two largest in this latter group are Buriat, a Mongolian language with some 318,000 speakers, and Yakut, a Turkic language with 363,000 speakers. Other languages with significant speaker

---

[2] Data for the local languages is taken from Neroznak (1994) and Vakhtin (2001); for Altai, Buriat, Tuvin, and Yakut, see Grenoble (2003b); and Grimes (2000). See also Kibrik (1991) for an overview of endangered languages in the USSR.

base and status are Tuvin (Turkic; 206,000 speakers) and Altai (Turkic; 71,600 speakers, including both Northern Altai or Teleut, and Southern Altai or Oirot).

Of the local languages, almost all are endangered to varying degrees, with Nenets the most vibrant, in large part because a major portion of the Nenets continue to maintain a traditional lifestyle. Unlike other Siberian languages, it has a relatively high fluency rate (77.1 percent in 1989) and approximately 20 percent of the population is monolingual (in Nenets). Fluent speakers are found across all generations and retention is very high. Dolgan is the other Siberian language which may not be disappearing; children continue to learn the language as a first tongue, and it enjoys special status as a regional lingua franca in the entire Taimyr region. Yet it is unclear how long this situation will continue, as the percentage of ethnic Dolgans who consider their first language to be Russian has grown to 35 percent, while 62.5 percent consider Dolgan their first language.

Dolgan and Nenets are, however, exceptions. Almost a century after the 1917 Declaration of Rights of the People of Russia proclaimed "the free development" of the national minorities and guaranteed native-tongue education, the overwhelming majority of the Siberian indigenous languages are disappearing or nearly extinct. The downfall of the Soviet government has brought increased freedom in education and in language use, yet these new freedoms are accompanied by increased economic hardship.

To see how past policies merge with the present situation, we focus on Evenki, the most populous of the Siberian Tungusic groups. The ethnic population is estimated at some 30,000, with Evenki living throughout much of Siberia. The largest portion – approximately 42.5 percent of the total Evenki population – lives in the Republic of Sakha. Another 12 percent live in the territory of the former Evenki Autonomous District, 13 percent in the Khabarovsk Territory, and the remaining 33 percent is scattered in the Regions of Amur, Chitin, Irkutsk, Sakhalin, and Tomsk (Bulatova et al. 1997:15). Thus the relatively small population is further divided by tremendous geographic distances. Language vitality and interest in language revitalization vary greatly from region to region. In general, the language is most vital at a local level only in those villages where Evenki live in relatively dense groups *and* have maintained a traditional lifestyle. Such villages have populations of about 200 or so. At a regional level, Evenki living in Sakha, for example, have shown a strong tendency to shift to either Yakut, the regional language, or Russian, the national language. A 1992 survey showed that only 16 percent of Evenki living in Sakha (about 600 people) still used Evenki. Of those aged 30–50 in the Aldan region, for example, some 50 percent claimed not to know Evenki at all; 30 percent claimed knowledge of individual words; and only 20 percent claimed passive comprehension (Myreeva 1993:72–3, cited in Vakhtin 2001:180–1).

The Evenki situation is representative of Siberian language attrition, and so informative about the region as a whole where national level variables, and increasingly extra-national ones, have such force that it is difficult to counteract their impact. In order to understand the obstacles that Evenki revitalization faces, it is important to understand what led to the decline in use of the Evenki language. The 1926 Soviet census shows a population of 37,545, with just under 64 percent claiming fluency in Evenki (a.k.a. Tungus) at this time.[3] Due in part to very high illiteracy rates in Siberia (nearing 100 percent for some groups), selected local languages were targeted for "development." This involved a monumental effort to document and describe the Siberian languages. In the first two decades of Soviet history, teams of linguists were sent, primarily from Leningrad, to undertake the work. This decision was made by the central government, without local consultation, which was, of course, characteristic of the Soviet government, but it meant that from the local perspective linguists simply arrived in communities uninvited and started working.

In January 1932, the issue of the development of alphabets and writing for the Siberian languages was considered at the first All-Russian Conference. At this point, preference was given to Roman-based alphabets, as opposed to Cyrillic, for a number of reasons, including that Cyrillic was seen as representing the tsarist, Russian regime. Soviet language policy makers set as one of their goals the creation of a single "Northern" alphabet for all languages of the North, resulting in the Roman-based Unified Northern Alphabet (*edinii severnii alfavit*), first adopted in November 1929, with further amendments and ratification in 1931. This single alphabet was created with the hope that it would simplify the literacy process and unite the speakers of Siberian languages, both with one another and with their counterparts living abroad (e.g. Saami in Finland and elsewhere, and the Aleuts in the United States, who were already using a Roman-based orthography). It is perhaps noteworthy that we support this kind of rationale for the development of writing systems (Chapter 6), but that in the Siberian case the decision was made without local consultation or input of any kind.

One of the languages targeted for development was Evenki. In 1931 a written language was established for Evenki using the Roman-based orthography on the basis of the Nepa dialect spoken in the Irkutsk region.

---

[3] These figures are somewhat unreliable, as there were a number of classification problems with the census. For example, Negidal were grouped together with Evenki, and Manegirs were treated separately, so these figures should be taken as ballpark estimates.

In the years 1936–7, the alphabet was changed to Cyrillic, with minor modifications of Russian Cyrillic; this was part of a general shift in policy which affected alphabets for almost all languages in the USSR. In 1952, the dialect basis of the standardized language was shifted to a slightly different variant, again a decision made by people external to Evenki communities, not by the Evenki themselves. In both cases, the dialects chosen were selected by virtue of being spoken in a geographically central area and for relative mutual intelligibility with other dialects. There is no published explanation for the shift, but the overall impact appears to have been negligible.

More important than minor changes in the standard language, however, was the fact that it had failed to become established as a norm which cut across dialects. In large part this has happened because Evenki literacy was never very successful. In the early Soviet era, during the major thrust for local literacy, those living a traditional lifestyle had no need to read and write Evenki. In addition, the geographic center of spoken Evenki began shifting away from the Baikal region, where language loss was far more pronounced than in Sakha and the Amur basin. Therefore, the literary norm is based on dialects which are no longer spoken.

The change from a Roman-based orthographic system to Cyrillic would certainly have had a major impact when it occurred. Clearly, use of Cyrillic facilitated acquisition of Russian literacy, although it would be an exaggeration to think that this alone caused language shift. At present, orthographic inconsistencies in the Cyrillic used for Evenki sounds not found in Russian make reading and writing challenging, in particular when taking into account that many of the literacy learners are in fact second-language speakers. There is a striking mismatch between some of the published pedagogical materials, such as textbooks (e.g. Bulatova 1992; Bulatova et al. 1989), the standard school bilingual dictionary (Kolesnikova 1989), and an alphabet practice book (Maksimova 1995) on the one hand, and published Evenki prose and poetry (e.g. Keptuke 1991; Oegir 1987) on the other.[4] Particular difficulties arise in the different ways of writing two different sounds, the velar nasal and a pharyngeal fricative, as well as in the marking of vowel length. Vowel length is phonemic; when it is marked orthographically, it appears either with a macron or, less frequently, with a doubling of the vowel letter. More often, it is not marked. Such inconsistencies can be readily tolerated by fluent speakers, but for second-language learners they are problematic.

---

[4] Often such decisions were based on the availability (or lack) of certain characters at the press. The more widespread use of computers and camera-ready copy may alleviate this problem, or it may lead to an even greater proliferation of fonts.

Despite these difficulties, orthography is not really the central cause of the lack of Evenki literacy (see Grenoble and Whaley 2003). It is, rather, symptomatic of the failure of Evenki literacy to be established as a viable, living practice. One problem already noted has been the failure to create a standard variety that is intelligible and acceptable to the speakers who might use it. Even more critical is the failure to create a context for the use of written Evenki. Instead, it has remained an artificial construct, taught in the schools to a limited degree. The language of writing is Russian.

One ongoing contradiction which mitigates against the use of Evenki is the nature of language instruction in schools. In theory Evenki is taught in all village schools, though in areas where the language has largely been lost language instruction is often perfunctory and awarded little time in the curriculum. Furthermore, teaching methods have not been adapted to the shift in the knowledge of the language, where children must now learn Evenki as a second language. In such schools the teachers themselves may not be proficient in Evenki; Evenki "language" classes in some regions are conducted entirely in Russian.

In areas where Evenki thrives, the situation is different. The school population consists roughly of three groups of children: those children who use little or no Evenki in the home; those children who speak Evenki in the home and live in the village; and those children whose families continue to live with the herds. Children in this last group are raised with Evenki as their first language and may have had little contact with Russian (or Buriat or Yakut) before entering the school system. When they reach the age for formal schooling, their parents face two options. One is to place the children in boarding schools,[5] and the other is for the parents, or often just the mothers, to move to the village to live with the children during the school year. Because the schools are Russian-language-based, these children tend to do poorly academically, at least until they have learned enough Russian to get by. A few regions have experimented with home schooling, or "taiga schools." Children are placed in boarding schools for the first few grades and are then allowed to return to the herds, where their parents educate them. Teachers visit the herds periodically to check up on the progress of the children and to work with children and parents more directly. One such school is centered in the village of Ust'-Nyukzha. Despite initial successes, the school has had

---

[5] The boarding school system is a carry-over from the Soviet push to educate the native Siberian population. As in the United States, the boarding schools were prime facilities for language loss. Children of different ethnic groups and different languages were frequently placed in boarding schools together, in such a way that Russian was the only possible lingua franca amongst them.

difficulties maintaining the taiga school system due to a lack of financial resources, which has made it impossible for teachers to travel to the herds. Where language revitalization is taking place in Siberia, it is often dependent upon the commitment of individual community members. In the village of Iengra (Sakha), for example, key leaders in the community are working to reinvigorate the language curriculum in the local school and day care, and have written their own pamphlet with Evenki phrases. The success of these programs depends on the energy of a few critical activists in the community.

Such efforts are often hampered by confusion of the roles of the federal government, the regional government, and the local community. This situation itself is a legacy of the Soviet era, when the federal government exercised control over every aspect of life. In fact, language rights are made explicit in the country's constitution, and the ongoing roles of federal and regional governments are dictated by law. Article 68, section 1 of the Constitution of the Russian Federation makes Russian the official state language of the Federation and all of its territory. Each republic has the right to instate its own official language, to be used alongside Russian in administrative and state business (Article 68, section 2). Section 3 states that "The Russian Federation guarantees all its peoples the right to the preservation of [their] native language, [and to] the creation of conditions for its study and development" (*Konstitutsiia Rossiiskoi Federatsii*, ratified 12 December 1993). The education law of the Russian Federation gives citizens the right to native-tongue education, and to the right of choice of language of education "as feasible" (Article 6, section 2). Moreover, it mandates that the federal state bear some responsibility for training specialists in those languages of the Federation which do not have their own government (Article 6, section 7). While this division of responsibilities may appear clear on paper, in reality it is murky. Consider the Republic of Sakha, where the largest concentration of Evenki currently live (42.5 percent of the total population). As part of the Russian Federation, residents are obligated to know the national language (Russian). Technically the Republic has authority over education in its own regional language, Yakut (also called Sakha). This leaves the education of Evenki, in Evenki, to the local communities for children, in day-care centers and in the schools. The federal government technically oversees programs in higher education aimed at training teachers and other professionals, such as at the Gertsen Pedagogical Institute in St. Petersburg, but provides little oversight and few resources.

One more telling piece of information comes from the realm of higher education. Relatively early in the Soviet period, Leningrad became established as the center for the education and training of peoples of the

North.[6] The decision to locate the center of Siberian studies outside of Siberia, in the European part of Russia, though not surprising in the context of the highly centralized Soviet governmental system, was indicative of the schizophrenic nature of language policy during that era. Remnants of the system remain with the Institute of Peoples of the North,[7] a part of the Gertsen Institute. However, the mission of the Institute has shifted significantly over the last few years, and the numbers of Northern students interested in receiving training in their own languages has been in decline.

The course of study lasts five years. Students from all over Siberia are eligible to attend. In the academic year 2003–4, the total enrollment was 331, representing 30 different ethnic groups.[8] Of these, two groups are not indigenous to Siberia (one German student and one Ukrainian), and two of the other ethnic groups (Buriat and Yakut) represent "large" minority groups within Siberia. Their languages have official status within the Republic of Buriatia and of Sakha, respectively. Of these 331 students, only 11 are specializing in their native language and literature, as opposed to 77 who are specializing in Russian language and literature. Moreover, teachers at the Institute report a noticeable shift in the language abilities of their students. Whereas entering students were formerly fluent in the local languages, now only the Nenets students matriculate with a strong knowledge of their language. With rare exceptions, other students need to learn the language while enrolled at the Institute, and accordingly graduate with less than full fluency. The combination of a general lack of interest in specializing in the local languages, along with relatively low knowledge of them, reflects the rate at which they are disappearing.

The Siberian languages have inherited the effects of nearly a century of centralized language planning that, at best, superficially recognized their needs and, at its worst, was deliberately hostile toward them. The result is that Russian has become the dominant language throughout Siberia; local languages thrive only in isolated villages and among people living a more traditional lifestyle. In some areas, the pressures to master a regional language (e.g. Buriat or Yakut) are enormous and, in cases of

---

[6] For the history of the development of Northern studies in Leningrad, see Forsyth (1992) and Slezkine (1994).

[7] The Faculty of Peoples of the North (*Fakultet narodov Severa*) was renamed in 2002 as the Institute of Peoples of the North.

[8] The different groups and exact numbers of students are as follows: Nenets (44); Khanty (31); Even (33); Evenki (28); Yakut (28); Mansi (18); Nanai (18); Chukchi (17); Dolgan (17); Veps (16); Koryak (4); Gilyak, also known as Nivkh, (7); Saami (20); Selkup (10); Buriat (8);Yukaghir (5); Itel'men (4); Ket (3); Udege (3); Nganasan (2); Oroch (2); Soyot (2); Orok (1); Ulch (4); Chuvanets (1); Komi (1); Tuvin (1); Udmurt (1); as well as German (1) and Ukrainian (1).

intermarriage, the local language (such as Evenki) virtually always gives way to the regional or national language. In addition, young people in particular are interested in learning an international access language (English), for all the reasons outlined in Chapter 2. The watchgroup for Siberian local communities, the Association of Native Peoples of the North, has a largely symbolic role with some limited funding for language and cultural projects, but does not have the resources to play a significant role in language revitalization and does not have much influence over the federal government. Thus the language pressures on local populations, which largely stem from external policies and attitudes, make it difficult to create the kind of community-wide enthusiasm and commitment needed for language revitalization. These factors, coupled with extremely limited resources and a lack of federal or regional support, make the long-term prospects for revitalization programs in Siberia quite slim.

2   Shuar (South America)

Only twelve of the thirty indigenous languages spoken in Ecuador at the time of conquest are spoken today (Klein and Stark 1985). Among these twelve is Shuar, a Jivaroan language. The Shuar minority in Ecuador provides one example of the complex link between language maintenance and revitalization on the one hand, and political organization and activism on the other. Their efforts to protect the land that they occupy, to control the education of their children, to lobby for minority rights in Ecuador and to preserve their cultural distinctiveness have been effective enough to earn the Shuar a reputation as a model for other ethnic minorities around the world, including as a model for language preservation. For example, Calvet (1998:152) writes: "[The Shuar success] shows us that the language empires that are slowly being established across the world, whether they speak French, English, Russian, or Spanish are not an inevitable misfortune and that it is possible to fight for a space for difference in a universe tending towards uniformity."

The bulk of the Shuar population, currently estimated to be anywhere between 30,000 and 100,000 people, remained relatively isolated from Spanish speakers well into the twentieth century due to their geographic remoteness in *El Oriente* – that is, the rainforest region east of the Andes mountains in Ecuador (see Harner 1984 for a helpful overview of the history of Shuar people). The Shuar famously resisted Spanish attempts to tax them and use them as laborers in goldmines during the sixteenth century, and the Spanish only managed to establish one permanent settlement of whites – the town of Macas. Efforts to found Catholic missions in Shuar-speaking areas failed repeatedly until the 1920s.

Eventually, the gold deposits, rubber, and land of *El Oriente* attracted miners and farmers from the Ecuadorian highlands, and in their wake came improved transportation routes and a greater flow of migrants into the region. In patterns typical of colonization, epidemics decimated the Shuar population as new diseases arrived with the settlers, and conflicts over land use arose as farms were cut out of portions of the rainforest that the Shuar used for hunting. Ironically, the Shuar, who had strongly resisted Christianization for three centuries, now took an active interest in the Christian missions, which provided them with some measure of protection against the loss of their land and furnished them with better access to trade goods (Rubenstein 1995).

In 1958 the Federación Independiente del Pueblo Shuar del Ecuador (FIPSE) was created in the town of Macuma with considerable assistance from the Gospel Missionary Union, an evangelical Christian organization. Initially, the purpose of FIPSE was to obtain land rights for the Shuar, though over time the role of FIPSE expanded to developing an educational system, providing improved health, and exploring economic opportunities for Shuar families. A second federation, FISCH (Federación Interprovincial de los Centros Shuar), was established in 1964 completely independent of FIPSE. Under the supervision of Salesian missionaries, FISCH also was formed for "the social, economic and moral improvement of its members, and as a coordinating institution for colonization projects undertaken by the government" (Federación de Centros Shuar 1974:3, cited in Salazar 1977:26). The growth in the number of members and the influence of FISCH has greatly eclipsed FIPSE over time (over 80 percent of Shuar families belong to FISCH), though both organizations still exist, as does a third organization, OSHE (Organización Shuar del Ecuador), which was formed in 1985.

Considering the fact that individual Shuar households traditionally were not bonded together by any formal political structure, and large distances were intentionally placed between houses, it was no small task to bring Shuar families into associations such as FIPSE and FISCH. To help overcome these difficulties, the federations created strongly hierarchical organizations. For example, FISCH created local units called Centers (in 2001 there were 490 such units), which group together Shuar families in a particular region and are run by a council elected from among its members. A group of Centers together form an Association (there were thirty-five in 2001), each of which is run by a local president. There is an annual General Assembly that elects a Federation President and Board of Directors for FISCH. While local issues are dealt with at the level of the Center or Association, most of FISCH's business falls under the purview of the President and Board of Directors, who are stationed in FISCH's headquarters in Sucúa. The introduction of this non-traditional structure into Shuar society has not been without its critics: in interviews carried out with the leaders of FISCH, FIPSE, and OSHE in 2001, they estimated that 10–15 percent of Shuar currently choose not to affiliate with any of the organizations. Yet there is no doubt that the hierarchical organization has provided the legitimacy and political muscle necessary to negotiate with the government of Ecuador over the past fifty years. And there is no doubt that, as a result, FISCH has played an instrumental role in giving voice to Shuar concerns at a national level.

Another significant decision made by Shuar federations and their missionary patrons was to employ radio as a means of communication and a means of education. Given the highly dispersed settlement of Shuar families and the poor infrastructure in *El Oriente*, radio was recognized to be the only feasible means for the federations to communicate with their members over long distances. Already in the late 1960s, the Shuar established a radio broadcasting station that aired programs in both Spanish and the Shuar language. Though it is not clear that in the original conception the use of Shuar on the radio was intended to promote the use of the language, this became a explicit goal soon thereafter.

In 1968, this initial effort to promote knowledge of the Shuar language was supplemented by the foundation of bilingual schools using the radio to transmit lessons. The development of these schools was based on a set of principles which included a commitment to teaching Shuar culture along with the language (similar to the Mohawk case described in section 3), the idea that any language can be adapted to deal with modernity, and the conviction that Shuar should not compete with Spanish as a unique language option for Shuar individuals.

Prior to the formation of the radio schools, the only option for most Shuar children to attend school was to go to one of the dozen or so mission schools, which tended to be many days' walk away from Shuar homes (Macdonald 1986:18). The language of instruction in these boarding schools was Spanish, and the curriculum contained little content drawn from Shuar culture. Consequently, children who went away to school often found themselves caught between two cultures. Spending so much time away from their homes meant that they did not adequately learn Shuar history from elders, nor did they attend to traditional activities such as hunting and fishing, all of which caused difficulties when they tried to reintegrate into Shuar communities. At the same time, even with a typical Ecuadorian education, the Shuar students who attended boarding schools did not find an abundance of opportunities awaiting them in non-Shuar areas.

Education through the media of radio was seen by the federations as a way to provide schooling to a greater number of Shuar children without requiring them to leave their communities. FISCH's program, the Shuar Bicultural Radio Education System (SERBISH), achieved official recognition from the Ecuadorian government in 1972, at which time it broadcast to thirty-three schools. The SERBISH schools were originally small huts, built to be the schools for some of the Centers affiliated with FISCH. Students connected to a particular Center would come to the school for several hours, Monday through Friday. Over time, the bilingual education was expanded to cover all levels of primary education, and Spanish-only instruction was provided for the first three years of secondary education. FISCH (and other federations) also dedicated funds to send promising students to high schools to complete their secondary education and, in some cases, to go on for degrees in higher education.

SERBISH developed rapidly in both size and sophistication. By 1980, there were over 150 schools, and by 2000 the number had approached almost 300 schools serving approximately 7,500 students. Many of the huts were replaced with more substantial buildings and, in the course of this expansion, the Shuar also developed a two-tier system of teachers. A so-called *teleauxiliary* was placed at each of the schools to assist the children in their radio lessons, as well as to work with students from one grade level when the broadcast was geared towards students of a different level. When possible, the teleauxiliaries were recruited from the Center where the school was located, though this was often not possible. In such cases the teacher would be brought in from outside. Those Shuar with higher levels of education served as *telemaestros*. Their duties included training the teleauxiliaries, traveling to the schools on occasion to provide oversight to the education going on there, and to prepare the textbooks that were used in the schools (Macdonald 1986).

In the period during which SERBISH was evolving, it became gradually evident to Shuar leaders that a greater percentage of Shuar were primarily speaking Spanish and that there was a general erosion in the knowledge of cultural traditions and practices. As a result, it became an overt goal to promote the use of the Shuar language and to incorporate a greater focus on Shuar culture into the school curriculum including folklore, local plant and animal life, songs and traditional crafts. The inclusion of such material, however, did not entail a decrease in the time spent on literacy, math, basic science, and Spanish, since SERBISH was conceived on the principle that the Shuar need to be able to negotiate Ecuadorian culture successfully as a matter of political, economic, and social survival. Therefore, class time was extended to five and a half hours per day, and adult literacy programs were added.

By the year 2000, SERBISH had a proven track record in educating Shuar people. Before the onset of radio education, only about 40 percent of Shuar children attended school, and only 28 percent completed a primary level of education (Macdonald 1986:19). The latter number jumped to 80 percent with nearly all of the primary graduates going on to the secondary level. Illiteracy has dropped to about 5 percent of the population. Significantly, the problem of cultural dislocation created by the boarding school system has been eliminated; there is now a generation of Shuar who are equipped to interact with non-Shuar in the economic and social sphere, to protect their land rights (the more recent threat has come from large oil companies), and to lobby for national policies that are favorable to their unique situation. Indeed the government of Ecuador adopted SERBISH as "a model for other bilingual and bicultural programs in the eastern part of the country" (Davis and Partridge 1994:39).

A new chapter in the Shuar efforts towards bilingualism and biculturalism is now being written. Though the educational accomplishments of SERBISH have been obvious, the program was plagued by two ubiquitous problems. First, the level of education and training for the teleauxiliaries was highly variable among schools, and in many locations these "assistant teachers" simply were not qualified. This meant that the students were not always receiving adequate instruction. Second, due to the medium of instruction, with the telemaestros teaching via radio broadcasts, the SERBISH system could not accommodate variation in the speed at which children learned material, different learning styles, and localized problems such as bad weather, a crisis in the community, or the sickness of a teleauxiliary. This, combined with the fact that teleauxiliaries only had minimal training, led to a situation where the education techniques being employed with the students at the schools were not as effective as they could have been. For example, Spanish was taught using a direct translation method in which a Shuar word (or phrase) would be given followed by its Spanish equivalent. The students would repeat the Spanish version and then move on to the next word.

Therefore, with considerable pressure from the Ecuadorian Ministry of Education, SERBISH was closed in 2001, and the radio schools were replaced with more typical face-to-face instruction. According to Pablo Tsere (p.c. 15 March 2002), the President of FISCH in 2002, teachers are given formal training in education in one of three locations (in the cities of Macas, Pugu, and Sucúa) and then sent to one of 200 or so schools. These schools are held in the same buildings that had been utilized by SERBISH, and the curricula developed by SERBISH are still employed.

The newly implemented system is seen to have several advantages (Raphael Vega, former health director for FISCH, p.c. 16 March 2002).

First, the quality of instruction has improved, with over 60 percent of the teachers being certified to teach and all teachers having achieved at least a secondary school education. Second, there is much greater flexibility in decision making for individual teachers as they confront the challenges unique to their situation and students. Third, bilingual education has now been extended into the secondary grades as the number of qualified bilingual teachers has increased. (Note, however, that in the current approach this means that the material is taught in both Spanish and Shuar, which is not only cumbersome but also does not ensure that an individual student actually knows both Shuar and Spanish.) Significantly, these improvements have come without losing some of the original benefits of the SERBISH system: Shuar input into the curriculum, schools that are relatively close to Shuar homes, local control over schools, and the ability to communicate with FISCH (and other federations) through the established organizational hierarchy.

Not surprisingly, the new system has also introduced its own set of challenges. Teacher certification and the improvement of teacher training has necessarily brought the Ministry of Education of Ecuador more directly into the picture. Increasingly, materials introduced into the school curricula come from the Ministry of Education, which has the funds to pay the teachers. The Ministry of Education also must approve all the materials used in teaching. At this point, the relationship between the Shuar federations and the Ministry of Education appears to have been highly cooperative, but the more intricate connection also decreases the ability of the Shuar to make their own independent decisions about education. Another problem is that, as in the past, the teachers who are sent out to relatively remote regions are not always keen to be there, so teacher absenteeism is a perpetual problem. And in some locations, teachers, who are not always truly bilingual, scuttle the use of Shuar and teach primarily in Spanish.

As with any change in a community, the act of dropping SERBISH in favor of the newer approach to bilingual education has provoked the gamut of reactions from strong support, to cautious optimism, to skepticism, to outspoken dislike. These reactions, however, are intensified because it is evident to many Shuar, particularly those living in close proximity to monolingual Spanish speakers, that the use of Shuar is in decline. And in some areas (most notably Zamora Chinchipe), there has been an overt switch from thinking about maintaining the Shuar language to recognizing the need to revitalize it. Though accurate assessments of Shuar fluency are even less likely to emerge than population statistics (recall that these vary by the tens of thousands), anecdotal information abounds about children having great trouble understanding the language and families moving increasingly to Spanish in the home. These accounts stem primarily from Zamora, where contact with Spanish has been more extensive, but portend the future of Shuar elsewhere.

For this reason, the fate of SERBISH has become symbolic of differing attitudes about the role of the Shuar language in the lives of Shuar people. As became clear in our interviews with Shuar individuals, many believe that the termination of SERBISH represents a tip toward Spanish that will doom the language, and they feel that the radio schools should be reinstated to help "recover" and "rescue" the language. Others much prefer the newer system, though believe a different approach to bilingualism should be pursued in which Shuar is taught as a formal subject in schools where Spanish is the medium of instruction. For example, Juaquin Najandey (p.c. 18 March 2002), president of FIPSE, argues that although "we, being Shuar, must value the language," the Shuar are placed at a disadvantage in Ecuador by not having more education in Spanish. Along with many parents, he promotes the idea that school be primarily a "Spanish space", while other cultural spheres (home, church, traditional religious practices, local subsistence activities, etc.) be "Shuar spaces." To this end, FIPSE was working on a campaign for "All Shuar to speak Shuar" when we interviewed President Najandey in 2002. Finally, many people are content that Shuar is fully vital, evidence to the contrary notwithstanding, and see little need for Shuar to be used in the schools at all. A move to education in Spanish is welcomed because "the best education is Hispanic" (Marco Najamtai, OSHE official, p.c. 18 March 2002).

As has been discussed here, efforts to sustain and bolster use of the Shuar language of Ecuador can be traced back to the early 1960s, which proffers an historical perspective of four decades, far longer than is available for most language maintenance or revitalization programs. Their case is worth examining for this reason alone, but other aspects of the situation make the case particularly instructive. First, the use of technology was instrumental in meeting the challenge that Shuar communities were, and are, widely dispersed throughout the Ecuadorian rainforest, often living in areas inaccessible by car or train. In order to accomplish the remarkable feat of linking these communities together via the airwaves, two basic obstacles had to be overcome – the need for organization and the need for financial and technical resources. For historical and political reasons, the Shuar did not look to the government of Ecuador for assistance in overcoming these obstacles, and in this way, they serve as a potential model for minority groups looking towards revitalization of a local language without the aide of a national government. Rather the Shuar first turned to the missionaries working in the region, and through their consultation and support were able to develop the organizational structure of the federations and to implement their radio programs. For example, the Salesian missionaries paid for two members of the Shuar community to receive radio training and helped them to garner support from UNESCO, as well as charitable organizations in Europe, to set up a radio station (Calvet 1998:147).

Despite the fact that the Shuar relationship with missions agencies and NGOs has been mostly amicable, the connection with outside groups has had continuing ramifications for the Shuar, not the least of which was the fact that hierarchical social structures such as the federations and technology like radio were breaks with traditional cultural patterns. Breaks were made with tradition that were deemed to be necessary for survival. Once introduced, the federations became increasingly significant institutions and are very much part of modern Shuar identity. These institutions are connected to power and privilege, and at times they become focal points for tensions among the Shuar. For example, FIPSE and FISCH originated under the patronage of Protestant and Roman Catholic missionaries respectively, a division which continues to hold today (this despite the fact that many associated with the federations are only nominally Christian). OSHE, for its part, was originally a splinter group from FISCH, making its break over the belief that FISCH was being poorly run and primarily benefiting the small privileged group that was in power. More often than not, these three federations work cooperatively, but each promotes a slightly different vision for the Shuar people, and they cannot help but compete when it comes to attracting members and securing grants from funding agencies.

A second noteworthy feature of the Shuar case is that their efforts at language maintenance/revival have always been interlaced with, and subsidiary to, political activism over certain other rights: land titles, economic self-sufficiency, control over education, and, most recently, protection from land-grabs by oil companies. Shuar political activism has been laced with a heavy dose of realism, and their working assumption has been that they need to be able to access and engage the Spanish-speaking culture that is slowly encroaching into their homelands. This often creates a pull in two different directions when it comes to decisions about the promotion of the Shuar language, in particular about how it will be used in the schools. While in the short run the radio school system effectively protected the use of Shuar language and culture since children did not have to leave their homes to receive a formal education, in the longer run SERBISH created the infrastructure for a rapid spread of teaching exclusively in Spanish. Whether this will eventually happen under the current system remains to be seen, though it is the clear trajectory. Moreover, an argument could be made that the type of bilingual training provided by SERBISH helped perpetuate the attitude that Spanish is the language of modernity and progress, relegating Shuar to traditional activities and discourse realms, just the areas of Shuar life which are currently coming under increasing assimilatory pressures. Already in the early 1980s one observer noted, "for the most part the Shuar today are an acculturated people" (Bottasso 1983:22), which does not bode well for the Shuar language to the degree that it is associated with uniquely Shuar activities.

One final observation should be made regarding the Shuar situation. Their various successes in fighting to maintain an identity distinct from greater Ecuadorian culture, including the formation of SERBISH, was almost certainly possible because of the low ethnic diversity in the region where they live. Only one other minority, the closely related Achuar, inhabited *El Oriente* at the time of conquest. This fact has allowed the Shuar to mount their efforts for measures of autonomy without competing voices in the same region of Ecuador. Despite a relatively small population relative to Ecuador as a whole (and relative to many other Ecuadorian minorities), the Shuar still dominate most portions of *El Oriente*, which makes it easier to lay claim to it being *their* region of the country, to attract missionary attention in the area exclusively to *their* issues and so on.

3   The Mohawk Immersion Program in Kahnawà:ke (Canada)

The Mohawk immersion school in Kahnawà:ke is a relatively long-standing full-immersion program, established over twenty years ago in Québec, Canada. It is also considered to be one of the more successful attempts at renewing local language use. Though there is much to be learned from the experiences surrounding the development of the school, we highlight here three items in particular. First, the achievements of the program have depended heavily upon individuals with the persistence to develop community commitment and participation. Second, this process has involved navigating between different attitudes about the school coming from within the community. Finally, prior to the institution of this program, Mohawk was an unwritten language, and so this program has faced many of the codification issues which are inherent in establishing a standard language.

Before 1970, there was no Mohawk language instruction in the Mohawk school system of Kahnawà:ke, Canada. The impetus for creating the language immersion program came as the result of two separate factors. First of all, data made available by Statistics Canada showed a 76 percent decrease in the number of Mohawk speakers since 1959 (cited in Blanchard 2003). The Mohawk community had been relatively complacent about language vitality, not realizing that they were already in a state of accelerated language loss. The statistic spurred people to action. With the beginning of the 1970 academic year, Mohawk language instruction was introduced into the regional schools for fifteen minutes each day, increasing to thirty minutes per day over the next couple of years. Three community members served as the language teachers, receiving a small salary through a grant from the Federal Department of Cultural Affairs. Although they had no formal training and no pedagogical materials, they were dedicated and committed to the idea "that this was something that had to be done" (Jacobs 1998:117). This initial program laid the foundation for the Kahnawà:ke Survival School, which was to open several years later, in direct response to other political events.

The second major event came with the passing of Québec's Language Law Bill 101. When the Parti Québecois came to power in 1976, the party leader René Levesque began negotiating for the separation of Québec from the rest of Canada. Part of this negotiation involved Bill 101: The Charter of the French Language. Although Bill 101 may have been intended to enhance the revival of French in Canada and the Québec separatist movement, it had a major impact on indigenous people because it made French the sole official language of Québec, thus severely restricting services and education in languages other than French. Moreover, it limited access to English-language schools to indigenous children, though many of these children's parents had attended English-language schools.

Bill 101 is a prime example of a policy constructed with one specific goal (in this case the revitalization of French in Québec), which had unanticipated repercussions in local communities. Perhaps needless to say, the Mohawk correctly interpreted the legislation as ignoring their specific rights and needs. One of their complaints was that Bill 101 treated them as immigrants on their own land. In this Bill 101 was a direct violation of the Two Row Wampum Treaty, ratified in the 1600s, which guaranteed Iroquois authority over Iroquois lands so that the Mohawk viewed Bill 101 as directly undermining their sovereignty. The Mohawk stance is very clearly articulated on the website for the Kahnawà:ke Survival School:

Bill 101 Violated The Two Row Wampum Treaty. Bill 101 was a direct violation of the Two Row Wampum Treaty. It attacks the sovereignty of the Mohawk people. The Mohawk people felt that if they signed the application for a license for an English education, they would be recognizing the right of the provincial government to legislate culture and education for native peoples. This was unacceptable to the people. (http://www.schoolnet.ca/aboriginal/survive/history-e.html)

As is clear from this excerpt, the response from the Mohawk community was unequivocal, and they issued strong objections, in principle, to the law on the grounds that it gave the Québec government the right to legislate the culture and education of the Mohawk people. This came at a time when the community was already engaged in a battle with the government to regain what it had lost in terms of respect, land, legal rights, and cultural sovereignty. The establishment of the Kahnawà:ke Survival School was a response to Bill 101, which had the unintended effect of uniting parents, students, educators, and other community members against the Quebecois government. Thus perhaps ironically, legislation aimed at strengthening French led to a revitalization of Mohawk, albeit at a high cost.

Under these circumstances the Kahnawà:ke Survival School, the first native-controlled school in Kahnawà:ke, opened in September 1978[9] as an English-language high school. The name was chosen to symbolize the belief that the people of Kahnawà:ke needed to establish their own secondary school, under their own control, so as to survive as a people. After its first few years of operation, it was moved outside of the town to a site on the eastern boundary of Kahnawà:ke, i.e. Kanatakwenke, a location settled by the Mohawks (Kahnawakeronon) in 1696 and so of great historical and symbolic significance. The program has grown gradually and incrementally. The high school is dedicated to the study of native culture and history alongside the more traditional curriculum supported by the Québec Ministry of Education. The school complex, in addition to athletics facilities, arts, and carpentry studios, includes a Mohawk Language Center and a teacher resource center.

In conjunction with the survival school movement, a language immersion program was being developed for the younger children. In September 1979, a pilot project was begun at the nursery school, using a total-immersion approach. Children graduating from this class went on to a partial-immersion kindergarten and then a partial-immersion first grade. As this lead class graduated from grade to grade, a partial-immersion program developed along with them, through the fourth grade. Then in September 1984, a total-immersion program was developed in the pre-school, kindergarten, and first grade. This was gradually extended to encompass the third grade, and then partial immersion was added in the fourth through sixth grades. English instruction is introduced in these latter grades for half of the school day, and French is also introduced. The program was revised in 1994 to include full-day, total immersion in the kindergarten through fourth grades, while the partial-immersion programs of the fifth and sixth grades were revised to be maintenance programs. Since then, the program has expanded with the inclusion of a middle school (grades 7 and 8) and what is called a senior school, grades 9 and higher, which includes Mohawk (and French) language classes in its regular curriculum.

---

[9] Hoover (1992:270–1) states that the school opened in 1979; the school's website at http://www.schoolnet.ca/aboriginal/survive/index-e.html gives the date as September 1978.

Developing pedagogical materials and teacher training were critical to the success of the program; the lack of appropriate classroom materials is cited as "one of the biggest challenges" facing the development of the school (Jacobs 1998:120). These materials have been created gradually over time. When the teaching of Mohawk was first instituted in Kahnawà:ke in 1970, it was made possible thanks to untrained community members whose knowledge of the language and commitment to teaching made the program viable. The school administrators immediately saw the need to create an orthography and standardized language because, as the school's principal has described it, every teacher was writing idiosyncrati- cally, using a system developed by the Jesuits in the eighteenth century (Jacobs 1998:118). And so in 1973, a linguist, Marianne Mithun, working with five student teachers, developed a standardized orthography for Mohawk. Close collaboration with a linguist who knows the language and is sensitive to community concerns was critical to the success of this project. This collaboration has resulted in a linguistically sound grammar workbook which has become a source for teachers. This descriptive gram- mar was first published in 1976 in the form of a "workbook," and has subsequently been published in revised editions at the Kanien'kéha Cultural Center (Deering and Delisle 1995).

A grammar workbook (*She:kon Wa:ri*) was produced as a summer project in 1972 by a group of linguistics students working with com- munity members. Several years later, in 1976, a different summer project resulted in the creation of primers, charts, games, and so on, created through a collaboration of university students under the direc- tion of one of the Mohawk teachers, Karihwénhawe Dorothy Lazore. But the creation of pedagogical materials went hand-in-hand with the development of the program for a number of years. For example, when what had been the initial preschool immersion class (i.e. the class which had entered the program in September 1979) reached what was then a partial-immersion first-grade class, the teachers quickly developed classroom materials, and so on in the second through fourth grades. Initially the materials were directly translated from English texts and workbooks, and so they were awkward in the Mohawk setting. Then, in 1983, a permanent curriculum office was created with a staff of seven, including a coordinator, an artist, an editor, and two production people. Crucially, the staff included two writers/translators who were also resident elders. The school has two major goals, as defined on its website:

(1) To promote and preserve Kanien'kéha language, culture, values and history.
(2) To develop the academic and technical skills needed to live and work in today's world. (http://www.schoolnet.ca/aboriginal/survive/index-e.html)

These goals were first developed on the basis of two separate studies published in the 1970s. These are the National Indian Brotherhood's *Feasibility study on Indian control of Indian education* (1973) and the *Kahnawà:ke feasibility study of local control of education* (Beauvais and Deer 1976), which was commissioned by the Kahnawà:ke Combined Schools Committee. The goals are reinforced in a study by the Assembly of First Nations published in 1988 (*Tradition and Education: Towards a Vision of the Future*), which stated that "(1) education should prepare children to gain the necessary skills for successful living and to contribute to community and (2) education should reinforce the student's cultural identity." This emphasis on cultural education, an approach that informs students about their ethnic heritage and is consistent with its traditions and customs, is a very strong component of the Kahnawà:ke school system and may well be one of the factors which has contributed to its great success. The curriculum includes traditional skills and knowledge (such as drumming, dancing, singing) and a Student Council whose structure mirrors that of traditional governance systems, such as the longhouse, and so on. At the same time, the academic skills taught are within the standards established by the Québec Ministry of Education.

The program is voluntary and parents may opt to enroll their children either in the Mohawk immersion school or in an English-based school. Initially only a small percentage of parents determined to send their children to the native school, but this has changed over time. Enrollment as of 1998 was roughly half in one and half in the other; a lack of qualified Mohawk teachers has limited enrollment in the immersion school, keeping the enrollment lower than demand (Hoover 1992; Jacobs 1998). Demand is in part high because the Kahnawà:ke group has been one of the most successful at creating a comprehensive program in terms of curricular and cultural development, such that it reaches throughout the community.

One unforeseen result of the program's success is the creation of a middle generation, the parent generation, which does not speak Mohawk. Thus "it is not uncommon in Kahnawà:ke to hear people conversing with their grandchildren in Mohawk, then switching to English to speak to their own children" (Hoover 1992:271). That said, even non-fluent speakers of Mohawk are now reported to use Mohawk greetings and phrases in what are otherwise English conversations.

Evaluation of the program was conducted in 1990 through a survey of the community (Hoover 1992). Students from the Survival School distributed a questionnaire to every household in Kahnawà:ke in the summer of 1990 in an effort to determine the impact of the Mohawk immersion program. One clear conclusion by the survey is a generational reversal of language shift. The highest percentage of each group which spoke

Mohawk was found in the oldest generation, i.e. those aged 60 and older, with 88 percent speaking Mohawk. At the same time, the lowest percentage was that group in their twenties and thirties, with only 20 percent of the group able to speak Mohawk. This trend is reversed with the generation aged 19 and under, showing more than 50 percent able to speak Mohawk. At least as telling is the survey of attitudes toward Mohawk: "there were no differences among the age groups on this factor: people in all age groups overwhelmingly felt that the language was central to their identity as Mohawks" (Hoover 1992:278).

The connection between Mohawk identity and the language is clearly a central component of reversing language shift. Several other factors should also be identified, such as extensive teacher training. Teacher training is done both locally, within the community and within the school system, and under the auspices of the federal government. The school maintains a 15:1 faculty-to-student ratio, and finding adequate numbers of qualified teachers is an ongoing challenge. Notably, the immersion efforts were initiated before teacher training began, and the needs of the immersion schools have driven the extent and nature of the training.

Another commendable aspect of the Mohawk efforts has been a shrewd approach to the development of a written language and of pedagogical materials. At all points, the program has made due with the best available resources, while simultaneously looking to improve the materials for the future. Thus, the work on Mohawk standardization which was begun in Kahnawà:ke in the early 1970s has continued for several decades. It achieved a new level of codification in the 1990s with the Mohawk Language Standardization Project. This was an effort with the aim of creating an orthography for use among the six different Mohawk communities and to establish a system for writing the linguistic (dialect) differences between these communities, and it brought together representatives from all six Mohawk nations: Tyendinga, Ahkewsahsne, Wahta, Ohsweken (Six Nations) Kahnawà:ke, and Kanehsata:ke.

The project culminated in a conference held in Tyendinaga in August 1993, where the group made its final recommendations.[10] Prior to this meeting, however, the group consulted broadly in each of the Mohawk nations, inviting elders, teachers, linguists, and all fluent Mohawk speakers to work with them. On the basis of these discussions, they made five

---

[10] The conference report is available in English at http://www.edu.gov.on.ca/eng/training/ literacy/mohawk/mohawk.html and can be accessed in Mohawk through this site. It was submitted by Dorothy Karihwenhawe Lazore to the Mohawk Language Steering Committee, and translated and edited by Annette Kaia'titahkhe Jacobs, Nancy Kahawinonkie Thompson, and Minnie Kaia:khons Leaf.

basic recommendations for the writing of Mohawk, which are outlined in the conference report (Lazore 1993). These recommendations are: (1) use of the Roman alphabet consisting of twelve letters (A, E, H, I, K, N, O, R, S, T, W, and Y); (2) the use of diacritics to mark falling tone with length (`̀:`), rising tone with length (`́:`), rising tone stress (`́`), and the glottal stop (`'`); (3) the use of capitals; (4) the use of punctuation marks, including question marks, quotation marks, exclamation marks, commas, and periods; and (5) new words "are to be formed by function, activity or characteristic," and loan words may be taken from other languages. These principles in many ways articulate what had been the practice for many years already, but codify certain critical principles. These include a commitment to spelling conventions which reflect dialect differences, as in:

wátien   Wahta/Kahnawà:ke/Kahensata:ke
wákien   Ahkwesahsne/Ohswe:ken
wádien   Tyendinaga

The system is phonetically based; in the Tyendinaga dialect, for example, /t/ is voiced in prevocalic position, and so the letter *d* is written. As a general principle we advocate standardizing orthography and spelling (Chapters 5 and 6) more on a phonemic, rather than phonetic, basis. However, the Mohawk decision was made as part of a collaborative and extensive effort among these different communities and so represents the best solution for them. Moreover, the fifth principle – allowing for the creation of new words, including borrowed words – intrinsically recognizes the ever-changing nature of a living language. It is a realistic approach to language revitalization.

The Mohawk push toward control of their schools was not an isolated movement but rather occurred within the framework of a larger national context. A third factor in their success in developing immersion-based schooling was political skill in negotiating with the Canadian government on the one hand, and other communities of the First Nations Peoples on the other. In order to understand the developments at Kahnawà:ke, it is critical to view them in light of the document *Indian Control of Indian Education* (National Indian Brotherhood 1972). This is a policy paper presented to the Minister of Indian Affairs and Northern Development in December 1972, which resulted from the collaboration of Indian groups throughout Canada[11] who joined together to assert control over the education of their children. A central part

---

[11] The document specifically recognizes the members of the National Indian Brotherhood's Education Committee: John Knockwood and Peter Christmas (Union of Nova Scotia Indians); Barry Nicholas (Union of New Brunswick Indians); Larry Bisonette (Indians of Québec Association); Louis Debassige and Roland Chrisjohn (Union of Ontario Indians); Verna Kirkness (Manitoba Indian Brotherhood); Rodney Soonias (Federation of Saskatchewan Indians); Clive Linklater (Indian Association of Alberta); Teddy Joe and

of the manifesto is the demand for *local* control, that the authority and jurisdiction of Indian education be transferred from the federal government to *local* Indian bands. Furthermore, "whatever responsibility belongs to the Provinces or Territories is derived from the contracts for educational services negotiated between Band Councils, provincial or territorial school jurisdictions, and the Federal Government" (National Indian Brotherhood 1972:5). Local control in this document is seen as involving responsibilities ranging from administering the physical plant of the school, to hiring staff, determining the kinds of facilities needed to meet local needs, and overseeing curriculum development with special attention to Indian languages and culture. In February 1973, the Minister gave official recognition to the document and approved its proposals.

The document contains a special section addressing the curriculum and Indian values, and an additional section devoted to the question of the language of instruction. It is here that the National Indian Brotherhood makes the clearest statements about the central place of language to identity, and specifies the role of the school in language instruction. They underline the need for formal instruction in the local language, a task which must be taken up by the school system as it can no longer be done by the parents and the community without formal education. This formal instruction has two basic requirements: teaching in the local language; and teaching the local language.[12]

The document also underscores the need for teachers who are in fluent in the local language and, to that end, cites a number of ways to achieve this goal. These include the use of teacher aides who know the local language or, alternatively, working with what are called local language resource aides who can assist the professional teachers, and the waiving of rigid teaching requirements which prohibit Indian teachers from becoming teachers. Those community members who are fluent in the local language tend to be elders who are not likely to complete all the requirements for teacher certification, but are often the only community members who are qualified to use the language in a classroom. (This is an issue for Hawaiian revitalization as well; see section 4.) These issues are taken up again in a section devoted to teachers and teacher training: "It is evident that the Federal Government must take the initiative in providing opportunities for Indian people to train as teachers and counselors. Efforts in this

William Mussell (Union of British Columbia Indian Chiefs); David Joe (Yukon Native Brotherhood); James Wah-shee (Indian Brotherhood of the Northwest Territories); and Dr. Jacqueline Weitz (National Indian Brotherhood).

[12] The document refers specifically to teaching in the "native" language and teaching the "native" language, a term which we have avoided here as it implies first-language knowledge of the target language, which is clearly not what the writers of this document intended. Our use of terminology is defined in Chapter 1, section 3.

direction require experimental approaches and flexible structures to accommodate the native person who has talent and interest, but lacks academic qualifications" (National Indian Brotherhood 1972:18). The fundamental place of language in Indian education is reiterated in the summation of the document, where it is stated that "Indian children must have the opportunity to learn their language, history and culture in the classroom" (National Indian Brotherhood 1972:28). The National Indian Brotherhood thus sees it as the inherent responsibility of the federal government to provide the necessary resources and opportunities for teacher training.

A final factor which has contributed to the success of the Mohawk language program at Kahnawà:ke has been community commitment and community involvement. Community members of all ages have been active in the program since its beginnings: children by attending schools, parents by learning enough Mohawk to support their children's efforts, and elders by working in the schools with the teachers to help create a critical mass of speakers. Their support for a range of what can be called promotional schemes which help promote and facilitate the use of spoken Mohawk has been critical. In addition, there is strong support for further, increased efforts to strengthen Mohawk and a recognition that any successes will be achieved only through a sustained effort on their part (Hoover 1992:279, 281).

4   Hawaiian

The Hawaiian-language revitalization effort, which has been occurring for over twenty-five years, is among the best known in the world.[13] It provides an illuminating case study, as it illustrates a number of relevant factors operating at different levels. It is a prime case where governmental-level variables have hindered the development of the program and illustrates how program organizers have fought state and national regulations. As with the Kanien'kéha (Mohawk) language immersion program (section 3), the Hawaiian program owes its success to a group of dedicated individuals who were committed, from the outset, to revitalizing Hawaiian. It also

---

[13] The discussion in this section relies heavily on sources, including Kamanā (1990), Wilson (1998), Warner (2001), and Wilson and Kamanā (2001). Some of the current information on the school programs comes from the home website of Ke Kula Kaiapuni (http://www.k12.hi.us/~kaiapuni/) and the 'Aha Punana Leo website (http://www. ahapunanaleo.org). During the summer of 2003, Elizabeth Gannes carried out extensive interviews with individuals involved with Hawaiian language instruction, which resulted in an Honors thesis at Dartmouth College. We have also looked to her work in the writing of this section.

illustrates some of the complexities of dynamics within a community, underscoring our point in Chapter 1 that it is not only inaccurate but potentially hazardous to treat the community as a monolithic, homogeneous group without internal disagreement. Finally, it illustrates that the revitalization program itself can bring about an unanticipated kind of language change and shift.

At the time of first European contact in 1778, Hawaiian was spoken by hundreds of thousands of people, perhaps even approaching one million (Fuchs 1961; Heckathorn 1987). One result of this contact was rapid population loss through the introduction of diseases, so that some hundred years later the population had declined by nearly 60 percent to 47,500 (Schmitt 1968). Meanwhile, missionaries from the United States introduced Christianity in 1820, developing a Hawaiian orthography in 1826 and, with it, bringing literacy to the Hawaiian population. Incredibly, the literacy rate reached 90 percent, "the highest in the 19th-century world" (Whitney 1999:2). Hawaiian was established as the primary language of the government and of government-funded schools in 1840, although just one year earlier the first English-based school had been founded for the children of the Hawaiian monarchy. Despite widespread Hawaiian literacy and the use of Hawaiian in the public schools, English was introduced into government-funded schools in 1854 and gradually replaced Hawaiian. The move towards English was all but ensured as the government began paying English-speaking teachers more than their Hawaiian-speaking counterparts (Warner 2001). Thus, the number of Hawaiian-medium schools went from 624 in 1848 to 200 in 1874, and were eliminated altogether by the turn of the twentieth century (Reinecke 1969). Though education through Hawaiian had effectively ceased anyway, English dominated instruction was codified in law by the government of Hawai'i in 1896 and was reinforced by the signing of the Organic Act in 1900, which decreed English to be the language of government business. It also required that English be employed for at least 50 percent of the time in schools.[14]

By 1920, Hawaiian Creole English became the language of most younger Hawaiians, serving as a lingua franca among native Hawaiians, white Hawaiians, and the influx of immigrants from Asia. Hawaiian newspapers, which had abounded in the nineteenth century, mostly disappeared. With the exception of the small Hawaiian community living on

---

[14] Note that this insistence on using English at least 50 percent of the time in the schools resurfaces in 1986 with revised set of statutes; although these permit use of Hawaiian in special programs with board of education approval, the half-time requirement for the study of English is stipulated for all other programs.

Ni'ihau, Hawaiian-speaking parents increasingly used English in the home such that few people used the language on a regular basis. Even the teaching of Hawaiian as a second language steadily declined. Consequently, the number of native speakers dropped to around 2,000 in the 1970s (Warner 2001:135–6, citing p.c. William Wilson), the majority of which were over 70.

The 1970s saw a "Hawaiian renaissance" (Benham and Heck 1998) in which there was a re-emergence of interest in Hawaiian culture by an increasing number of ethnic Hawaiians, particularly among college students. Language took on a special role in this movement as "teaching Hawaiian was the most easily supported area of Hawaiian culture because it was used both in ancient Hawaiian culture and in Europeanized Hawaiian culture, including Hawaiian Christianity" (Wilson 1998:98); that is, language served as a unifying feature during this time because Hawaiians of different backgrounds and interests could rally around its importance. Ultimately in 1978, a major symbolic victory was attained when Hawaiian was designated as an official language of the State of Hawai'i, together with English.

In the early 1980s, Timati Reedy, a graduate of the University of Hawai'i at Mānoa who was then the Chief Executive of the Department of Māori Affairs, returned to Hawai'i and discussed the concept of the language nest model from his experience with Te Kōhanga Reo (Chapter 3, section 2.1). A group of people, mostly fellow graduates from the University of Hawai'i at Mānoa, decided to establish a similar type of preschool immersion experience for their children.[15] Thus, in its first phase, the Hawaiian revitalization program was built on the language nest model of the Māoris, Te Kōhanga Reo. The group began by establishing a nonprofit organization with a dedicated corps of volunteers under the name 'Aha Pūnana Leo ('Organization of Language Nests' – hereafter 'APL). The first Pūnana Leo center opened in Kekaha (Kau'ai) in 1984, followed by two more in 1985: one in Hilo (Hawai'i) and one in Kalihi (O'ahu).

The program ran into legal difficulties before it even began (Warner 2001 provides a succinct overview). Not only was the 1896 ban on Hawaiian in the schools still in effect, but also there were a variety of state regulations about staffing, school-day length and building codes that made the implementation of Pūnana Leo schools a practical impossibility. Ironically, many of these regulations would not have been applicable to the schools if Hawaiian had been considered a "foreign" language," because according to law Hawai'i had no jurisdiction over foreign language

---

[15] Some among them, most notably, Kauanoe Kamanā and William H. Wilson, had determined to raise their children with Hawaiian as a first language, a remarkable achievement given that Kamanā and Wilson were not native speakers themselves.

schools. However, the Department of Social Services and Housing argued that it was not a foreign language because the language was not treated this way in the departmental structures at the University of Hawai'i. The 'APL was unable to change the laws in its initial attempts in 1984, yet opened the first Pūnana Leo in September of that year while the organization continued its battle on the legal front. Some success came in 1985 when staffing regulations were eased, and in 1986 the ban against Hawaiian in the public schools was lifted with the passing of revised legislation (see Section 298–2, *Hawai'i Revised Statutes*). Ultimately, eleven language nest sites were created on five different Hawaiian islands.

Shortly after the establishment of the Pūnana Leo schools, the first group of children had reached the age of kindergarten and first grade. Therefore, the 'APL, as well as other interested parents and teachers, began to work for Hawaiian-language immersion schools, which were officially launched in 1987 by the Hawai'i Department of Education as a pilot program, Papahana Kaiapuni Hawai'i ("Hawaiian-Language Immersion Program"). The program was initiated at two different sites, Keaukaha (Hawai'i) and Waiau (O'ahu) with a combined enrollment of forty students. The program, which drew inspiration from French immersion programs in Québec, steadily evolved to meet the needs of the oldest group of students, and in 1992 the state Board of Education passed a resolution allowing for Hawaiian-medium education through the twelfth grade with one hour of English instruction each day starting at grade 5. The first senior class of Hawaiian-immersion students graduated in 1999, some 110 years after the law banning Hawaiian-medium education had been put into effect. Papahana Kaiapuni Hawai'i, along with four public charter schools that employ Hawaiian-immersion education, now enroll more than 1,500 students.

Funding such an enterprise has been a continual concern. In early phases, money came from donations, tuition, and fund-raisers, but the program rapidly grew beyond what these sources could support. Therefore, beginning in 1990, the 'APL began to receive federal funding of about $1 million. By 1999 the 'APL was receiving $18 million (Warner 2001:137). In order to obtain these levels of funding, members of the 'APL contributed significantly to the drafting and eventual passage of the Native American Languages Acts of 1990 and 1992. Though these acts were in themselves insufficient to fund the Hawaiian-immersion schools, let alone the numerous other programs in the United States, they represented an important step in attaining larger levels of federal funding.

As this brief overview of the history of Hawaiian language revitalization indicates, a major factor in the successes has been the personal commitment of a handful of people dedicated to the idea of making education in

Hawaiian available to those who want it. The investment of time and energy has been great as members of the 'APL (and many others in the community) have had to function in all manner of different roles: lobby-ists, fund-raisers, curriculum writers, janitors, teachers, to name just a few. For most of the people involved this was done during "free-time," in the hours and minutes between the demands of jobs and raising families. This point is a crucial one to underscore in any discussion on language revita-lization: few programs have any hope of succeeding without an individual or individuals who are willing to sacrifice greatly over many years' time. While outside support in the form of money, expertise, or moral support can be valuable (as in the Shuar case in section 2), it does not make revitalization happen. Rather, nascent programs must be nurtured by individuals who not only have a personal stake in the outcome but also have the time, health, and energy to do so.

The Hawaiian revitalization movement was fortunate to have several such individuals, and it demonstrates just how much can be accomplished in the face of overwhelming odds. Recall that the primary founders of the 'APL came from the University of Hawai'i. Student-based political move-ments were not uncommon in the United States in this period, but this focus on local language rights, developing into an actual educational program, was highly atypical. The 'APL leaders were not native speakers of Hawaiian; rather they learned it as a second language in the schools. With few exceptions (e.g. 'Ilei Beniamina), the student activists also did not come out of the Ni'ihau community, where they might have had easy access to native speakers to reinforce their learning of the language. On the contrary, they had relatively few spheres of activity, other than the ones they created, where they could turn to use Hawaiian. In many ways, then, the 'APL leadership was an unlikely group to have success in creating a Hawaiian-immersion program, yet this is precisely what they managed to accomplish.

The Hawaiian case is also notable in that it provides another example of the need for political organization when revitalization is linked to state or federal educational structures. The 'APL arose at an early stage in order to negotiate with various government offices, to raise money, to bring legiti-macy to the revitalization effort, and to enact changes to legislation that stood in their way. Much like the Shuar case described in section 2, changes had to be made in the sociopolitical context in order to gain some measure of control over the local education system, and, much like the Shuar (as well as the Māori), a measure of their success must be credited to the fact that there were not other indigenous groups in the region laboring for legal and political reform to achieve their own ends. While minority groups often have common cause and can effectively pool their efforts to effect mutually beneficial change (see section 3), the reality for language revitalization movements is that the greater the number that arise in a given polity, the less responsive governments are to unique needs and circumstances of specific groups.

Another reason for the success in bringing Hawaiian-immersion education back to the Hawaiian islands after a century hiatus has been the willingness of the 'APL to adapt to new challenges, particularly in their interaction with the state of Hawai'i. Though the 'APL and teachers have had oversight of the curricula used in the Pūnana Leo and immersion schools, the schools remain part of the public system, typically being located at the same sites as English instruction schools, and so come under the auspices of the state Department of Education (DOE). Frequently, the goals of the DOE are in tension with those interested in language revitalization. For example, before the first immersion school had opened its doors, some members of the DOE advocated excluding Hawaiian literacy from the schools, grounding their argument in the traditional orality of Hawaiian. This position did not find community support, as the educators and parents alike were committed to literacy as essential for the ultimate vitality of Hawaiian.

Now that the immersion schools are established, a major ongoing issue is student performance on state assessment tests. Prior to the fifth grade, immersion school students do not receive formal training in English, which puts them at a potential disadvantage in taking assessment tests that are written in English. While the DOE has permitted schools to translate the tests into Hawaiian, there is disagreement, not only among educational officials, but among teachers and parents at the immersion schools, whether this is a good idea. Graduates of the immersion schools enter a world dominated by English, and there is concern for many people that delaying testing that is carried out in English may mask inadequate fluency in the language. This, of course, cuts right to the heart of the philosophy of the immersion school curriculum, which is predicated on the idea that waiting to include English in the school day until grade five will not disadvantage students in their English abilities in the long run. The debate has been exacerbated by the recent No Child Left Behind program in the United States, which includes federally mandated testing of students (see Chapter 2, section 2.2.3).

The Hawaiian-language revitalization efforts, like many around the world, have focused on language learning through formal education. As a result certain issues have risen to the fore. First, since there was not widespread fluency in Hawaiian when the schools were formed, there has always been a heavy reliance on people who have learned Hawaiian as a second language to teach. Moreover, because the DOE has a vested interest in teacher training and certification, many fluent speakers are ineligible to work in the schools, and semi-fluent speakers must be hired. This is particularly true at the higher grade levels, where specialization in math, science, or some other subject, is required. Consequently, the 'APL reports that at times the teachers are less fluent than incoming students. Administrative and staff requirements for Hawaiian are even looser, as these contracts fall under union constraints, and the schools have even less control over them. Thus, ironically, the Hawaiian-language schools may also be administered by staff who do not speak Hawaiian fluently.

The fact that almost 100 percent of teachers and staff are second-language learners of Hawaiian, speaking English or Hawaiian Creole as their first language, and have varying degrees of proficiency, has obvious effects on the form of Hawaiian being taught in the schools. It is clear that the Hawaiian being spoken by immersion school students differs from the Hawaiian being spoken by the native speakers who remain. Quite apart from the need to develop new words to make Hawaiian suitable for teaching modern school subjects,[16] there are differences in pronunciation, in morphology and syntax which result from imperfect learning, a reliance on written materials from the nineteenth century in constructing curricula and heavy English influence (Warner 1999a).

Not surprisingly, this has engendered debate over whether the immersion schools are producing authentic Hawaiian speakers (Wong 1999), which in turn has played a role in who should control the future development of the Hawaiian schools and language revitalization more generally. The small community which has preserved Hawaiian language and traditional cultural practices lives primarily on Ni'ihau, a privately owned island, and a rural part of Kau'ai, the island closest to Ni'ihau. The relative isolation of these families has facilitated the preservation of Hawaiian, but it has also put them on the periphery of the language revitalization movement. While the language of the community might have served as the basis for the Hawaiian revival, it did not, and so the future relationship between the Ni'ihau families, the 'APL, the immersion schools, and other native Hawaiians remains unclear.

At this point the center of gravity for Hawaiian-language revitalization remains in Hilo, where most of the 'APL activity occurs, though it should be noted that a second locus is found in Mānoa, where one of the Pūnana Leo founders, Sam L. No'eau Warner, serves as a professor at the University of Hawai'i. Warner has been a significant factor in language revitalization, though he has engaged in sometimes acrimonious debate

---

[16] The Hawaiian Lexicon Committee was formed in 1987 for this purpose.

with people in Hilo (most notably William [Pila] Wilson) over the direction that the movement should take. Of particular concern for Warner is whether other aspects of Hawaiian culture have been overly neglected in the drive to establish schools, whether native speakers should play a more central role in revitalization, and whether too much emphasis has been placed on the immersion schools and not enough on working to extend Hawaiian language use outside of the schools (Warner 1999a, 1999b, 2001).

This final point is clearly of concern, and not just for Warner, because the ultimate marker of success in Hawai'i will be the degree to which Hawaiian becomes the dominant language in spheres of activity outside of the schools. Since children in the program acquire Hawaiian in schools, not at home or in interacting with their neighbors, English is the language that they are using most often outside of their school day (and often dominates non-classroom time at school, such as on the playgrounds). Therefore, parents are asked to learn Hawaiian so as to support their children's use of the language at home, and classes are free for the parents at most of the immersion schools. There are also classes offered at both the Hilo and Mānoa campuses of the University of Hawai'i and at community college. Yet this kind of change is easier to suggest than to implement, and adult speakers inevitably find it difficult to learn a second language, let alone change their primary language of communication. Similar difficulties have arisen in the Māori revitalization program (or the revitalization of Irish; Benton 1986). One result is that the domain for Hawaiian usage continues to be centered primarily in the schools.

That said, the 'ALP and others have responded creatively to foster the use of the Hawaiian language outside of school. One of these is the creation of Hawaiian-speaking softball and volleyball teams (Warner 1999a:320; 2001:141). Another has been support of Hawaiian artists, which has now seen the emergence of Hawaiian playwrights and the creation of a native Hawaiian journal, 'Oiwi. Hula dancing, which is a prominent part of Hawaiian culture, has represented another domain in which efforts to promote the language occur. Finally, beginning in the mid-1990s, Hawaiian-language content began to appear on the internet on various sites. For example, Leokī, a Hawaiian electronic bulletin system, was launched as a way to provide "a total immersion computing experience in Hawaiian" (Warschauer and Donaghy 1997). Though at this point it is impossible to predict how successful any of these endeavors will be, the fact that such a range of different sociocultural domains has been targeted points to the gains made by Hawaiian revitalization in the last thirty years.

5   Literacy

1   Introduction

One of the most complicated issues in language revitalization is literacy. It is often assumed that literacy is a necessary first step in language revitalization programs: developing literacy in a local language can imbue a greater sense of prestige to it; most school-based revitalization programs typically require literacy; literacy in a local language makes it suitable for use in many modern social domains; and so on. At the same time, it has also been argued that literacy can actually facilitate acquisition of a majority language, thereby accelerating the loss of the very language it was instated to protect. Instituting literacy can be very divisive as decisions are made about what the standard form of a language should take, decisions that inevitably promote the use of one dialect over others. Literacy bears a complex relation to other features of culture, and so it usually involves reshaping a non-literate culture to some degree, and it inevitably poses a challenge to the place of oral tradition. It assumes a literate group within a culture who can serve as teachers, and the development of this group requires outside expertise and, possibly, outside funding. These influences add another level of complexity. Such considerations point to the more central issues in language revitalization. Is literacy necessary for revitalization in today's world? What are the potential benefits and what are the potential detriments to a local culture with the introduction of literacy?

In this chapter, we argue for multiple literacies in revitalization situations; that is, we take the position that communities are best served by literacy in both the language of wider communication and the local language, though we recognize that there will, of course, be exceptions to this general stance. The basic argument for literacy in a language of wider communication rests on the rights and needs of a community to communicate, equitably, with its regional and national governments. The inability to communicate effectively puts individual members of a community, as well as the community as a whole, at a disadvantage in a number of ways, including access to health care and economic equity. Our argument that there should also be literacy in the language being revitalized is based on the conclusion that the local language must have its own literacy domains in order to compete with the language of wider communication.

Within this general stance, it is critical to keep in mind that literacy, whether this be literacy in the local language or the language of wider communication, cannot be implemented without support from the local community. Most failed attempts at literacy are associated with outsiders who insist on an orthography, a standardized form of the language, reading materials, pedagogies, or even a view of literacy, that are unacceptable to the people being asked to adopt them. Ideally, literacy will be the product of a grassroots kind of movement, coming from within the community itself and involving community participation in all phases of development. In preliterate communities, the need for outside technical and supervisory support will be extensive, but even in such cases local ownership of the literacy efforts are a prerequisite to long-term success.

Given the complexities of literacy within revitalization movements, it is important to begin the chapter with a brief overview of some common notions about literacy. Then we outline in more detail some of the pros and cons of literacy in revitalization work. Finally, we outline the basic steps in initiating a literacy program.

2   Models of literacy

Literacy is not neutral but is embedded in multiple cultural contexts and receives values through those contexts and other cultural values. In most industrialized societies, for example, written language is held with "higher" value than spoken language; the written word has supremacy. Not surprisingly, most linguists and activists approaching revitalization tend to adopt this same view toward writing and reading, and so interpret literacy in a relatively narrow sense, as what can be called *traditional literacy*. Traditional literacy is intrinsically associated with formal, Western-style education and has only one basic goal, which is the teaching of reading and writing. In this, literacy is viewed as a goal in and of itself, as a self-justified activity which is worthy without further justification (Bhola 1994:30). While such attitudes are prevalent in many places in the world, this kind of thinking is insufficient to justify the teaching of local literacy, as there is no inherent need for it. Unlike literacy in a language of wider communication, in most cases there is no context which requires local literacy. Thus the narrow view of traditional literacy is too restrictive for revitalization, if it is to include local literacy. Literacy in the language of wider communication may be an end in itself, but local language literacy requires a context or contexts for usage. It cannot be presupposed to be an end in its own independent of a larger educational curriculum.[1]

Modern theoretical understandings of literacy go beyond the traditional to encompass a broader range of meanings and situations. Some familiarity with this corpus of scholarship is helpful in deriving a framework for local language literacy. In this section we are neither exhaustive nor balanced in our discussion. We do not discuss all models of literacy such as *literacy for education* (see Stubbs 1986; Williams 1977 for a critique), which has historically been very influential but is not currently at the forefront of thinking with regard to literacy programs. Rather we focus on several types or understandings of literacy of particular relevance to endangered languages: functional literacy, "autonomous" literacy, and the New Literacy Studies, the latter of which includes both local literacy and social literacy. Note that these labels are used with a variety of meanings in the vast literature on literacy. *Functional literacy*, for example, is commonly used as an umbrella term for different notions of literacy (distinguished as *social literacy*, *functional literacy*, and *local literacy*, in the present work). In order to avoid misunderstanding, we are careful to define each term, but with the cautionary note that the potential for terminological confusion is high.

2.1   Autonomous literacy

The autonomous model of literacy centers around that notion that literacy is a technical skill that can be separated from social context; it is thus seen as existing independently of the culture in which it is used. In this view, literacy is an *autonomous technology* (see the seminal work of Goody and Watt [1963], which is further developed in Goody [1968, 1977, 1987, 2000]; Olson [1994a, 1994b]; Olson et al. [1985]; Ong [1982] and others). The model has been enormously influential in shaping views of literacy, education, and cognitive development.

Early work in autonomous literacy identified literacy itself as a *cause* for social and cognitive change. Goody and Watt (1963), for example, argue that the acquisition of alphabetic literacy causes fundamental changes in human cognition, or as Olson (1977:258) puts it, "[t]here is a transition from utterance to text both culturally and developmentally and that this transition can be described as one of increasing explicitness with language increasingly able to stand as an unambiguous and autonomous representation of meaning." A critical component of this model is a binary division between preliterate

---

[1]   The UNESCO literacy project frames this in terms of functional literacy, which is addressed here in detail in section 2.4.

(and therefore undeveloped) societies, and literate (and therefore developed, modern) ones. This binary division is often called the Great Divide, referring to the presupposition that societies are divided by literacy, i.e. that there is a gulf which separates literates from preliterates. This gulf is manifested on several levels. On a cognitive level, it is argued that literacy is necessary for the cognitive development of certain skills, such as scientific reasoning, logic, abstract thinking, and the ability to distinguish between literal and metaphorical meanings. Preliterates, so the model says, are deprived of these higher-level functions and, in the extreme view, it becomes the collective moral responsibility of literates to bring such cognitive advancements to them. On a social level, a certain standard of literacy is viewed as a pre-requisite to economic development, which would allow one access to the benefits of modernization and industrialization. Furthermore, preliterate people are socially disadvantaged and *de facto* denied access to political power and rights, as well as social mobility. Thus literacy/illiteracy separates people into two groups: the privileged and the disadvantaged. To attain political, economic, social, and cognitive equality, one must be literate.

The claims about the Great Divide in the cognitive realm are widespread in the literature on literacy, either implicitly or explicitly.[2] Olson outlines his theory in eight basic principles which relate literacy to cognition. The most relevant for the current discussion are the following:

1. Writing is responsible for bringing aspects of language into consciousness, that is, writing provides a model for speech. Writing turns aspects of language into objects of reflection, analysis and design.
2. What the script-as-model does not represent is difficult, perhaps impossible, to bring into consciousness. What is represented tends to be seen as a complete model of what there is.
3. Once a script-as-model has been assimilated it is extremely difficult to unthink that model and see how someone not familiar with our distinctions would perceive language.
4. Once texts are read in a certain way, "nature" is read in an analogous way. Epistemology is applied hermeneutics.
5. Once the illocutionary force of a text is recognized as the expression of a personal, private intentionality, the concepts for representing how a text is to be taken provide just the concepts necessary for the representation of the mind.

Olson (1994a:136)

The essence of this is that, without writing, certain aspects of language (such as words, sentences, etc.) are not in consciousness. Indeed, writing is argued to have been "basic to the formulation of a clear distinction between what was said and what was meant or intended by it" (Olson

---

[2] For a detailed critical review of this line of thinking, see Street (1984, 1995).

1994a:137). Furthermore, "the formulation of a theory of grammar or of logic is constructed in terms of the categories brought into consciousness by the means of the script" (Olson 1994a:138). Thus Olson's claims are that literacy alters the very nature of how people think.

Opponents to the Great Divide stress that there is a continuum rather than a discontinuity between oral and written language and, similarly, between "traditional" and "modern" societies (Finnegan 1988; Maybin 1994; Street 1993). In particular, Street (1984, 1994, 1995) criticizes this approach for using as evidence claims from anthropologists based on an imperfect understanding of the people and cultures they are describing. As just one example, citing Levy-Bruhl (1926/1966) and Evans-Pritchard (1956), Olson (1994a:139) claims that a number of preliterate groups are found not to understand the difference between the literal and metaphorical meanings of expressions. Though such claims have been almost universally discredited, and though even some proponents of this earlier strong view of the autonomous nature of literacy have more recently come to refute it (Goody 1987), the prevalence of these ideas remains such that illiteracy in language has become stigmatized. That stigma brings a wealth of social problems with it; it also makes implementing any kind of literacy program all the more complicated.

2.2   Vai literacy as a counterexample to autonomous literacy

The monumental study of Vai literacy published by Scribner and Cole (1981) has had a significant impact on models of literacy. Their work demonstrates that it is not literacy *per se* but rather formal education which affects thought processes, and so this study is frequently cited as a response to advocates of autonomous literacy. Because the Vai were literate but had not received formal schooling, Scribner and Cole were able to test explicitly for the development of abstract and logical reasoning as linked specifically to literacy, the claim of the autonomous school (e.g. Goody and others). They sampled five areas of intellectual activity (abstract thinking, taxonomic categorization, memory, logical reasoning, and metalinguistic, or reflective, knowledge about language [1981:114]); these domains were chosen for testing because they frequently figure in the claims of the impact of literacy. Based on these studies, they concluded that Vai syllabic literacy, as well as Arabic alphabetic literacy in which many Vai were trained, were "not associated with what are considered the higher-order intellectual skills" (1981:132; see 113–33 for a full discussion of their experiments and conclusions). But the significance of their work extends beyond that important piece of it, because of the nature of Vai literacy or, more accurately, because of the multiple literacies used within the Vai community, which illustrate this in a very concrete way.

Scribner and Cole conducted fieldwork with the Vai people of Liberia in the 1970s.[3] The Vai had developed their own syllabary in the 1820s or 1830s, and that syllabary was very much in use when Scribner and Cole conducted their research (and is still used today). Consequently, Vai literacy presented a nearly unique opportunity as it was an indigenous literacy, informally taught to other community members, providing the researchers with the chance to interact with literate people who not been schooled. Interestingly, while Scribner and Cole understood literacy to be both reading and writing skills, the Vai insisted that literacy be assessed solely as a reading skill.

Literacy in the Vai community takes place in three different venues and three languages – Arabic, English, and Vai (Scribner and Cole 1981). Arabic is learned in Qur'ānic schooling, starting at the age of 5 or 6 and continuing for several years. Arabic is a foreign language for these children and, unless they have an exceptional teacher, remains so. They do not learn to read or write but rather to decipher the Arabic script sufficiently well to be able to pick up the Qur'ān and begin to read at any point in the text. Their teacher provides an overview of content. Thus, by and large they "learn" Arabic without comprehension, although there are some exceptions. English is associated with formal education in Western-style schools. At the time of Scribner and Cole's study, Vai children had limited access to such schooling and, as a result, the average village child had enough knowledge of English to read a basic letter but not much more. In addition to the two modes of schooling, there is a system of "traditional socialization," whereby women educate the girls and men the boys in traditional knowledge, including subsistence skills, and traditional culture and folklore. This is all done in Vai.

There is general agreement among scholars that the Vai syllabary was created in the 1820s by Dualu Bukele, who claimed to have been inspired by a dream. This account is recorded by a German-born philologist who came to Cape Mount to write a grammar of Vai (Koelle 1854, cited in Scribner and Cole 1981:265). Vai elders, however, tell somewhat different stories, and it is quite likely that the script underwent several stages of development, perhaps at different times and places. In all likelihood, it was based on an pre-existing graphic writing system which was developed to a very sophisticated syllabary (Dalby 1968). Although both the Arabic and Roman alphabets were known in the region by the 1820s, they do differ markedly from Vai orthographies by virtue of being alphabets, as opposed to syllabaries.

---

[3] At present, there are approximately 105,000 Vai living in Liberia and Sierra Leone combined; 20 percent use English, 10 percent Mende, and 5 percent Gola as a second language (Grimes 2000).

When Scribner and Cole visited the Vai in the 1970s, the syllabary was taught only tutorially, outside of the system of formal education.[4] It is worth noting, however, that 150 years prior to their work Koelle (1854) reported that Vai schools had been established to teach the Vai writing system to the people (Scribner and Cole 1981:267). The uses of Vai reading and writing are not as immediately obvious as English and Arabic; public and government signs, government documents, and official records are in the latter two languages. But families and business associates write letters to one another in Vai; funeral records are recorded in Vai; diaries, family histories, and so on, are written in Vai (see Scribner and Cole 1981). In the Vai case, the sustained coexistence of literacy in more than one language is found, which led Scribner and Cole (1988:69) to argue explicitly that their "evidence indicates that social organization creates the conditions for a variety of literacy activities, and that different types of text reflect different social practices."

One of the enduring findings of this study was empirical evidence that literacy does not exist as an autonomous technical skill which, when introduced into a society, deterministically transforms the way in which members of that society think. Instead, Scribner and Cole (1981) demonstrated that literacy is a social construct, which itself can be affected by the people who create and use it. (For a variety of views on literacy as a social construct, see Cook-Gumperz 1986; Heath 1983; Finnegan 1988; Street 1984, 1995).

2.3   New Literacy Studies

The term New Literacy Studies is used to refer to the work of such researchers as David Barton, J. P. Gee, S. B. Heath, and (notably) Brian Street, and will be used here as an cover term to encompass more specific formulations of the New Literacy Studies, including what are called local literacies and social literacies. New Literacy Studies are in part a reaction to "autonomous" approaches to literacy. (Street in fact coined the term to refer to the work of Goody, Olson, Ong, and so on.) The central tenet of New Literacy Studies is the insistence that literacy is not autonomous and cannot be considered outside of its social context. The practices of reading and writing are not just technical skills but are socially shaped. People make use of reading and writing in a variety of ways, with different purposes in different circumstances.

---

[4] Since Scribner and Cole's work, Vai literacy has been introduced into some Liberian schools; for example, as of 1993, to the Lott Carey Baptist Mission school in Brewerville, outside of Monrovia (Asumana 2004).

New Literacy Studies have highlighted some of the reasons that literacy programs may be unsuccessful or even detrimental to the communities where they are instantiated. These insights can guide future programmers as they develop literacy projects that might more effectively aid people whose languages are endangered. Once literacy is viewed in its larger context, planners can more effectively try to understand which type of program would be most effective in a particular setting. Not surprisingly, the New Literacy Studies therefore stress that it is important to do careful ethnographic work prior to establishing a literacy program so as to understand the local context and be in touch with needs of individual situations.

2.3.1 Local and social literacies

In earlier sections, the term *local literacy* has been used to mean literacy in a local language; that is, a language used in a community (or group of communities) that is not used widely in the region or nation in which the community is found. New Literacy scholars commonly employ the term in a slightly different sense, one which allows them to draw attention to the complex manner in which literacy is used in a culture. For example, for Street (1984, 1994) *local literacy* entails the way literacy is uniquely practiced within a particular setting, with an awareness of how that literacy shapes one's community identity. This understanding leads Street to identify different types of local literacy. One kind of local literacy involves regionally dominant languages/dialects (which may have different orthographies) in the same nation. Literacy practices in one or the other language establish a connection to the particular region where they dominate. A second type, "vernacular literacies," does not involve different languages or orthographies, but unique uses of literacy particular to a community that develop outside formal education. (An example of vernacular literacy is the writing of Philadelphia adolescents; see Camitta 1993.) Still a third type, "invented local literacy," consists of developing literacy for a community in their language (either one that is still widely in use in spoken form or was previously so used) in response to the colonizing literacies.

Though the last of these categories most clearly depicts the type of local literacy in the majority of language revitalization cases, it is the general philosophy underlying all three types that offers insight into how successful literacy programs can be developed. Most significantly, literacy is not taken to be a uniform and strictly technical skill but is a *practice*, or a set of practices, differing depending upon the context in which it is embedded. The creation of an orthography, primers and the construction of a school are insufficient, in and of themselves, to create a local literacy. In addition, one must pay careful attention to the ways in which writing will be utilized on a regular basis, to what are called *literacy events* (Barton 1994a).

Without the existence or development of such events, local literacy is not likely to take hold when it is introduced because it has no practical or cultural value associated with it.

Because literacy can function in a wide range of domains – the practice of religion, artistic endeavors, bookkeeping, informal communication, formal correspondence, chronicling, to name just a few – different literacy events can be associated with different literacy practices, which is to say that there are *multiple literacies*. Therefore, prior to the question of *whether* literacy should be a central part of language revitalization, the question of *how* new literary practices will function in a community must be addressed, as does the question of *who* will use the new practices.

At the heart of much of the writing in the New Literacy corpus is the conviction that all literacies, including local literacies, are *social literacies* (Street 1995). More than a bounded set of technical instructions on how to form letters, connect written symbols with words, and derive meaningful utterances from written texts, literacy is a practice that is deeply embedded in social networks and other cultural practices. This fact underscores the potential power of local literacies: "Literacies in local languages and cultures imply creation of socio-political and economic conditions in which members of a hitherto exploited group can explore all the possibilities of the languages and traditions that constitute their verbal and cultural repertoire and decide upon the literacies they would like to sustain" Agnihotri (1994:47). It also underscores the potential that introducing literacy has to disrupt other cultural practices, e.g. performance of stories, that may have played a prominent role in a community. Finally, the fact that literacies are best seen as *social literacies* serves as a powerful reminder that introducing new forms of literacy into a community immediately confronts the challenge of altering social practices.

2.4   Functional literacy

The last type of literacy to be discussed before moving more specifically to issues surrounding literacy in language revitalization programs is that of *functional literacy*. This is a term used in a wide variety of ways, most frequently to refer to adult education programs (see Levine 1986:25–35 for an overview of the history of the use of the term), and it is commonly associated with UNESCO's worldwide literacy campaign (see Bhola 1984, 1994; Street 1984).

At its first General Conference in 1946, UNESCO launched this campaign with its goal being adult functional literacy, defining a literate person as one who has the reading and writing skills needed to participate in that person's own society. Although the early years of the campaign did not produce the promised results,[5] their programs are far-reaching and have the potential to have a major impact on the way local communities view literacy. Though the UNESCO plan asserts that each individual literacy program must develop its own operational definition of literacy, it is clear that, for UNESCO, literacy involves both reading and writing. Furthermore, their use of the term *functional literacy* is generally tied to very specific economic functions. The thought is that literacy should be introduced to adults with the goal of them being able to access opportunities for socioeconomic development and growth, as well as to avoid potential exploitation (Bhola 1994:37).

The UNESCO plan has three core curricular components: literacy, functionality, and awareness. The *literacy component* centers on reading and writing. It is designed so that each individual program sets its own standards for the level of skills it needs to attain. That said, UNESCO does advocate what they have dubbed *sustainable literacy*. The notion here is that, in order for literacy to be useful to a community, its application must extend beyond the classroom. Technical skills in literacy are not something that should be forgotten and should go beyond the ability to sign one's name. Rather, UNESCO sees a fourth-grade reading level as generally retainable and thus sustainable. Sustainability must, of course, be supported by literacy events that require literacy practices on a regular basis, to borrow terminology from New Literacy Studies.

The *functional component* of the UNESCO literacy program focuses on economic skills which are a core aspect of functional literacy. Economic skills are intended to be taught within the context of "income-generating" projects that will enable participants to earn money. Finally, the *awareness component* encompasses what could be called cultural and civic literacy with respect to social, cultural, and political life. Thus functional literacy involves not only reading and writing, but content within a context. Ideally teaching awareness is understood as instructing people how to take control of their lives, not just personally but socially and politically. Moreover, its intent is to foster pride in one's own culture. Awareness includes social participation in the business of running the community, including an awareness of civil rights and social responsibility. It can also include other social responsibilities such as the environment, sanitation and public health, and pollution, to name a few (Bhola 1994:37–8).

In this conception, functional literacy is potentially empowering for local communities which, in most of the modern world, are embedded in literate cultures. At the national and/or global levels, social and political

---

[5] By 1975 only 12 percent of the one million people targeted for functional literacy had attained it (Levine 1982).

decisions are made by literate individuals. It is undeniable that members of local communities also need to be literate in order to participate in political processes that direct their futures. At the same time, UNESCO has been criticized for placing too great an emphasis on economic development and for failing to recognize the complexities of literacy. Critics point out that literacy is a complex cultural dynamic; attempts to single out economic functionality and give it primacy lead to a false dichotomy between economics and life as a whole (Freire and Macedo 1987; Street 1984). Criticism notwithstanding, UNESCO's program continues to flourish because it promises comparatively substantial gains "by equipping individuals with an ill-defined but relatively modest level of competence" (Levine 1986:35).

There is one final point to make with regard to UNESCO's promotion of functional literacy. In general, the organization upholds the importance of mother-tongue literacy, arguing that the acquisition of literacy is a primary goal, and that meeting that goal is facilitated by literacy in one's native language. This attitude is articulated in the definition it formulated in the 1960s of literacy as "the ability to read and write in the mother tongue" (Bhola 1994:29). This definition stems in part from a political reaction to colonizing powers who created literacy programs in the colonizing languages, not in the local languages. At the same time it is based on the belief that learning literacy is in and of itself enough of a challenge that it need not be coupled with learning a new language. Thus the assumption of the need for literacy is married to the pragmatic notion that introducing a new language into a community adds an extra obstacle to the attainment of literacy.

This marriage, however, presupposes that one's mother tongue will be equated with the heritage language and that the most problematic issue once mother-tongue literacy is established will be "handling the transition from mother-tongue literacy to literacy in the official or the national language" (Bhola 1994:56). In other words, their concept of mother-tongue literacy is ultimately *transitional literacy*, a position consistent with UNESCO's desire to protect individuals from exploitation and to improve their prospects for employment, but one that runs counter to the goals of literacy in revitalization efforts, which are premised on the ideas that bilingual literacy is sustainable and is critical to long-term language vitality and maintenance.

Herein one finds one of the thorniest issues in language revitalization. What is the goal of literacy? In most instances where particular communities are ceasing or have ceased to speak a local language, speakers have done so under assimilatory pressures from the outside. They are in regular interaction with, if not embedded within, a society where economic, religious, educational, and/or entertainment opportunities are intimately connected to a regionally, nationally, or globally dominant language, and so individuals opt to use and teach these languages instead of the local language. Functional literacy has as its goal access to the opportunities, so it can only move people – in the short or long run – toward greater use of languages of wider communication. Local literacy, when used as a way to bolster or spread the use of a local language, is geared to move people away from the use of languages of wider communication, at least in some domains. Of course, given the view expressed in the previous section, there is no reason in principle why multiple literacies that stake out different cultural domains cannot co-occur and coexist, but it again raises the very practical question of how this can be done. Indeed, putting aside the issues of developing a written form (or forms) for the local language (issues which are by no means trivial), the major ongoing challenge in revitalization is establishing domains for the use of local literacy. When the written form of the language of wider communication is well entrenched, this is a monumental task, as there may appear to be few, if any, domains where the language of wider communication cannot serve the same functional purpose as the local language, and so local literacy is superfluous. One of the greatest challenges in creating local literacy is establishing useful and sustainable domains for its use. We take up this issue in section 3.

3   Literacy in language revitalization

In the context of local language revitalization, literacy needs to be considered from the perspective of communities which have the active use of at least one language, i.e. the language of wider communication, and are hoping to revitalize another, the local language. Such situations differ fundamentally from those where there is no encroaching or dominant language of wider communication. The local literacy is, or will be, in competition with literacy in the language of wider communication, which is more widely used and better established. This has been called "special diglossia," a term used to refer to what might be called a specialized use of literacy for local languages, having to do with the relationship between writing/reading and the domains and functions of literacy (Spolsky and Irvine 1982).

In undertaking revitalization, communities need to consider the impact of having and using two (or more) literacies. Some of these communities are completely preliterate; others have literacy in at least one language of wider communication; and still others have literacy in both a language of wider communication and the local language. Thus we can identify three basic types of situations. In the first, the concept of literacy is itself new, and its introduction will have certain ramifications. In the second, the concept of literacy in the language of wider communication is established, but the idea that local literacy is possible or desirable may be new. In the third, literacy in the local language has been established but needs reinvigorating. These are broad categories and each individual situation presents variation, but can serve to illustrate possible outcomes here.

Representatives of the first category – completely preliterate societies – are becoming increasingly rare in modern times; in many nations in the world there has been a prolonged attempt to introduce literacy to all ethnic groups within national borders, and in most nations where this has not occurred it is due to a lack of resources rather than the absence of a desire to do so. Where entirely preliterate communities exist, it is possible to imagine the introduction of literacy in both the language of wider communication and the local language, in tandem and on a par with one another. This is an idealistic view, however, because the two languages are not equal, socially or politically. In fact, historically this kind of simultaneous, balanced introduction of multiple literacies has been problematic, with the local literacy sooner or later giving way to the language of wider communication. A well-documented example is the introduction of literacy to New Zealand by missionaries in the early nineteenth century. The missionaries brought with them English literacy and created Māori literacy, but when Māori literacy rates outpaced those of the English-speaking cohort, local literacy was banned from the schools (see Chapter 3, section 2.1). Even today, although English and Māori are both official languages of New Zealand, they do not exist on a par.

More frequently we find examples of the second category, where there is no written form of the local language but literacy in the language of wider communication is at least familiar, and perhaps well established. This is not to say that literacy is an integral part of community life or even recognized as valuable, but rather that it is not an alien concept. In such cases the community may associate literacy and writing with the language of wider communication, and not with the local language. This attitude is a commonly reported stumbling block to initiating local literacy programs because it requires people to reset their thinking to conceptualize that local literacy is possible and useful. In such situations, it is important to assess the overall literacy levels in the language of wider communication.

The acceptance of local language literacy is largely dependent upon two sets of interrelated factors. One is that existing beliefs in the culture need to be compatible with the values of reading and writing. The other stems from the fact that local language literacy is more readily acceptable in those domains where written language existed prior to its introduction. Although this may suggest that local literacy will be successful only if it comes after literacy in a language of wider communication, such a view is too restrictive. The shift from orality to literacy is one kind of transition, and the shift from orality in a specific language is quite different when the concepts and use of literacy have already been established. In language endangerment situations, special diglossia is often seen in a division of languages for written and oral use. In Navajo communities, for example, Navajo use is largely restricted to oral domains and functions, whereas English is used as the language for written communication (Spolsky and Irvine 1982). The challenge for a local literacy is to shift that pattern so that there are domains for its use. Ideally, these would be domains which would not, could not, be occupied by literacy in the language of wider communication. Such domains exist but tend to be limited. The most obvious are religious and spiritual domains where the concepts involved are not readily translatable (see Jocks 1998) and so are often the last existing domains for use of the spoken language, assuming there are no taboos on their use. Other domains include traditional stories and folklore, and aspects of the practice of traditional culture or lifestyle which can be recorded in writing. A number of linguists (e.g. Nettle and Romaine 2000) have argued for the close interconnection between local languages and traditional knowledge, especially botanical and medicinal information. Manuals, guidebooks, and explanations of flora and fauna and their uses, or of the practice of traditional medicine, can be created to serve as domains for local literacy. Note that beyond a few obvious exceptions, such as religious and traditional texts, the domains need to be willfully created for local literacies; they cannot be expected to develop simultaneously.

This leads to the question of when, if ever, a local literacy is necessary. As noted in the introduction to this chapter, it is often assumed that literacy will be a fundamental component of revitalization. But this assumption must be examined critically, because no language revitalization efforts, with the exception of Hebrew, have been in existence long enough for us to have empirical data indicating a correlation between success in the program and local literacy. There are, it should be said, certain situations where local literacy clearly is not warranted. First, there are abundant cases in which there are too few speakers of a language to make developing literacy in that language worthwhile. Second, the lack of resources for implementing literacy training may render it impractical. There may be insufficient expertise within a community to create pedagogical and reference materials or, even if the expertise is available, the time needed for such activities may not be. There may be insufficient financial resources to train and pay teachers or to write training materials. Though, in some communities, outside help in these endeavors may present itself (through international agencies, national governments, NGOs, or missionaries), even here the assistance will have to take the form of a long-term commitment in order to bring a literacy program to fruition.

Third, and most important of all, efforts toward local literacy do not make sense in cases where there is a lack of desire or commitment from a critical mass within a community to develop a program and to learn. Often, people have been conditioned to think that only a language of wider communication is "worthy" of a written form, that it suffices for all purposes, and that the local language does not merit writing. For example, in the Quechua community of South Peru, literacy is highly valued but also associated exclusively with Spanish; Spanish is the language for reading and writing, and Quechua for speaking. The high regard for literacy in turn only further adds to the greater prestige of Spanish since the two are seen as inextricably linked (Hornberger 1988:85).

Such attitudes may be explicitly stated in national or regional policies and laws, or may be implicit, but are by no means infrequent. There are numerous anecdotal accounts from the field telling of people who think that they do not have a "real" language because it is not written. If it were not for the significant number of programs which have failed for lack of considering attitudes towards local languages, it would seem to be a matter of common sense that "buy-in" for literacy is critical to implementing a literacy effort. However, particularly in language endangerment situations, where there is some urgency in finding ways to protect the language from disappearing altogether, there is an obvious danger of someone, from within a community or from outside, deciding that literacy in the language is essential, yet failing to assess how widely that view is shared.

Having mentioned some of the more evident reasons for not initiating a literacy component, we turn in the next section to a summary of some of the arguments for it.

3.1   Why literacy?

Two of the most compelling reasons for including local literacy in language revitalization are the prestige that it can inspire for a language and the potential empowerment that it brings to a community that has literate members. In the latter case, local literacy generally does not represent the direct cause of empowerment but an indirect one, as it facilitates access to literacy in a language of wider communication.

3.1.1   Prestige
The mere existence of literacy can have an impact on the way people view their own languages. Having a written form of a language can elevate perceptions of its prestige. Alternatively, lack of a written form is often interpreted by local communities as signaling that their language is not a

"real" language, that it does not merit writing. If reading and writing are valued at a regional or national level, not having them in a local language can, unfortunately, lead to the idea that the language is inherently deficient. It is not a long leap in many people's minds to extend this sense of deficiency to the people using the language rather than the language *per se*.

Even small-scale local literacy can have profound effects on how a language is viewed, and even programs that are relatively unsuccessful in creating domains for the use of literacy can be effective in destigmatizing a local language. As domains begin to arise where the local language is preferred, the process of changing perceptions moves beyond only removing negative attitudes to the point where writing in a local language becomes a marker of identity or pride.

3.1.2   Empowerment

Literacy typically has a political dimension to it: it is empowering (recall, as described in section 2.4, that this is the basis for UNESCO's promotion of functional literacy). The ability to read and write means participation in social activities that are denied to those who are illiterate. Where only local literacy is involved, these activities may not constitute direct empowerment with respect to institutions operating in the regional or national contexts, though they may help mitigate against outsiders perceiving community members as unintelligent, hopelessly backward, or socially inferior.

In the modern world, however, literacy in a local language that is being revitalized is nearly always bound up with literacy in a language of wider communication. Either speakers of the local language are already widely literate in the language of wider communication (in which case, empowerment through literacy is not an issue) or they are preliterate (or semi-literate) yet acquainted with the advantages that come with literacy in a non-local language. In most instances of this second sort, interest in local literacy is grounded in the perception that it represents a step towards greater ease in interacting with power structures outside of the local context. (Note that this link between local and non-local literacies has been raised as a potential downside of having a literacy component in language revitalization, an issue that we return to below.)

Just as literacy leads to empowerment, illiteracy can be a mechanism to ensure the subservience of local communities. In an examination of these issues in India, for example, Agnihotri (1994) argues that the lack of local literacy is part of a deliberate effort on the part of ruling officials. Officials with power in rural areas do not want literacy among the local people at all, since this could lead to a challenge to their political power, while officials in urban areas want local peoples to acquire just enough literacy in the national language(s) to be effective members of the workforce. Both the complete lack of literacy and limited literacy thus become a means of control over local groups.

3.1.3   *Literacy as a basic human right*

As the empowering function of literacy has become more clearly articulated, the concept of literacy as a basic human right has emerged (see especially Phillipson 1992; Skutnabb-Kangas 2000). With this fundamental claim, Skutnabb-Kangas advocates mother-tongue literacy be instated on a global level.[6] The essential argument is that, first and foremost, access to education is a basic human right. Effective education is only possible when students are fluent in the language of instruction. Therefore, globally accessible education is possible only by having instruction in mother tongues. Finally, since formal education presupposes literacy, mother-tongue literacy becomes essential to guaranteeing this fundamental human right.

Again, with respect to languages requiring revitalization, the matter of linguistic rights and access to education is murkier since the local language often may not be the mother tongue of a significant portion of a community, including those who identify themselves by it. As Bhola (1984:191) warns, developing literacy exclusively in a local language may "doom those involved to a limited, parochial and marginal existence." Therefore, the concern must be to develop multiple literacies, including literacy that empowers people in their association with institutions external to their immediate environment and literacy that emboldens people to use a local language both by creating social spheres where reading and writing the local language is expected. In the ideal, the emergence of these local literacy domains also increases the social and economic advantages for literate speakers.

3.2   *Arguments against literacy*

Though the motivations for literacy are compelling, there are also a number of arguments that have been raised against literacy regardless of the particulars of the local context (Robinson 1994). With the exception of the first, most of these arguments are grounded in factors external to the community where language revitalization is occurring.

3.2.1   *Shifting from an oral to a written culture*

Perhaps the most powerful argument against developing literacy in a local language, particularly in the case of preliterate societies, is its inevitable

---

[6] Here we distinguish between mother-tongue literacy and local language literacy, with the former used for literacy in any mother tongue, including national level languages.

impact on the culture into which it is introduced. Many oral societies are reported to have highly developed modes of wordplay; many place high value on the verbal skills of expert storytellers; others make a connection between the spoken word and connection to spiritual realms. With the onset of literacy, the special value assigned to spoken language can deteriorate, being relegated to a secondary place behind the written form. To the degree that this happens in different language domains, major culture shifts occur. Traditional wordplay may disappear. The role of stories, and accordingly of the elders or other authority figures who tell them, can be transformed, which has attendant effects on social hierarchies. The connection between speech and spirituality can be loosened, and so on. Thus, while literacy may be found to buttress an endangered language, it may simultaneously alter aspects of traditional culture. Where language revitalization and reclamation of traditional culture were seen to be concurrent goals, literacy is often a wedge forcing them apart.

It is also important to note that oral and literate societies tend to view one another differently. One obvious danger is the potential for a literate outsider to view the oral society as primitive or backward, an attitude which has repeatedly been documented historically as outsiders came to save oral societies from themselves by introducing writing.[7] A perhaps less obvious hazard is the attitude of oral cultures toward writing and the people who write. Canger (1994) records the experience of publishing a book in a Nahuatl variety spoken in Coatepec Costales, Mexico, that had not been previously written. Although the book was positively received by the community, it was viewed as an authoritative text, authoritative in the sense that the linguistic choices made in recording and writing the speech of one individual took on a prescriptive nature. The publication of the text had inadvertently imposed a standard that did not previously exist for the native speakers.

Though to this point our focus has been on the introduction of literacy to preliterate societies, the same dynamic arises when local literacy is being introduced to those who are already literate in a language of wider communication. The erstwhile oral language may have been associated with specific cultural domains (e.g. the performance of songs, learning hunting or cooking techniques not practiced outside the community, and speaking

---

[7] A few examples should suffice to illustrate this point: the literacy campaign of the Soviet Union in Siberia was, in large part, an effort to bring "civilization" to native peoples and increase their numbers in the industrial workforce (Grenoble 2003b); the British introduction of writing to native Māori in New Zealand (Mühlhäusler 1990; 1996); and the introduction of literacy to Native North Americans by US officials (Zepeda and Hill 1991).

with members of an older generation). Though such domains may be limited, they are, at least, clearly defined. Once local literacy is developed, the pattern of using the language of wider communication for "modern" things, or activities shared with those outside the community, versus using the spoken local language for "traditional" things, is broken. The local language now has a written form, making it potentially utilizable for just about any social activity. The boundary line for its functions is no longer clear, and so neither is the boundary for the language of wider communication.

Clearly, assessing the impact of literacy on the full range of social domains is critical when making decisions about whether to include literacy in language revitalization. Yet we do not see the fact that literacy will transform culture (which we take as a given) to stand as a general principle against doing so. In the first place, the creation and use of a written form of a local language need not necessarily replace all oral heritage. Stories, rituals, and other traditions can be written down and still remembered and transmitted orally. In other words, a written tradition does not necessarily preclude an oral one. More important, warnings of the danger of cultural shift brought about by literacy ignore the fact that, for endangered languages, a major cultural shift is already underway. Language use is shifting in a way that indicates no social domain will obviously remain exclusively connected to the local language. The problem facing endangered languages is not that a new equilibrium between a local language and a language of wider communication is being negotiated but that the language of wider communication is threatening to eliminate the local language altogether. Often, this is partly due to the insistence that citizens in a nation, whatever language they may speak, should be literate. Ultimately, many local communities may face the decision of literacy in a language of wider communication and the local language, or just in the language of wider communication.

Therefore, if the alternative to internal, local shift in cultural practices is language extinction, in most cases communities will rightfully opt for the shift. Obviously, a change to writing and literacy is not the only option in language revitalization, as programs may instead opt to return to a greater reliance on the oral language, a theoretically possible (albeit difficult) change to instate.

3.2.2   The lack of a written tradition
Somewhat related to the question of a cultural shift, the lack of a written tradition in the local language has been invoked as an explanation as to why it is either impossible or undesirable to create a written form of language. This is a simple argument: essentially, there is no need for writing as there is no written tradition. Alternatively, it is argued that the

existence of a strong oral tradition will impede the development of literacy (see Robinson 1994 for discussion). The value of the argument is that it correctly highlights the need to consider literacy in conjunction with other linguistic practices in a society. There is little doubt that the existence of a literary tradition can be helpful to introducing a literacy component into a revitalization program (as was the case, for example, with Hawaiian; see Chapter 4, section 4). Not only does a corpus of literature in a local language provide resources for the teaching of local literacy, it also offers a point of connection with the past, which is a critical feature of language revitalization.

However, the lack of a literary tradition, or the presence of a strong oral tradition, does not serve as a principled argument against the concept of introducing local literacy, because it is based on the false premise that oral and written uses of a language (or oral and written traditions) are in conflict. This assumption is driven by a view of orality as a merely developmental stage en route to literacy, an idea prevalent both in Marxist thought and in the Western tradition more generally. Empirical evidence contradicts it. For example, Finnegan (1988) reports that in the South Pacific both oral and written traditions work in tandem. The technical aspect of writing was used to augment the innovative oral process; she argues that the recording of oral traditions was not neutral but a "formative and creative act," that orality and writing were not "separate and opposed modes but, both now and in the past, form part of one dynamic in which both written and oral forms interact" (Finnegan 1988:122).

It must also be noted that the introduction of local literacy in an endangered language is typically intended, in the first place, to protect a local language from infringement by other, more dominant languages. That is to say, the greatest tension exists not between literacy and orality in the local language, but between the use of a local language in literacy and orality versus the use of a language of wider communication.

3.2.3   Transitional literacy

Another argument against local literacy is that, for most communities, it is by its very nature always a transitional literacy and so a gateway to acquisition of the regionally prevalent language. This occurs in practice both from pressures internal and external to a specific community. Externally, literacy in the local language is typically seen as a bridge to facilitate language learning of the language of wider communication. Therefore, local literacy is tolerated or encouraged because in the longer term it represents a way to foster use of regional or national languages. Internal to the community itself there may be little motivation for literacy in the local language other than the possibility that it may leverage opportunities to acquire skills in the language of wider communication.

Ironically, local literacy can be the conduit for languages of wider communication to eliminate the use of local languages. As one case in point, Peter Mühlhäusler reviews the language policies of the island communities of Melanesia, Micronesia, and Polynesia, and concludes that "the most general long-term effect of literacy in the vernacular has been language decline and death" (1990:190). Mühlhäusler outlines the history of literacy in these regions, arguing that it has had a detrimental effect on local populations who were manipulated and taken advantage of by the colonizing populations. This is almost certainly the case, and there is much to be learned from an examination of the history of this region so as not to repeat the same mistakes.

At the same time, it is unclear that the fate of these languages would have been significantly different if literacy had not been introduced, and in the case of endangered languages the short-term advantage of supporting the use of language through local literacy may be the most effective way to protect against imminent moribundity. Regardless, there is an important lesson to be learned about assessing the role of local literacy in particular circumstances. Literacy is an instrument for social and linguistic change, and the effects of local literacy are connected to the goals and attitudes of those working for the changes. When introduced by governments, literacy is usually part of a larger-scale program for social and/or economic development. (This is the case with the introduction of literacy in the former Soviet Union, for example; see Grenoble 2003b.) Literacy introduced by missionaries is often part of a larger campaign for spreading their religious ideals. Literacy introduced by humanitarian organizations is often part of a larger vision of political reform. In each of these cases, cultural change is being sought through local (or non-local) literacy, and the potential consequences to a local language and traditional cultural practices are a subordinate consideration.

Though the complexity of literacy makes it nearly impossible to estimate all the varied ways in which it will reshape culture, tying local literacy primarily to the goal of language revitalization may lessen its transitional nature significantly. Under the control of members of a community committed to language preservation, local literacy can be assessed, and adjusted, with respect to that end.

4   Instituting local literacy

In previous sections, we have examined some models of literacy, as well as some arguments for and against local literacy. These have served as necessary background to our fundamental claim of this chapter; namely that local literacy should play a role in language revitalization efforts. This is not intended to be an absolute claim: there are ample situations where efforts at local literacy might be seen as a subversive act by a national government; there are instances where too few speakers exist to make literacy a reasonable consideration; and there are cases where lack of resources (of time, money, or expertise) render literacy impractical. Readily granting such caveats, we contend that most languages in need of revitalization[8] would be well served by efforts in achieving local literacy. In this, the final section of the chapter, we comment on what we see as the foundational considerations in implementing a literacy program in revitalization contexts.

4.1   Attitudes

As has been mentioned at several points previously, the single most important consideration in developing the right sort of literacy program is the attitude of the community toward its own language and toward the act of writing. Language attitudes as a whole are shaped by a complex set of sociolinguistic factors. At the same time, patterns of language use have an impact on language attitudes. What emerges, then, is a set of reciprocal relationships between language use, attitudes, and sociolinguistic factors; indeed many of the very same factors which can influence language shift and loss.

Specific external factors include the widespread use and prestige of the language of wider-communication as promoted by governmental policies which favor it and discourage use of the local language. Alternatively, we have seen that a change toward positive national policies can have a positive effect on attitudes at the local level (Chapter 2, section 2.2.1). Increased contact with speakers of the language of wider communication is another prime factor; such contact may come through educational policies, immigration (of language of wider-communication speakers) into the community, or emigration of community members to urban areas, and the spread of the majority culture. In the modern era, the media plays an extensive role in the spread of culture, not only of the national culture, but also of transnational cultures, further enhancing the prestige of international access languages (Chapter 2, section 2.1). Of prime import among these factors is the strong economic pressure for literacy in a language of wider communication, which is often a formidable deterrent to local literacy.

---

[8] Note that this excludes languages that are vital, but may be endangered in the sense that the small overall number of speakers makes them vulnerable.

Thus we see that the same factors which have an impact on language endangerment are involved in the success or failure of a local literacy program (see Williams 1981 for corroborating evidence). Given the very complicated nature of these factors, and the critical role of community attitudes in determining the future of a program, assessment of those attitudes is an absolute prerequisite to developing a literacy program (see Chapter 7, section 1.4). The first question that needs to be asked is whether the community truly supports creating a local language literacy. This needs to be honestly answered; the commitment to local language literacy is often superficial and therefore such literacy fails (Dauenhauer and Dauenhauer 1998). Yet another pitfall is the attitudes, or beliefs, about what a literacy program can achieve. The reasons for wanting literacy in one's local language may be *intrinsic* (Hofman 1977: 278–9; McKay 1982:108) or *affective*, rather than *extrinsic* or *instrumental*. For example, in a survey of 27 adult Kunibidji speakers (Maningrida, Australia), although 85 per-cent (or 23 people) of those interviewed supported developing Kunibidji literacy, a full 74 percent (20 speakers) could not propose any uses for such literacy (McKay 1982). While this positive view towards local literacy reflects a healthy desire for increased domains of language use, a literacy project would not be likely to succeed without an accompanying vision of the role Kunibidji literacy would play.

Though the reason for assessing attitudes about a local language and literacy should now be obvious, this does not change the fact that carrying out such an assessment is not easy. It involves talking honestly with people who are thoughtful observers of a culture (whether they be members of the culture or outsiders working in it) and synthesizing a variety of perspectives. In the end, it involves some guesswork because the potential causes for success or failure of a literacy program are not often obvious at the onset. Some communities, such as the Chuj in Guatemala (Williams 1981), accepted literacy quite readily, while others (the Quiché) have shown little to no interest despite many years of work (Henne 1985, cited in Walker 1988).

As noted in the previous section, one cause for failure can be a conflict in goals between the external agents for literacy and the community members themselves. The work of Dyer and Choksi (2001) with the Rabaris of Kachchh, a nomadic group from the western part of India, illustrates this point very well. Kachchh is a semi-desert region in Gujarat State, bordering Pakistan in the northwest and Rajasthan in the southeast. Historically the Rabaris were camel breeders; today most herd sheep and goats, with only a few still breeding camels. Access to the land and water needed for their livestock has become increasingly problematic due to growing development by sedentary farmers. The Rabaris have come to see themselves as in a disadvantaged negotiating position with the sedentary farmers and governmental officials, due to their lack of education. Consequently, their views on the needs for literacy were based on the recognition that they needed greater abilities to negotiate with outsiders, ranging from reading signs on public transportation to writing letters to the larger goals of communicating effectively for one's rights.

Given the Rabaris' nomadic lifestyle, Dyer and Choksi proposed a peripatetic teaching program to tribal leaders so that the teacher(s) could travel with the Rabaris. Dyer and Choksi had relatively high hopes for the literacy program, hoping to include in their instructional program additional information about herding, veterinary medicines, and so on, "to see whether it would be possible to align Rabaris' practices of animal husbandry more comfortably within the wider, modernized context" (2001:34). These were not, however, the goals of the Rabaris themselves. In addition, the Rabaris strongly associated literacy with being sedentary, and so the idea for a peripatetic school failed conceptually for them. Dyer and Choksi found themselves repeatedly confronted by the attitude that people could not simultaneously learn to read and continue to migrate, and the Rabaris insisted that Dyer and Choksi stay in a village (where there already was a school for village children). They attribute the failure of their initial effort to the fact that they had misunderstood the community's own goals and beliefs about literacy and how these interacted with their expectations for a literacy program.

Extrapolating from this case more generally to language revitalization situations, one finds an even greater potential for a mismatch in the goals of literacy among community members. While some may see local literacy primarily as a mechanism by which to increase the use of the language, others may take literacy to be worthwhile only if it improves a child's ability to find a job, while still others may see local literacy as a means for power for certain individuals within the community. Since many revitalization efforts rely on outside assistance (for money, legal support, materials development, or linguistic expertise), the attitudes about literacy of outsiders must also be thrown into the mix.

Finally, certain attitudinal issues are likely among adult learners, a particularly important constituency in language revitalization since they may represent the only fluent speakers of a language. Even when one has succeeded in convincing adult learners of the merits of literacy, they may want quick and easy results. This is particularly common when the program essentially promises not only literacy but a critical knowledge that comes with literacy, and the accompanying improvement in one's standard of living. On the one hand, the connections between the literacy program and its functionality may at best be indirect. Bhola (1994:47) cites the example of information about good health habits which can be learned in a functional literacy class. Even if those good habits translate into improved health and, accordingly, lowered doctor's fees and medicines, the literacy learners may not directly connect the two. On the other hand, the functional content of literacy classes is not always provided as promised, chiefly due to inadequate teacher training and materials.

4.2   Assessing the prospects for successful local literacy

A set of core criteria has been identified for determining the ultimate success for the introduction of literacy to a preliterate culture (Ferguson 1987; Huebner 1986; Spolsky et al. 1983), and these can be extended to the introduction of local literacy more generally. Presupposing a generally positive disposition towards literacy in the local language by members of a community, the criteria for success are: (1) the approval and recognition of traditional community leaders (e.g. elders, politicians, or religious leaders) to the usefulness of literacy for the community; (2) the formation of local functions for literacy; (3) the continued widespread use of the local variety as a spoken language; and (4) the support of the maintenance of local literacy by an educational system under local control (Ferguson 1987:234).

The last two points are potentially problematic in differing ways. In respect to point (4), local control over education to the degree where individual communities make decisions about what languages and literacies are taught is not likely in many places in the world, so "control" must be interpreted in relative terms. Even so, the reality is that most revitalization movements that plan to include literacy programs must concurrently have the resources available to fight for educational rights from regional or national governments. In respect to point (3), there is an assumption that a necessary precondition for the development of literacy is the widespread use of the local language (e.g. Spolsky et al. 1983). Without a doubt, widespread use of a spoken language facilitates the development of literacy, but in the case of revitalization programs the concern is precisely with those languages whose use is not only widespread, but is in fact declining. In this we are presented with an interesting apparent contradiction, since the creation of literacy is often touted as a ready solution for language revitalization. It is important to see that creating literacy will not, in and of itself, revitalize a language. Instead, the creation of domains for the potential use of literacy is a clear step toward enhancing use of the language itself. We must accordingly pay particular attention to creating a set of circumstances to help compensate for the lack of use of the language.

4.3   Creating a context

Literacy is not clearly beneficial unless there is a context and need for its use. In preliterate societies, it is generally necessary to create that context *ex nihilo*. Regardless of the theoretical approach, there is widespread agreement among linguists and specialists in literacy that, in order for literacy to succeed, a context for its usage must exist. This claim is supported by the work in local literacies which shows that literacy programs succeed when they are perceived as needed by the community and when the acquisition of literacy has some direct application to life in the community (Barton 1994; Street 1994). This fundamental view also lies at the basis of UNESCO's functional literacy program, although how one goes about creating a literacy context differs in the two approaches. Consider one example. The Jharkhand Mukti Morcha's literacy campaign was successful because it took place in the larger context of major cultural changes: "literacy constituted an integral part of cooperative farming, afforestation, eradication of dowries and child marriages, drinking, mental gymnasiums, reconstruction of places of traditional activities and an overall struggle for a distinct political and regional identity" (Agnihotri 1994:49). Local literacy grew up with these cultural innovations.

Measuring the success of programs is, however, a complicated enterprise. Hualapai, for example, currently has approximately 1,500 speakers; a survey conducted in 1995 showed that only 50 percent of the children in kindergarten through grade eight were fluent in the language, an obvious indicator of a threatened language. Prior to 1976, there was no written language for Hualapai; intense community efforts have created one. Watahomigie and McCarty (1997:95) assert that it is thanks to this literacy program, the development of literary texts, and Hualapai instruction in the schools that the language has not eroded even further. Conversely, Hualapai literacy could be argued to be a failure, because it has not been able to achieve domains outside of the school where Hualapai literacy is used. But this would be an overly simplistic evaluation. Survey data show that, with very minimal exceptions, community members agree that Hualapai is as important as English and that the people should read and write in the language.

This represents a dramatic reversal of attitudes from the time prior to the literacy campaign when, due to years of repression, parents opted not to teach their children Hualapai so that they would not undergo the same kinds of humiliations and punishments they themselves suffered. Yet, if Hualapai literacy is not used outside of the schools, does it serve any clearly identifiable purpose? Watahomigie and McCarty (1997:107–8) argue that there are four main ways in which Hualapai literacy is significant. First, it serves as an affirmation and expression of indigenous identity. Second, it represents local control over such agencies as the schools, which have historically played the role of suppressing the local language by promoting English only. Third, it serves as a proactive "bridge" between the local children and the larger society, as the bilingual educational program has improved the children's success levels in the school. And fourth, the existence of the Hualapai literacy program has fostered other measures for cultural vitality and maintenance. Thus, the program has had a significant impact on the revitalization of Hualapai even if it has not established Hualapai literacy as a central part of the community's daily life outside of the school. Rather, it has succeeded because it has gone beyond creating an awareness of the importance of the language to gain the commitment of the community members to its maintenance and support.

A very different case is that of Diyari (spoken in south-central Australia), where the introduction of literacy is documented from the beginning in the fieldnotes and diaries of German Lutheran missionaries who settled the region in the late 1860s.[9] At this point, the Diyari culture was oral and highly multilingual. Enough different linguistic groups came into contact that knowledge of several languages was more the norm than monolingualism. Two missionary pastors (trained in the Hermannsburg seminary school in Hanover, Germany), together with two lay missionaries, went to Diyari territory to set up a mission, which they named Hermannsburg. The mission functioned for fifty years (1867–1917) despite a very turbulent start, due to general physical hardships and cultural clash between the Aborigines and the early missionaries.

The missionaries were committed to learning Diyari and within two short years had already established a school and printed a primer in Diyari. Literacy was a cornerstone of their lives and of their mission policies. The missionaries used printed versions of the Bible, wrote out their sermons, wrote both formal and informal letters, and many kept journals. As Ferguson (1987:227) points out, the literacy practices of their wives and of the non-ordained "must have been at least as salient to the Aborigines and quite likely more directly influential." Their wives kept records of various types, including financial records, inventories, names and addresses, and temperatures and daily weather. There were a variety of books, including medical remedies, and a number of the women kept journals.

---

[9] The discussion here is taken largely from Ferguson (1987), which draws on Proeve and Proeve (1952). Ferguson provides a thorough overview and reconstruction of the introduction of literacy.

At least initially, reading and writing were viewed by the Diyari as unimportant for themselves. Recognition of the importance of literacy probably emerged on two fronts. When some Diyari accepted Christianity, they came to value reading the Bible. And, as some Diyari found work at the missions or at farms away from their families, they found writing and reading useful for sending communications to their relatives, keeping up with community news, and so on. The point here is that no context for Diyari literacy existed when the Lutheran missionaries arrived. Despite what seem to be good-faith efforts, in many ways they failed to create domains for specifically Diyari literacy; rather, they created new cultural domains in which literacy would operate.

Though Diyari literacy lagged until the Diyari converted to Christianity and sought culturally imported forms of work, in many cases it is indigenous religions that provide the single domain in which the local language survives and even thrives. Thus religious, ceremonial, and traditional uses of language are prime domains for literacy, and new literacies may begin by recording some of these in written form.[10] If the local language continues to be used exclusively in any particular domain, this may well be the place to start developing domains for writing and reading. Standard sources for writing local texts are folklore, customs, stories, myths, and oral histories.

For literacy to be a truly vital part of the community, however, it should extend beyond traditional cultural domains. Creating contexts for local literacy requires creativity and commitment on the part of the community and its members. One relatively obvious domain is the use of writing for personal needs, such as writing messages, letters, notes to oneself, keeping lists, writing diaries or journals, and so on. This kind of writing requires a personal investment on the part of the writer, as well as a commitment on the part of the recipient of any message, to use the local language in this kind of writing.

4.4 Standardization

Creation of a written language requires a certain degree of linguistic standardization, and in this section we examine the necessary processes involved. Because the issues of standardization are so large, we separate the overall discussion into two parts, and focus on orthographic standardization in Chapter 6, though we recognize this is a somewhat artificial distinction as many communities will need to consider creating or

---

[10] Of course there may be taboos about writing some texts; this decision needs to be made by the community.

standardizing the writing system in conjunction with linguistic standardization. Standardization is a natural part of the development of any written language, but in the case of unwritten languages or languages without a recent written tradition – just the sort of languages typically involved in revitalization – the establishment of a literary standard represents an abrupt, and often controversial, step. A certain amount of variation exists in the speaker communities of any living language. Standardizing the written language does not eliminate such differences, but rather creates an additional variety which should be maximally comprehensible to all speakers. An important question thus arises when differences among given speech varieties are so great that no single standardized variety can be comprehensible to all speakers. When such differences occur, it is generally better to consider the differences between such varieties as more language-like than dialect-like and, moreover, usually important to create more than one standardized variety. If the differences between local speech and the standardized written form are so significant that speakers are, in essence, asked to master a second language in order to acquire literacy, a separate standardized variety needs to be created for these speakers. Of equal importance, though, is shaping a standard form of the language that is acceptable to a wide range of speakers on social grounds. Often, if a standard is seen to privilege one dialect of a language over others, it poses an obstacle to literacy. Similarly, if the standard written form is seen to depart too much from spoken varieties (or, conversely, not enough), there may be resistance to accepting it as an authentic representation of a language.

We presuppose that standardization is a necessary part of creating local language literacy, and therefore is a critical part of many language revitalization efforts. It cannot be overemphasized that the standard does not supplant language varieties or dialects, but rather offers an additional form. Without standardization, writing becomes idiosyncratic and cannot be interpreted by a large enough body of speakers. As we have seen, one of the critical aspects of a successful revitalization program is the creation of an active body of language users. The written language can be a powerful tool toward achieving this goal if all, or a large number of speakers, can read and understand it.

Creating a standard literary form for unwritten language is typically an intentional and explicit process best carried out by those with a high level of metalinguistic awareness or specialized training in linguistics. In this way, it is very different from the manner in which standard linguistic forms have emerged in widely spoken languages where the production of materials in and about a language, as well as technological developments, have pushed standardization. In the sixteenth century, for example, Martin

Luther's translation of the Bible played a critical role in the standardization of German,[11] as did the publication of the authorized version of the King James Bible in 1611 for English. Books about language have also been instrumental in creating standards such as the publication of Samuel Johnson's *A Dictionary of the English Language* (1755) and Robert Lowth's *A Short Introduction to English Grammar* (1762).

The practical needs of publishing only one variant of a book, as opposed to multiple versions in multiple dialects, which historically drove the need for standardization, still hold today. In language revitalization situations involving local literacy, one of the core activities is creating materials to teach the language in a written form, i.e. the publication of books, pamphlets, and handouts. In such cases standardization not only serves the purpose of unifying a local community (or group of communities) around a common form; it also has the practical value of limiting the need to replicate the same set of materials for closely related dialects.

The kinds of variation one encounters in a language vary among specific languages, and so the process of standardization will involve different decision-making processes from situation to situation. Variation can involve any linguistic level: phonetics/phonology, morphology, syntax, and the lexicon. Certain choices for the literary standard may not require a choice between dialects. For example, in North Slavey, an Athapaskan language spoken in North America, /zh/ can be pronounced as [zh] or [y], and /gh/ as [gh] or [wh] (Rice 1995:79). In designing a written language for North Slavey, it makes sense to write /zh/ and /gh/ consistently, regardless of the way that they are pronounced by individuals. Speakers of the different dialects can then learn to pronounce what is written as they themselves say it, in much the same way that English speakers pronounce /ʍ/ in the word *which*, either [w] or [ʍ], depending on their own dialect. However, other choices for a standard form will favor one linguistic variety over another. For instance, the English negative form *ain't*, which appears in many spoken varieties, has been rejected for use in the standard literary form.

It must be stressed that intelligibility is only one factor in decisions about the dialect basis for standardization. A key factor for the ultimate success

[11] Luther translated the New Testament in 1521 and the Old Testament in 1534, i.e. at a time when Germany was divided into a number of states without strong political or linguistic unification. Luther's translations had a unifying effect because he was able to integrate features of both northern and southern dialects to create what was to become a single standard. Full standardization of German is generally attributed to the publication of the *Duden Handbook* in 1860, which included full grammatical and orthographic rules. It was not declared to be the standard authority until 1901. See the articles in Linn and McLelland (2002) for the specifics of the development of standardized languages for Germanic.

of a written language is its acceptability to the community, and so social and political issues almost always enter into the equation. The case of Éwé (Niger-Congo) in Togo provides an example. Togo has forty-two languages, three of which serve as official languages – Éwé, Kabiye (a related, Niger-Congo language), and French. Éwé speakers constitute the largest segment of the population at 20 percent, and Kabiye the second largest at 14 percent (Grimes 2000). When the decision was made to develop literacy for Éwé in the 1970s, two different missionary groups (the Norddeutsche Missions-Gesellschaft from Bremen and the Roman Catholic missionaries), together with the German colonial powers, were involved in determining which dialect would serve as the basis of the written language (see Ansre 1974; Robbins 1992). The Bremen group favored the Anglo dialect, which they had used for over a century in Bible translations, textbooks, and dictionaries. In contrast, the Roman Catholic group had used the Anexo dialect (also called Gen-Gbe or Mina) in its catechism since 1858. Both dialects were more or less equally suited to the task, but economic and political factors were significant. In terms of geographic distribution, the Anexo dialect was spoken on the coast and the Anglo dialect more centrally, which historically had meant that Anexo was more central to trade. The shift of the capital from Little Popo (Anexo-speaking) to Lomé (Anglo-speaking) also entailed a change in the center of commerce and political power.

The combined support of the German authorities and the Bremen mission for the Anglo dialect proved to be decisive. Robbins (1992) reports that Anglo Éwé is no longer taught in public schools although it continues to be used in the mission schools. There is some anecdotal evidence that it is currently associated by Gen-Gbe (Anexo) speakers with the church and is treated as a separate language, although these speakers can understand it with little to no difficulty. Thus it appears that its use has been confined to a relatively restricted domain and written Éwé has not taken on the unifying role one might have expected.[12]

Therefore, choices among dialects for use in a written language must be made with careful attention to how they will be received by the full range of people who are being targeted for training in literacy. If speakers of a particular regional dialect find that their peculiar dialect features do not occur in the standard written form, whereas those of a different regional dialect do, they may very well resist learning it, or reject it altogether. If

---

[12] There were other issues involved in the division between the Anglo and Anexo speakers, as well as other dialects: the position of Éwé in Ghana (Obeng and Adegbija 1999:355) and regional stereotyping and prejudice (Amonoo 1989, cited in Obeng and Adegbija 1999:361).

linguistic markers associated exclusively with elderly speakers are selected, younger speakers may find the written form of the language poorly suited for informal uses with each other. Such occurrences are problematic in any sort of literacy, but they can be disastrous for efforts at local literacy in an endangered language. It is challenging enough to create or protect cultural domains for people to use a language which is in danger of disappearing. When any of these domains becomes a source of contention, the revitalization effort suffers a setback. Though the social factors in each situation are different, the guiding principles for choosing one dialect feature over another are: (1) choose the feature which will maximize the intelligibility of the written form among those likely to use it; (2) choose the feature which emblematizes the domains where writing will be used (e.g. if writing is likely to be perceived as a high-prestige, highly formal activity, then linguistic features associated with low prestige or informal activities are dispreferred); (3) choose the feature most closely associated with expert speakers of the language; (4) choose the feature which is not associated exclusively with one segment of society (e.g. gender-specific linguistic features, which may cause unease for members of the opposite sex to use); and, perhaps most importantly, (5) do not choose between features if it is unnecessary, i.e. a written standard can admit a certain degree of variation and still have a high degree of usability, even for those in the process of learning to read and write.

Of course, in order to make choices such as these, those developing a written form of a language need to have an awareness of where the variation in language arises. The variation may have clear regional connections, or speakers of different varieties may be intermingled in the same location. Variation may be followed along gender lines or be based on familial relationships (i.e. different clans within a community may have linguistic features associated with them). Given the complexities and subtleties of variation, developing a written standard is generally best done corporately. In instances where a non-native speaker is central to a literacy initiative, this becomes essential.

5   Literacy teachers

Several points need to be considered about the position of the literacy teachers within a community. Literacy teachers are critical to the success of a literacy program and can have great influence in the community in terms not only of educating members in reading and writing, but also in affecting their attitudes about literacy and their language. Motivations for taking on the role of literacy teacher should be included in a literacy program from its initial phases. Many of the teachers work in rural areas for little or no pay.

Indeed, in some places significant social status is attached to the role of a teacher; Bhola (1994:14) points to the very high respect for teachers in Tanzania and notes that this position may elevate one's status within the community such that teachers find themselves invited to parties, festivals, and other social events. This cuts multiple ways. One needs to realize that the potential status of teachers may be a factor in attracting talented individuals. Clearly, teaching ability and a commitment to teaching must figure into decisions as to who will teach, yet potential social status can be a factor in teachers self-selecting or being appointed by communities to teach.

Particular aspects of local culture may be decisive in determining who is better or less well suited to becoming a teacher. In many parts of the world, education is uneven for both sexes, and there may be resistance to having a woman teacher oversee the education of boys. Or there may be strong pressure to educate men and boys first, and then attend to the needs of women and girls. If local conditions dictate separate education for the sexes, then literacy education needs to be constructed in such a way as to meet the local culture. Outsiders may object to this attitude, but our stance is strictly practical. We do not see that one can simultaneously institute literacy and equal opportunity for education if the latter does not exist, nor do we see it as the role of the outsider to determine how a community chooses to provide education to its members.

Literacy teachers may face a variety of problems depending upon local variables. In some communities, teachers have been recruited from urban areas and sent into the villages. Iran provides one such example. The Ministry of Education in Iran set up a program which deliberately trained urban teachers to move out to village schools (Arasteh 1962; Gharib 1966, from Street 1984). The philosophy behind this was that the village lifestyle and way of thinking needed to change as a necessary part of the education system. Thus the teacher was an inherent outsider and not part of the community; instead, the teacher was a government-supported instrument of change. In the extreme, the teachers were attempting to take the children out of the village and urbanize them. The social network of Iranian villages rests upon a complex reciprocal relationship of dues and obligations, with village members creating positions for themselves where they could make demands based on services rendered. Thus this system of teachers from the outside was fundamentally disruptive and opposed to the ways of the local culture. The failure here was a focus on literacy as the teaching of technical skills, as opposed to understanding the ideological shift which literacy education involves. At the same time, such village teachers only invested a half-hearted effort in the village schools. These teachers saw their chances of upward mobility as resting within the central educational system and viewed teaching in the village schools as temporary, as a hardship post of sorts. Moreover, many lived in urban centers and commuted to village schools, often teaching there part-time to earn supplementary income. Their lack of success seems to have been predetermined by the failure to take into account the needs and goals of both the community and the teachers themselves (Street 1984:198).

6   Conclusion

We have repeatedly argued throughout this chapter that local literacy should generally be considered a positive step in language revitalization, and have recommended its implementation in many (but not all) cases. Despite the benefits that a written language and literacy can bring, there are a number of potential costs. The overall negatives need to be weighed against the positives in order to determine whether literacy is appropriate in any revitalization program. Even the basic assumption that literacy is needed stems from a bias of the dominant cultures of the world, which presuppose that in order to function a society must be literate. We can challenge this assumption in its own right. This Western bias can be further detrimental because Western ideas of "civilizing" are then embodied within the literacy programs and may lead, directly or indirectly, to language loss. One example is when literacy in a language of wider communication is more valued than local literacy simply because of the high prestige attached to the language of wider communication; a frequent result in such cases is that the local literacy simply becomes a bridge to the language of wider communication. Another possible cost to literacy is a loss of linguistic diversity, which may accompany the creation of a standardized language.

At the same time, however, it is clearly true that in order to function in a globalized world one does need to be literate. Four different kinds of support are needed to begin creating literacy in a preliterate community: technical, local, administrative, and supervisory support (Bhola 1994:69). Local support can be created, initially, by bringing in popular leaders to encourage local leaders and people to see the advantages of literacy and to participate in its creation. This initial step should be followed through with continuing collaboration on the part of local leaders; their participation is crucial to the program's ultimate success. The local leaders are also among the group which needs administrative support, a kind of administration which is viewed as enabling leaders and teachers to do the actual work of teaching and implementing literacy. Supervisory support may come from within the community or without, but critically anyone involved in a supervisory role should be facilitating the program, serving as mentor and advisor as opposed to overseer or manager. The term *technical support* covers an array of different kinds of support and almost necessarily will involve help from outside of the community. Technical support includes the creation of lexicons, grammatical descriptions and reference grammars, the creation of orthographic systems, as well as the creation of teacher and pedagogical materials, tests, evaluation materials, and so on. Specialists are needed to train both teachers and supervisors. In addition, support is needed for any use of technology (Chapter 7).

6   Orthography

1   Introduction

The decision to include local literacy as part of a language revitalization effort often entails the creation of a written form of the language, either because no such form has ever existed or because it has fallen into disuse, as noted in Chapter 5. In this chapter, we move to what is perhaps the chief consideration in standardizing language, the development of an orthography. Though some of the same general issues mentioned in the previous chapter are also relevant to orthography development and will need to be revisited, we have opted to devote a separate chapter to orthographies for two main reasons. First, since the creation of symbols to encode a spoken language is a precondition for any literacy in that language, many people involved in nascent language revitalization efforts find themselves confronted with the practical questions of how to go about creating an effective orthography. They have decided to make the first steps towards developing literacy in a local language, but are unsure of how to create materials for reading and writing. Second, most of the available resources on language revitalization do not contain more than cursory discussions about orthography (Hinton and Hale 2001 is a notable exception), even though they identify local literacy as a commonly desired aim of revitalization efforts.

One of the most important aspects of orthography development is the recognition that, beyond purely linguistic considerations, there are a range of social, psychological, economic, political, and historical issues involved in making decisions about how to write a language. Because situations vary dramatically, no single orthographic system can be prescribed as best for all situations. At the same time, some broad conclusions can be made about the process of developing an orthography.

The importance of sociological factors cannot be overstated. Regardless of how linguistically and technically sound an orthography might be, its initial (and continued) acceptance by the people for whom it is designed is critical in determining its eventual effectiveness and use. Therefore, local leaders and native speakers must be integrally involved in the process of developing an orthography regardless of their supposed linguistic aware-ness; the creation of a writing system by an outside linguist or single com-munity member acting independently, without continual local input and feedback, easily leads to a failed orthography. As just one of many exam-ples, two attempted orthographies for Coreguaje did not succeed in large part because of a lack of consultation with Coreguaje speakers who were semiliterate in Spanish (Gralow 1981).

An orthography must also be acceptable to authorities (including reli-gious leaders, familial or clan heads, and civil leaders) who have influence over the educational practices of a community. Endangered languages are nearly always spoken by communities embedded in literate (and domi-nant) societies whose members have tremendous influence over the use and development of the local language. Orthographers must take into account how national regulations and laws affect orthographic choices, including choices about script or the marking of tone. They must also be aware of conventions, such as spelling or punctuation, that are used in the national languages or other languages in a region, because local opinion might call for either conformity with, or divergence from, such conventions. Therefore, an ideal orthography will be acceptable not only to members of the local community but also to speakers of the language of wider communication who are involved with the community, particularly in the areas of language planning and education. Similarly, it is important to recognize that the various groups invested in the culture and language of a local community – professional linguists and anthropologists, aid work-ers, missionaries, and native speakers of the local language – may have competing motivations for representing a language in a given way (see Gordon 1986).

In addition to such sociopolitical considerations, linguistic, cognitive, economic, and technological factors can play important roles in the choice of the written form given to a language. Some types of orthographies are easier to learn for newcomers to literacy (see section 3). The technologies that will be used for local literacy (e.g. typewriters or computers) may restrict the symbols that can be employed. Though computers are increas-ingly able to reproduce a range of symbols that might be used in ortho-graphy, one must consider whether computers are readily available to those who will be writing the language. In some cases, an orthography which is poor on technical linguistic grounds may be more effective than a linguistically sophisticated one for the simple reason that people can recreate it on widely available typewriters, thus integrating the literacy into a formal cultural domain.

2   Writing systems

In developing an orthography, one of the first decisions that must be made
is to choose which writing system to adopt; a vast array of different types is
currently in use. Four main types of writing systems can be identified
throughout the world: *logographic*, *alphabetic*, *semi-syllabic*, and *consonantal*. In addition, there are a number of mixed systems found across the
world. Japanese writing, for example, combines a logographic system with
a semi-syllabic one.

Alphabetic systems use single symbols to represent individual phonological
segments. The Roman and Cyrillic alphabets are the most common alphabetic systems in use, with the Roman alphabet being used throughout much
of western Europe and in other areas of the world that have been influenced
by European colonists. The Cyrillic alphabet is used where the influence of
the Eastern Orthodox Church has been strong, as in Serbia, Bulgaria, and
Russia. Generally, alphabetic systems are preferred for the introduction of
literacy in a local language because they tend to use fewer symbols than semi-
syllabic or logographic systems, they are more likely to be compatible with
typewriter and computer keyboards, and they tend to be used in the languages of wider communication that surround the local language.

Consonantal systems, really a sub-type of alphabetic writing, use symbols to represent only the consonants of a given word, with vowels marked
optionally, usually being indicated by diacritics. Because Arabic employs a
consonantal script, local literacy programs in Islamic regions of the world
may find a consonantal system derived from Arabic script to be an effective
orthography.

Semi-syllabic writing systems use single symbols to represent syllables.
The oldest of these scripts is the Brahmi script of India, which spread
through Asia as the influence of Buddhism also spread. Many semi-syllabic
scripts, or syllabaries, have been developed elsewhere, often by individuals
in their desire for a unique written form for their languages. These include
Cherokee (North America), Vai (Liberia), Djuka (Suriname), and the Ol
Chiki syllabary for Santali (India). Syllabaries are well suited to languages
where there is a relatively small number of possible syllables, and there is a
high correspondence between a syllable and a morpheme – that is, where
syllable and morpheme boundaries tend to coincide. Syllabaries typically
require more symbols than alphabets. For example, the Cherokee syllabary
has eighty-five symbols, but could be written with an alphabet of only
eighteen letters (Unseth 1980). Therefore, they should be selected only
with the understanding that they tend to take longer to learn.

Logographic systems, rather than representing a sound or a syllable,
make use of graphic signs or logograms to represent words or morphemes.

In this system, even if two morphemes are pronounced identically, they will be represented by distinct symbols. The most widely recognized logographic system in use today is Chinese (though many languages in East Asia, such as Japanese and Vietnamese, also make use of logographic symbols borrowed from Chinese). Historically, Chinese logography was very widespread, and through the eighteenth century over half of the world's books were published in Chinese (Sampson 1985:145). Today, Mandarin speakers outnumber any other language by far, and a total of approximately one sixth of the world's population speaks some variety of Chinese. In the People's Republic of China alone, where Mandarin is the official language, there are roughly 200 living indigenous languages, many of which are endangered (Grimes 2000). Thus a significant number of language revitalization efforts which may develop in the near future have contact with the Chinese logographic system, and will need to consider this fact in creating standardized written forms.

That said, logographic systems are particularly difficult to adapt to new languages because the writing does not correspond to the sound system in any way. Moreover, the underlying principle upon which these systems are based (one symbol = one morpheme) is unwieldy for languages with extensive morphology. Finally, the morpheme inventory in any language is much greater than the phonemic inventory, so that the total number of symbols which a learner needs to read in a logographic system can take many years to master. (The characters number in the thousands for Chinese, although some estimates suggest that a total of one thousand may be enough for basic reading.) Accordingly, we do not recommend creating logographic systems for unwritten languages. At the same time, one must be aware of the possible influence they may have on speakers' perceptions of the act of writing and reading, as well as on their expectations of what an orthographic system should look like.

3   Linguistic and cognitive considerations

It has generally been the working assumption among literacy workers and linguists that the "best" orthography is an alphabetic orthography, specifically one in which every sound is represented by one symbol. The development of new orthographic systems has more often than not relied on the basic guiding principle of sound–symbol correspondence. In other words, one symbol should be designated to represent one (and only one) sound, and one sound should be represented by one (and only one) symbol. While this seems eminently reasonable, there is a thorny theoretical issue of what counts as sound and which sounds in a language should be represented.

The view that has come to dominate takes the position that orthographies should be based on phonemic representation. A particularly useful source in this regard is Rogers (1995), which provides the basis for the discussion here. The idea is that phonemes and morphemes should be represented consistently, even when their pronunciation differs from word to word, as can be illustrated with the English example *electric*, *electricity*, and *electrician*. Though the pronunciation of the letter *c* is quite different ([k], [s], and [ʃ]), the root is represented identically in the writing system. One advantage, then, to phonemic representation is that the semantic relatedness of words is easy to ascertain. Furthermore, the phoneme system of a language tends to change more slowly than do surface phonetic representations, and so in this sense phonemically based alphabets are more stable. Finally, the same or very similar phonemic systems tend to be found in closely related dialects; therefore using a phonemic system as the basis for the orthographic representation can help resolve the issues of dialect differences (Chomsky 1970; Klima 1972; for a discussion of the issues associated with dialect diversity, see Chapter 7, section 1.3).

While sound–symbol correspondence based on an underlying level of representation is a solid basic principle for orthography development, it is by no means the only consideration. In languages with a high degree of homophony, for example, a rigid sound–symbol correspondence will bring the lexical ambiguity of the spoken form of a language into the written form. A second principle, that different morphemes should be represented differently in writing, should be employed in conjunction with the first. This principle, for example, might sanction the alternate spellings in *blue* versus *blew* for English despite the fact that the words are pronounced identically.

Clearly, this second principle should remain subordinate to the first since such spellings are ultimately arbitrary from a synchronic standpoint. Representing all homophones distinctly in some languages could create an unwieldy system for those learning to read and write. Even so, there is plenty of evidence to support the idea that arbitrariness in a writing system that is used to lessen ambiguities is highly effective for those who have become literate. Traditionally, writing has been viewed as a representation of a language's sound system. Current research on reading, in contrast, suggests that writing is better viewed as embodying the *entire* linguistic system, meaning that it connects with and represents other parts of the language – such as morphology, syntax, or semantics – and not just phonology. Instead of devising an orthography simply by identifying the contrasting phonemes of a language and assigning symbols to each one, written language needs to be viewed as encoding much more than just the sounds. One result is that an orthography should be designed so as to present a relatively low level of lexical ambiguity and a high degree of consistency of morpheme shape (Gordon 1986). This approach entails attention to the larger-scale encoding of meaning and structure, greater attention to conventional aspects of capitalization, paragraphing, and punctuation as they relate to higher-level units (that is, phrase, clause, sentence boundaries, and so forth).

When considering the way in which written texts encode meaning, it is also important to consider how readers at different proficiency levels decode such meaning. It has been argued that beginning readers are thought to read primarily by decoding sounds, while more advanced readers are thought to read primarily by recognizing larger units of meaning such as the word or phrase (Dawson 1989; Gordon 1986; Rogers 1995). If this is the case, beginning readers learn and use a strictly phonemic system more readily, while more advanced readers benefit more from a morphemic or morphophonemic system with its consistency of morpheme shape. An ideal orthography would capture both; it would be transparent phonemically while also minimizing ambiguity. That is, the spelling system would enable beginning readers to sound out words, i.e. to read phonemically, while advanced readers would be able to capture meaning units quickly.

Yet actually achieving this balance is difficult. Given the complexities of introducing literacy to oral cultures, we suggest that the phonemic representation should have priority. This recommendation is based on a number of considerations. First and foremost, in many endangered language situations, the community is not literate in the local language, and may associate the notion of literacy with the culture of a language of wider communication. Added to this is the fact that in those regions where revitalization is necessary, there is generally at least some and often pronounced attrition, and so many users of the new orthography and literacy may well be second-language learners, who do not know the local language well. It is therefore important to keep the act of learning to read and write as simple as possible, and so orthographies for communities creating revitalization programs should be designed primarily with beginning readers in mind.

4   Social issues

As was noted in section 1, social, historical and religious associations cannot be ignored in the choice of scripts. Coulmas (1999), for example, highlights the historical association of scripts with particular religions, observing that the Arabic script is commonly connected with Islam and its influence in the Middle East, North Africa, Central, South, and Southeast Asia; the Indic-derived systems with Hinduism and its influence in South Asia, as well as with Buddhism and its influence in South and Southeast Asia; the Chinese-derived writing systems with Confucianism; and the alphabetic scripts (both Cyrillic and Roman) with Christianity and its influence in Europe, Africa, the Americas, and the Pacific. The importance of the religious associations of scripts can also be seen in Baker's (1997) observation that Christian missionaries have often deliberately avoided Arabic scripts and preferred instead local semi-syllabic scripts or the Roman alphabet in their work in countries in Africa and Southeast Asia.

The history of script usage in the languages of the former USSR also manifests the importance of political factors. Many groups in the late 1930s were forced by the national government to change the script used for their languages from Arabic or other scripts to the Cyrillic script used for Russian. This was mandated both to bolster national unity and to facilitate the transition to learning Russian. As a result, people had to relearn entirely how to write their languages, and in many cases serious difficulties arose in trying to develop adequate orthographies using just the Cyrillic alphabet. For example, in creating a writing system for the Kabardian language, digraphs, trigraphs, and even tetragraphs had to be used in order to overcome the limitation in the number of consonants available in the Cyrillic alphabet. In recent years, as groups are considering changing their scripts again, they are faced with a choice between what can be characterized as "pan-Islamic unity" in the selection of the Arabic script or "modernity and secularism" in the choice of the Roman script.

Besides scripts carrying certain religious and political associations, other choices in orthography are also often considered as markers of identity in different ways; choices in orthography reflect the desire of a group to distinguish itself from surrounding groups or, sometimes, to align itself with certain groups. Some Mayan groups have consciously distinguished their orthography from Spanish by including in it selected ancient Mayan glyphs in order to build a sense of pride and unity behind their alphabet (Henne 1991). They have also wanted to change their alphabet to be distinctive, in order to isolate themselves from the Western religious, intellectual, and economic influences which permeated their literature published in a Spanish-based orthography. Certain symbols can have particular significance for an individual group. For speakers of different Bamileke languages in Cameroon, for example, the shared tt symbol "iconifies the strong cultural unity of the group with respect to the languages outside the group" (Bird 2000:21). Quechua speakers who want to defend themselves against the influence of Spanish provide another example

(Hornberger 1995:198). Instead of making a five-way distinction between vowels, as in Spanish, they want only a three-way distinction to be made.

Besides orthographic choices in specific symbols, script choices can also be motivated by identity distinctions. For example, Coulmas (1999) points to the fact that so many groups have developed their own scripts, syllabaries in particular, as evidence of the importance of a script as a marker of identity. The Inuit of Canada exemplify this, having chosen a Cree-derived syllabary over the Roman alphabet for writing Inuktitut because of its symbolic power to mark identity. Script choice is particularly notable in India where, despite the government's efforts to use the Devanagari script as the national script or its efforts to enforce conformity with regional scripts, many groups still insist on using their own independent orthographies. Thus, many examples of choices made in orthography design reflect the importance of orthography as a marker of identity.

Just as two different writing systems can be used to distinguish two separate languages, different orthographies can also be used to distinguish two different communities who speak a single language. The term *digraphia* is used to refer to the use of two different graphical systems for writing one and the same language (Zimt 1974:58). Well-known examples are the use of Devanagari for Hindi and Arabic script for Urdu,[1] or the use of the Roman alphabet for Croatian and Cyrillic for Serbian. Both of these digraphic situations arose from a complex set of political and historical factors (see Robert King [2001] for Hindi-Urdu; and Magner [2001] for Serbo-Croatian). The differences underlying the choice of scripts are not trivial; as King (1998:84) points out, "[t]he power of language as icon must never be underestimated. Like it or not, the Urdu script *means* Muslim, and the Devanagari script *means* Hindu." These issues must not be ignored when developing a writing system.

Yet another issue is the orthographic conventions of the language(s) of wider communication used by the local speakers. Rice (1995), for example, cites the failure of the French-based phonetic alphabet developed for Athapaskan languages in part because the language of wider communication in the area is English, and Athapaskan speakers are more familiar

---

[1] India provides an example of country where a multiple number of scripts is used, and where one language is written using different scripts. There are 18 officially recognized languages in India and 398 total languages spoken (Grimes 2000; Singh 2001). The 18 official languages are written in a number of different orthographies. These include five varieties of the North Brahmi scripts (Bengali, Gujarati, Gurumukhi, Nagari and Oriya), and four varieties of South Brahmi scripts (see Singh 2001:66). Of the many languages spoken in India, 58 are taught as subjects in the schools but only 47 are used as languages of instruction (Annamalai 1991). These are the most frequently written languages, but publishing is carried out in 87 different languages (McConnell and Mahapatra 1990).

with English orthographic conventions (this in addition to its lack of adherence to the one symbol, one sound principle). Although in some cases, usually for purposes of identity, a local community may opt to use an orthography which is very different from that of the language of wider communication, in most situations similar orthographies are desirable. Speakers of endangered languages are commonly literate, or semiliterate, in the language of wider communication, and so adapting its orthography can spread the process of learning to read and write a local language. Moreover, because the very notion of literacy is often associated with the language of wider communication, it often makes good sense from the view of the community itself to use similar orthographic systems when possible.

There are several different ways in which the phonemic system of the local language may compare to the language of wider communication: (1) the orthography of the language of wider communication may contain a single symbol to represent a sound type[2] found in both the language of wider communication and the local language; (2) the language of wider communication orthography may use more than one symbol to represent a single sound type found in both languages; (3) the language of wider communication may use one or more symbols for sound type(s) not found in the local language; and (4) the local language may have phonemes not found in the language of wider communication. (Tone represents a particular instance of the fourth scenario and is discussed separately in section 6 of this chapter.) When the first case holds, it is generally advisable to use the symbol of the language of wider communication alphabet to represent the same sound types in both languages. In the second case, however, decisions are more complicated. If the language of wider communication uses multiple symbols to represent the same sound, which one should be selected for the local language? The decision should be based on a combination of factors. The most significant of these is the overall distributive restrictions of any given symbol, i.e. the symbol with few or no restrictions should be preferred over others (such as the letter *k* over *c* to represent a voiceless velar stop if the language of wider communication is English). Other issues include the overall transparency of each symbol in terms of the orthographic system as a whole, and the need to use the other symbols to represent other sounds in the local language.

---

[2] Here we use the term *sound type* to cover phonemes which are similar enough to one another to be treated as a single sound by speakers. For example, in one language the phoneme /d/ might be alveolar and in the other dental, but speakers of both languages would recognize either as /d/.

The situation is even more complex when there is a sound (or sounds) in the local language not represented by the language of wider communication orthography. Several choices arise in this case. These include creating an entirely new symbol (e.g. the introduction of *I* [the numeral 1] in the variety of Cyrillic used to write Chechen); borrowing one from another orthographic system (e.g. the use of the Roman letter *j* in Serbian Cyrillic to represent an alveopalatal glide); creating a new symbol through combining existing symbols into digraphs or trigraphs as needed (e.g. *gh* for the voiced velar fricative in North Slavey); using a diacritic (e.g. ' for the glottal stop in Hawaiian); or reassigning a symbol used for a sound in the language of wider communication which is not found in the local language, i.e. reassigning unused symbols of an alphabet to different phonemic values (e.g. the use of *q*, *x*, and *c* for click sounds in Xhosa and Zulu; Baker 1997). The advantages to this last method are that the symbols will be familiar and available in already-existing typesets, fonts, keyboards, etc. Difficulties have resulted from this approach, however, as documented in the creation of an alphabet for Coreguaje (spoken in Mexico). An initial alphabet used the symbols *b*, *d*, and *g* for unaspirated voiceless stops. When the alphabet was introduced to Coreguajes semiliterate in Spanish, the result was confusion (Gralow 1981); the redefinition of these symbols appears to have impeded, not aided, the acquisition of Coreguaje literacy.

Further comment is needed on the use of diacritics to provide additional symbols to represent phonemes, because this is commonly employed in the development of new orthographies. One should avoid "diacritic overload" on a given symbol with the goal of using no more than one superposed diacritic per letter. In situations where this ideal cannot be met, then particular care is in order to keep diacritic marks from interfering with each other. Though diacritics can be extremely effective in expanding an existing alphabet for use in local literacy, they can be the source of disdain towards a new orthography since it makes the language look "strange" or "complicated." In instances where people are using computers or typewriters in a local language, the need for additional keystrokes in order to write the language can cause annoyance.[3]

5   Underdifferentiation and functional load

Many local languages have relatively large phonemic inventories and phonemic systems that differ greatly from those of the contact language

---

[3] Boerger (1996:41), for example, notes the problems of diacritics in the Natqgu writing system which could not be easily typed on the English typewriters available to speakers.

of wider communication. In such situations the representation of each individual phoneme by a distinct symbol may be more than readers can handle (as in the case of Zapotec; see section 8). One solution is the *underdifferentiation* of phonemes in an orthography such that one symbol is used for more than one phoneme. Alternatively, one can limit the overall number of letters by simply not marking certain types of contrasts such as those that result from vowel length, stress, or tone (but see section 6). In an effort to limit the number of letters, it may even be desirable not to represent consonants and/or vowels. A key part of making the decision about whether to underdifferentiate in an orthography is to determine the functional load of a given phoneme in the language.

The classic definition of functional load comes from Charles Hockett's *Manual of Phonology*: "Assuming that two phonemes, x and y, can contrast at all, then the functional load carried by the contrast will be greater if both x and y have relatively high text frequencies than if one has a high frequency and the other a low frequency, and greater under those second conditions than if both x and y have low frequencies" (Hockett 1955). From the reader's standpoint, phonemes with a greater functional load are important to represent because they are crucial for distinguishing between different potential meanings. Accordingly, phonemes with greater functional loads should not be unmarked or eliminated by underdifferentiation. These theoretical discussions can be applied to create a more practical diagnostic for determining functional load, such that the following five factors should be considered (adapted from Gordon 1986; Powlison 1968):

(1) What is the level of contrast of the specific phoneme? With how many other phonemes does it contrast to distinguish words or morphemes? In a nutshell, the more phonemes with which it contrasts, the higher the functional load.

(2) What kind of feature or features distinguish the phoneme from the next most similar phoneme with which it contrasts? Generally, a difference in point of articulation indicates a higher functional load than a difference in manner of articulation; and either of these differences indicates a higher functional load than a difference in point of coarticulation.

(3) How many phonetic features distinguish the phoneme from the next most similar (contrastive) phoneme? The more differences, the higher the functional load of the phoneme.

(4) Does the phoneme contrast on one or more levels? In addition to distinguishing between words, phonemes may also distinguish utterances on a morphosyntactic level. An example comes from Bora, a language of Peru, where the tone in monosyllabic verbs with long vowels serves to distinguish between continuative and intensive

aspects (Gordon 1986). English weak verbs (*sing, sang, sung*) provide another example, where a change in vowel quality indicates a change in tense. If a phoneme distinguishes utterances on both lexical and grammatical levels, its functional load will be greater.

(5) What kind of contextual cues and redundancies exist to aid in distinguishing utterances, independent of phonemic contrast? The more clues given by the context, the less the functional load of a phoneme will be.

The idea of leaving phonemes unrepresented in an orthography is based on the fact that there is much predictability in the distribution and sequencing of specific lexical items. Thus underdifferentiating certain phonemic features does not necessarily hinder their recognition, particularly in languages with large phonemic inventories. Still, it must be recognized that underdifferentiation will create a variety of ambiguities in the written form of a language (Gordon 1986; Unseth and Unseth 1991). As an orthography is developed, the trade-offs of underdifferentiating and ambiguity must be weighed.

In addition to underdifferentiation, in certain cases it may be appropriate to *overdifferentiate* by using different symbols for allophonic variation or when speakers feel a morpheme should be represented uniformly (Simons 1994). Overdifferentiation may also be chosen intentionally so that an orthography can mirror the orthography of the national language or so that the orthography can be used by different dialects which may differentiate between variations of a form to differing degrees.

In working through decisions about underdifferentiation, overdifferentiation, diacritic use, and so on, tests can be developed to determine how a native speaker perceives contrasts and which contrasts are most significant for disambiguating an orthography (see, for example, Gordon 1986; Hampton 1989; Henne 1991; Mugele 1978; Unseth and Unseth 1991). While an outside linguist may judge certain contrasts to be minor and unnecessary for representation, these contrasts may be exactly the contrasts the native speaker looks for to disambiguate words when reading. In the same way, it is also extremely useful to test native-speaker reaction to symbol choice. Experience from literacy programs around the world has demonstrated how effective native speakers' intuitions are for determining symbol choices for elements such as consonant clusters, glottal stops, nasalization, tone, and vowel harmony. Although linguists, in their desire to develop orthographies that accurately capture the phonemic system of a language, may balk at involving speaker intuitions which may obscure the system, an orthography needs to be designed with potential readers in mind, and so needs to be suited to their needs and perceptions in ways that a linguistic account need not.

6   Tone

In the development of orthographies for languages in certain parts of the world, especially in Central America, Southeast Asia, and Africa, the question of how to mark tone is unavoidable, yet is frequently controversial. Tone languages are often spoken in regions where the language of wider communication is not a tone language, and so one question that often arises is whether tone should even be orthographically represented at all (see, e.g., Crofts 1976). Some of the sociolinguistic, linguistic, and psychological factors that affect the choices made will be discussed below.

Tone systems involve the use of pitch to distinguish units at the word level and at the syllable level. (This is often referred to as *lexical tone*, in particular in the literature on literacy and orthography for tone languages.) There are two basic tone systems for lexical tone. In the first, the tone domain, or the domain in which the phonological pitch operates, is the entire word. In the second, it is the syllable.[4] Probably the most familiar word-based tone systems are those found in Norwegian and Swedish; Slovenian also has a word-based tone. In syllable-based tone systems, each syllable has a relative pitch value, or tone. The marking of tone has often been neglected in the development of written languages. This is often due to the fact that colonizers or missionaries who have designed an orthography have failed to recognize the significance of tonal contrasts, since their own languages do not make such distinctions (Bird 2000; Cahill 2001). In addition, the marking of tone has been neglected because people have argued it was simply too difficult to learn or teach, that it caused texts to be too cluttered, or that it was too difficult to design a good enough system (Hollenbach 1978). These claims are offset by a number of studies which indicate that orthographies which do not indicate tone are harder to master by speakers of tonal languages (Bird 1999).

The issue of whether to mark tone is far from settled. As Baker (1997) points out, the tonal systems of many African languages have not yet been analyzed very thoroughly and that, even for those studied thoroughly, linguists may disagree among themselves about how tones should be marked. Nevertheless, Baker argues that tone should be marked when it is phonemic, and that it is important for there to be a provision for writing tone in any given tonal language, regardless of whether individual people choose to make use of such marking. Koffi (1994) also considers the

---

[4] See Pike (1948) for the fundamental work on syllable-based tone.

marking of tone to be necessary, stating that grammatical tone should definitely be marked and that lexical tone should probably be marked as well, though phenomena such as downstepping should not be marked. Wiesemann (1989) recommends that, for tonal languages, a minimum of one tone and a maximum of three tones should be marked. In contrast, Bird (1999) more seriously questions the effectiveness and necessity of tone marking, noting that in his own experience in sub-Saharan Africa, speakers have not achieved proficiency in reading and writing at levels analogous to speakers of non-tonal languages. Despite many assertions that a failure to mark tone results in too much ambiguity, he himself argues from his surveys of the Dschang language that "analysis showed that tone-marking degraded reading fluency, and did not help to resolve tonally ambiguous words" (1998:7). He also refers to the linguistic situation in Zambia, in which seven officially recognized indigenous languages of the country removed tone marking from their orthographies for the same reason, i.e. that it actually hindered reading. Based on the conflicting opinions of many who have experienced developing orthographies for tone languages, it is clear that decisions about whether to mark tone in the orthography – and if so, how and how much – should be made with attention to local attitudes and the specific circumstances surrounding a local language.

Just as people have questioned the claim that the best orthography is one in which each phoneme is represented by a distinct symbol, similarly people have questioned whether contrastive tones need to be marked in all cases. Some argue that tone distinctions should be underdifferentiated and that a native speaker will be able to disambiguate words from the surrounding context (especially, for example, if the ambiguous words would occur in different positions syntactically or if they would only be used in different registers). However, others argue that underdifferentiation causes rereading and a significant slowing down of the reading process, even discouraging persistence in reading because of the difficulty of decoding meaning. Again, the notion of functional load is relevant.[5] In fact, for documents such as sacred texts, speeches, radio addresses, and legal documents, additional tone marks are even added sometimes for people orally delivering these texts, to prevent them from stumbling over ambiguities (Baker 1997). For each language considered, it is important to determine whether tone carries a heavy functional load or whether it is not, in fact, a feature that speakers depend on for disambiguating context.

---

[5] For more detailed discussion of the implications of ambiguity for reading skills in tone languages, see Adegbija (1993), Gordon (1986), Unseth and Unseth (1991), and Wiesemann (1989).

In the same way that it is debatable whether or not it is necessary to mark tone at all, it is also debatable how much to mark tone if it is only marked partially. Bird (1999) describes several ways tone distinctions can be marked only partially. One suggestion for decreasing the overall number of tone markings is to collapse the distinction between certain tones such that a single symbol may mark more than one toneme. Another possibility is to leave some tonemes, such as the most common one or the one that changes the least, with zero marking. Alternatively, tone may be marked only on syllables where the tone changes, or only on syllables where the tone disambiguates one word from another (Bird 1999; Koffi 1994).

Another important consideration is how marking tone can best serve potential readers, especially if they have different proficiency levels in their reading skills. As discussed in section 3, beginning readers are thought to have the easiest time reading at a phonemic or phonetic level, whereas more advanced readers are thought to read at a morphophonemic level. For this reason, it has been suggested that if tone is only marked according to how it actually sounds on the surface, e.g. as it is affected by tone sandhi, it may serve a beginning reader better, but such surface-level marking may actually slow a more advanced reader, who reads for meaning units rather than for sound units (Snider 1992).

While these psychological considerations are important, there are other factors that may affect how native speakers use tone marking. For example, it is important to consider whether tone is best marked with superscript or subscript numbers, different types of diacritics (especially accent marks), punctuation marks, or otherwise unused graphemes from an alphabet. In making such decisions, it is important to evaluate how realistically the marks chosen will be able to be reproduced, particularly taking into consideration the type of technology available. Linguists working in North America, for example, tend to assume the availability of computer technology and photocopying machines, but in many places in the world communities have access to neither. Mimeographing or photocopying on old machines often results in texts which are hard to read, with faint or blurred diacritics.

7 Standardization of orthographies

There are many good reasons to advocate a single, standardized orthography for related dialects, or what has been called *multidialectal orthography design* (Simons 1994). Chief among these reasons is the potential for engendering a shared linguistic identity for communities that use different spoken varieties of a language. In language revitalization situations, where the number of people using a language is often small, cultural divisions stand as obstacles to success, and employing a single orthography offers a way to remove one division. The unifying effect of a common orthography finds compelling empirical support as illustrated (as just two of the plethora of examples) by the English alphabetic system and the Chinese logographic system. Despite the vagaries of English spelling and the difficulties of learning large numbers of Chinese characters, both systems can be read by speakers of vastly different varieties of each.

Regardless of the advantages of a shared writing system, there are potential pitfalls, such as the issue of "skewed systems," which arise in constructing a multidialectal orthography if the phonemic systems of some dialects differ. Since the phonemic systems have diverged for two or more of the dialects, a shared orthography cannot faithfully adhere to the sound–letter correspondence for all of them. There are two basic options: either one specific dialect can be selected as the basis of the standard and used as the model for writing, or one makes choices in developing an orthography which in one place is most closely matched to the phonemic system of one dialect, but in another place matches the system of a second or third. The resulting orthography will not represent the most psychologically real one for any single dialect, but can still be easily learned and used for all of them. Simons (1994) advocates the second option in all circumstances, because the first requires speakers of the non-standard dialects to learn at least some aspect of the orthography by rote memorization.

To show how an orthography can be created by drawing from multiple dialects Simons discusses the Dani language of Irian Jaya (based on the data in Bromley 1961). There are two main patterns for the stop phonemes in the eight dialects discussed by Bromley. Lower Grand Valley Dani has one pattern, with one stop series and two voiceless continuants, while the remaining dialects have two stop series. The difficulty in orthography design for Dani stems from the fact that there is not a one-to-one correspondence between the two series of stops in the majority of dialects and the stops and continuants of Lower Grand Valley Dani. This can be illustrated with representative data from one of these dialects, Western Dani. The voiced stops of Western Dani /b, d, g, g^w/ correspond to voiceless stops in Lower Grand Valley Dani /p, t, k, k^w/. The voiceless stops in Western Dani /p, t, k, k^w/ either correspond to the same voiceless stops in Lower Grand Valley Dani or to /s/ and /h/. More specifically, Western Dani /t/ can occur as /s/ in Lower Grand Valley Dani, and Western Dani /p, k, k^w/ to Lower Grand Valley Dani /h/. By comparing the phonemic level to their phonetic realizations, the correspondences become regular and predictable. Word-initially, the voiced stops in Western Dani are phonetically prenasalized and correspond to Lower

Grand Valley Dani voiceless, unaspirated stops. In intervocalic and final position, they correspond exactly between the two dialects (and are continuant and unreleased, respectively, in these positions). In Western Dani, the word-initial voiceless stops are aspirated and occur in Lower Grand Valley Dani as /h/ and /s/.

In creating a single writing system for all Dani dialects, there are two options. Bromley (1961), and Simons (1994) in turn, propose the following system:

b	d	g	gw
p	t	k	kw
ph	ts	kh	kwh

Readers would then learn rules as to how to pronounce these letters in their respective dialects, i.e. *ph* would be [h] in Lower Grand Valley Dani and [p^h] in the other dialects; *b* would be [p] in Lower Grand Valley Dani and [^{m}b] elsewhere.

In language revitalization, there may be practical considerations that override Simon's conclusion that a compromise orthography is the best design for multidialectal literacy. If there are significantly different levels of vitality among the dialects, one might decide to base an orthography on the most vital one. In a similar vein, if limitations on available resources (such as money or time) make it unfeasible to move between various areas where the dialects occur, the revitalization effort might be tied to one region, with the dialect of that region serving as the basis for designing an orthography. Often the urgency of starting revitalization while fluent speakers are still alive requires decisions for action that, with the luxury of more time, might be otherwise.

7.1   Motivations for standardization

One of the most common reasons for promoting a written standard is the desire for political or cultural unity. As Romaine comments, "Linguistic diversity is still seen as an obstacle to development" (1994:89). This belief in the unifying power of a common written standard has motivated many governments to enforce standards of script and orthography. One of the best examples of such a policy is in the People's Republic of China, where a common logographic script unites linguistically divergent and geographically distant dialects that are mutually unintelligible in spoken form but mutually intelligible in written form. While China has effectively united different groups through a common orthography, countries such as India have failed to do so, due to the irreconcilable split between the two scripts used for Hindi and Urdu.

Having a standardized written form with a single standardized writing system facilitates communication in a variety of ways. It is important in the distribution of medical resources, and can also be so in the development of infrastructure. A written standard often proves to be invaluable in education as well. Teachers need some way of guiding their students in making choices when writing, i.e. some form to teach their students, with the most obvious being a standardized form (Rice 1995; Schiffman 1998). Having a standard orthography can increase the functional domains of a language's use, which in turn increases its status within the community and reinforces community values (Adegbija 1993:167). Thus, standardization can play an important role in reinforcing a group's sense of identity, and may also enable a group to gain recognition and official status, thereby even further enhancing a sense of identity and pride (Schiffman 1998).

7.2   Implications of standardization

Although standardization has undeniable benefits, it does not come without its social consequences. One of the most apparent is the development of consciousness and belief about "right" and "wrong" forms of language. Prescriptive judgments about linguistic forms are introduced with the written form; native speakers tend to have fewer fixed notions of correctness before a language is written. In this sense an orthography constitutes a "normative idea that has no counterpart in the linguistic reality of the speech community" (Coulmas 1999:137). This is demonstrated in Canger's account of publishing a book in Nahuatl (Canger 1994). In initial attempts to elicit opinions about correct forms of speech, the native speakers' responses indicated much looser standards for correctness than after publication of the book. The linguistic choices of the written form were perceived as authoritative by the community.

There is an additional concern that the process of standardization actually leads to language loss in multiple ways. Standardization has been argued to contribute to the loss of linguistic diversity, as a written standard inhibits the amount of variability allowed in language and thereby inevitably causes some varieties to be lost. Mühlhäusler (1996:225–34), for example, argues that standardized phonemic writing systems can only help fossilize language and reduce variation, because they are inherently at odds with the accommodation of variation and change. In spoken communication, a wide range of dialectal variation can be maintained, but literacy favors standardized languages, and discourages variation, as seen in the principles presented in section 7.1. Moreover, standardized conventions for local languages are often expressly modeled after the writing conventions of national languages or languages of wider communication for the purpose of facilitating acquisition of these languages, which in turn can facilitate the loss of the original languages. As noted in section 4, an important consideration in the choice of orthography is whether or not it will provide a good bridge to a majority language. In order to resist such a transition to a language of wider communication and the loss of their own language, some groups have specifically avoided modeling their standardization choices after standards for national languages. Oko speakers of Nigeria, for example, while modeling some aspects of their orthography after Yoruba, have also conscientiously distinguished their orthography in order to avoid assimilation (Adegbija 1993:156, 161).

Standardization can also lead to language loss because of the status it gives to one variety over others. Because writing one variety of a language can elevate the status of that language, other surrounding languages or varieties may be lost because they lack relative prestige and thus are not preferred for use. The development of the Wemo dialect of Kate (Papua New Guinea) and of Yabem (Papua New Guinea) is a prime example (Mühlhäusler 1996; Romaine 1994). These two dialects of different languages were chosen above others by missionaries working in the areas; all other dialects of the languages have since seriously declined in use and are almost entirely lost as a result. Similarly, the Mbauan dialect of Fijian was chosen as a missionary lingua franca, which has consequently led to the decline of other languages and dialects with the spread of the written standard (Mühlhäusler 1996). In contrast, the speakers of dialects of North Slavey decided not to unify their dialects under a single orthography, even though their language committee was in favor of unification and standardization. They opted instead to insure that the linguistic and cultural identity of the individual groups would not be lost (Rice 1995).

Ultimately, the preference for one variety over another can lead to social stratification (Coulmas 1999; Mühlhäusler 1996; Schiffman 1998). People inevitably have unequal access to a standard form of a language; because standard forms are elevated in prestige, use of or failure to use standardized varieties can then begin to index social class, and thus standardization leads to certain forms of inequality. In countries such as Papua New Guinea, society was not historically stratified through the use of a standardized variety; rather, it was only after colonization that hierarchy in language, and correspondingly in society, was introduced. The imported models of a centralized government, wage economy, social and economic development, and Western-style education, have combined to result in a social hierarchy which is at odds with traditional culture and social organization in Papua New Guinea and is reflected in language use (Romaine 1991).

For local languages involved in revitalization, we note that social stratifications and power imbalances already exist, almost always to the detriment of speakers of a language, regardless of dialect. Therefore, while the introduction of a standard written form will produce new stratification within, and sometimes among, the communities where an endangered language is used, it has the greater potential to rectify the more obvious asymmetry of power that holds between members of the community and those outside it. The encroachment upon local communities of languages of wider communication and the cultures they represent, the ever-growing impact of globalization, means that local communities cannot afford not to consider a written language and, along with it, standardization, if they are to resist linguistic assimilation.

7.3   Process of standardization

Several factors should be in the forefront when standardizing an orthography. One of the most important factors is the political. Sometimes, governments have overt regulations governing choices in orthography, while at other times non-binding guidelines for developing a standard may exist. In the recommendations for standardization that were put forward by committees developing alphabets for African languages, for example, it is noted that the same sounds in different languages within a country or subregion should be represented with the same letters and that, if a single language is found in two different countries, the same symbols should be used for the same sounds in both countries (Baker 1997). Finally, there are often political implications implicit in orthography choices that must be recognized. Creating an orthography that is highly distinct from a regional or national writing system can be seen as subversive or defiant to the goal of national political unity. In certain parts of the world, there may be limited tolerance of such acts.

In addition to assessing external political implications of an orthography, the linguistic variation found in the language must be considered: people's attitudes toward different varieties; which variety has the largest number of native speakers; which variety is most widely understood; which varieties are mutually intelligible; whether people already consider one variety to be more prestigious; whether they consider one to be more "pure" or closer to the "original" language; where the varieties are spoken (especially if one variety is spoken in an urban center); and which varieties are used for religious or administrative purposes. Since several of these considerations deal with the perceptions of native speakers (or semi-speakers) and others with intuitions that can only be held by members of a local community or communities, it is essential to have them in the decision-making process. The best way to do so is through committees that are formed in order to make standardization decisions. In such committees, representative speakers from all varieties should be included (see also Schiffman 1998; Wiesemann 1989).

Committees can be inefficient, and they do not always operate as expected, particularly when cultural taboos or powerful personalities make truly cooperative deliberation difficult or even impossible, but they still represent the best way to reach a consensus on the nature of the orthography that meets local needs. When constructed properly, they also represent the best way to legitimize an orthography within and among communities. The negative evidence justifying this position is certainly abundant. In numerous cases around the globe, a lack of consensus about standardization or a lack of thoroughness in researching which variety to standardize has led to serious problems. As just one example of this, Mühlhausler (1990) and Henne (1991) illustrate the problems which have arisen when different missionary agencies have developed competing standards for a variety.

Once decisions have been made about which variety might serve best as a basis for developing a standardized orthography, language planners and community leaders need to consider what aspects of the orthography should be standardized. Namely, in addition to standardizing the choice of writing systems and the particular symbols within a system, it is also important to determine what other conventions should be introduced, such as capitalization, punctuation, and spelling. In most cases of language revitalization, provisions should be made from the outset for the introduction and standardization of loan words and neologisms. In all of these decisions, one should keep sight of the conventions used in national languages and languages of wider communication; the standards chosen may need either to reflect these or diverge from them in order to be acceptable to local native speakers.

Finally, the standardized orthography should be tested to determine whether the design works well and to make necessary adjustments. This is a potentially delicate moment in the process of creating an orthography. If reasonable decisions have been made from the outset, only rarely should major changes occur at this time. Early experimentation with the actual use of the writing system should indicate such things as whether particular symbols or diacritics cause confusion. Once a group has accepted a writing system, revision can be problematic. Though such changes are relatively minor in the abstract, actually making them can become challenging, as the conventions quickly take on symbolic value for individuals or constituencies within the speech community. For example, a diacritic mark may have been selected to distance an orthography from that of a language of wider communication. Even if the diacritic is then found to be technically undesirable, a suggestion to change it may meet with heavy resistance because it is seen as giving in to pressures to accommodate to a surrounding culture. Battles over orthography can become surprisingly passionate. While perhaps unavoidable to some degree, the potential for divisiveness can be lessened by encouraging people to see early decisions about orthography as tentative, and by constantly returning to the unifying vision of why the orthography is being created in the first place.

8   Recommendations

In summary, we offer the following recommendations regarding the development of an orthography in a language revitalization effort:

(1) *Alphabets.* Barring an overriding symbolic value that may be derived from the use of a syllabary or logographic writing system, alphabets should be used in creating orthographies. This is due to the particular nature of language revitalization. Revitalization is undertaken when a language is being lost, and so many of its users are semi-speakers, not fully fluent first speakers. A written language is thus by necessity instructive, and both teaches and reinforces a speaker's knowledge of the language. It is thus critical that the language's sounds be discernible from its orthography.

(2) *Learnability.* Learnability should be given high priority when designing an orthography. Thus with languages with extensive phonemic inventories one will need to strike a balance between such basic principles as one sound, one symbol and overall learnability. Learning to read and write is painstaking, hard work in any language. Motivation can easily be undercut if the writing system is difficult to learn. While extremely intricate orthographies, such as the Chinese logographic system, are learned by billions of people around the world, they are mastered only after a substantial dose of formal education with the active support of national governments. Languages in need of revitalization exist under a different set of circumstances, so maximizing the learnability of their orthographies greatly enhances the likelihood they will be learned and used.

Within the rubric of overall learnability, we include two subprinciples which support it: one sound, one symbol; and transparency.

One sound = one symbol. Alphabets should be constructed on the basic principle of one sound per symbol, one symbol per sound. In other words, an ideal alphabet would exhibit an isomorphic mapping between sounds and symbols. This is not always possible due to other factors. In Zapotec, for example, the phonemic inventory is considerably greater than in Spanish, which would suggest the need for a greater number of letters or symbols to write Zapotec (Munro and Lopez 2003). When written in accordance with Spanish orthographic conventions, a range of phonemic contrasts in Zapotec is not distinguished, yet many Zapotec prefer to do just that, under the influence of the prestige of written Spanish. Although most linguists would naturally prefer orthographies to be phonetically designed, on the basic principle that each individual phone should be represented by a single grapheme, local considerations can and sometimes should override this principle, as the Zapotec case suggests.

Transparency. Spelling conventions should coincide with those of the language of wider communication wherever possible. Note that this principle may be offset by desires to maintain a distinct identity from regional or national cultures, which is commonly of import in language revitalization situations. However, since local literacy either does not exist in these situations, or it exists on an extremely limited basis, it is typically best not to inhibit the learnability of an orthography for culturally symbolic purposes. Practically speaking, the symbolic value does not actually provide the intended benefit if people do not learn the writing system.

(3) *Acceptability.* As is mentioned repeatedly above, in order for a writing system to be successful it must be accepted by those who are being encouraged to learn it and use it. Therefore, acceptability stands above all other priorities in designing a writing system. Because of the tenuous state of many endangered languages around the world, an orthography created for local literacy must also be acceptable to the regional or national governments, depending on what level of control they exercise over education within the community, allocation of resources, access to media, and so on.

7   Creating a language program

This chapter provides a step-by-step account of how a community interested in revitalizing a language can assess its needs, commitment, resources, and goals, and then, based on these factors, how they can go about establishing the appropriate language program.

1   Preliminaries

Before beginning a revitalization program, we recommend as full an assessment as possible of resources available for the program, the status of the language, numbers of speakers, levels of knowledge of the language, levels of multilingualism, literacy, and so on. It should also cover an evaluation of community support, goals, and values, and the relationship with government agencies, including possible sources of financial support and relevant legislation. We recognize that a thorough assessment may take years to complete, and therefore may not be feasible in many cases of language revitalization, but some sort of preliminary assessment is needed in every community.

1.1   Assessment of resources

In the initial planning stages of any language revitalization program, it is important to identify the resources available to the program. In order to write about them more clearly, we have divided them into three categories: (1) financial resources; (2) language resources; and (3) human or emotional resources. By *financial resources* we mean the sources of money available within the community, the likelihood of obtaining external funding (from the federal government or humanitarian organizations, for example), as well as the kinds of resources available for education and programming, the use of media, etc. *Language resources* include access to existing language materials, such as grammatical descriptions and dictionaries, textbooks, pedagogical materials, written and oral literatures, and so on.

Moreover, language resources include available speakers of the language needing revitalization. *Human* or *emotional resources* refers to the number of people who might be involved in creating and promoting language revitalization, and the skills they could bring to the process. It also includes the general level of interest of community members, both speakers and non-speakers, to using, teaching, and learning the language. Finally, it refers to the availability of outside experts to assist in technical aspects of revitalization.

The degree and type of resources available obviously affect the model of revitalization project that is attempted (see Chapter 3 for an overview of different models). When, in relative terms, there are many fluent speakers of a language, clear sources of funding, community members who have some experience in the legal system, and broad enthusiasm for revitalization, it is possible to institute a larger and more formal set of programs. In most cases, however, some (or even all) of these are lacking and a quite different tack must be used, one which explicitly includes developing basic resources. The Hawaiian revitalization effort illustrates this point well (see Chapter 4, section 4). The initial approach was to get young children into a setting where they were immersed in the language, i.e. the founders of the Hawaiian language preschools decided to work on developing a crucial language resource, children who had a lot of exposure to the language. In addition, they invested energy in generating interest in the preschools (i.e. they saw the need for the development of human resources), and they sought to change laws that stood in their way and to sway the attitudes of educational authorities (both of which were necessary in the long run to make them eligible for federal and state money). Because their early efforts included the nurturing of different types of resources, the revitalization effort grew rapidly.

1.2   *Assessment of language vitality*

It goes without saying that when a group of people determine that a local language is in need of revitalization, they already have a general sense of how many speak the language, though interestingly this estimate is almost always on the high side. Our experience suggests that this arises for two reasons in particular. First, there is an assumption that if people have had exposure to a language at some point in their life, they speak the language. This assumption is often even stronger when the language is associated with a person's ethnicity or race. Therefore, so the reasoning goes, since someone was raised in a home where the parents spoke the local language, she must speak the language even if she is never heard to use it. Second, there is an assumption that if a member of a local community can respond to greetings or basic questions in a language, he can speak the language. However, in situations where local language use is in decline in favor of a language of wider communication, both assumptions are often wrong. What one finds in these cases is a high percentage of people who have limited abilities in a local language, so-called semi-speakers.

While semi-speakers can serve as a vital resource in language revitalization, their contributions will be of a different sort than fluent speakers. Consequently, before beginning any revitalization program, it is critical to have a clear sense of how many speakers there are of the language and their knowledge of the language. The assessment must be concerned with several aspects of the speaker population: the number of speakers; the age and generational distribution of the speakers; the correlation between age and proficiency levels; and perceptions that community members have about the degree to which a local language is known and used. As just noted, there is often a mismatch between perceptions of language vitality and reality, and educating community members about the actual threat of language loss may need to be a core part of the language revitalization efforts.[1]

For purposes of assessment, one should minimally assume four levels of speaking proficiency which can be placed on a continuum. At the one end are fully fluent speakers with native knowledge of the language. Such speakers comfortably use the language in all domains and can do so on a daily basis. Next we place speakers who, while not fluent, have a high level of communicative ability. These speakers may make some systematic grammatical errors and may have some lexical gaps in their knowledge of the language. Next on the continuum we place semi-speakers, i.e. those with some limited communicative ability and passive knowledge of the language. Finally, at the other end of the continuum are non-speakers, those people who do not know the language. They may know a few

---

[1] One of the difficulties commonly faced in language revitalization is the disbelief among many community members that there is a problem. The case of the Quechua community in South Peru provides an illustrative example. The sense of Quechua identity is strongly linked to language and culture; being Quechua entails being a member of a Quechua-speaking community and both "the language and the community are seen as permanent features" (Hornberger 1988:75). This belief is so firmly held that language loss is not viewed as an issue. It is further supported by what Hornberger (1988:76–7) calls the Quechua view of the "cyclical nature of life." This refers to the notion that the older generation certainly speaks Quechua and, although younger speakers currently use Spanish, when they become older they will use Quechua. Their beliefs about the resiliency and permanency of Quechua are firmly grounded in these two basic points. Thus, if one wants to address a downward trend in Quechua use with the community, it must be articulated in these – their own – terms. In this particular case, if one of two points can be made, that either youth are not learning Quechua or are leaving for Spanish-speaking urban centers and not returning, the basic premises of Quechua stability are destabilized.

commonly used phrases, but cannot create or interpret any new utterances. The continuum is thus as follows:

fluent speakers – highly proficient speakers – semi-speakers – non-speakers

We present this as a continuum to underscore its fluidity. With the exception of the two ends of the scale, the rankings are not discrete. The level of a given speaker's ability may vary with domain and topic, and may also be dependent upon the speaker's relationships with the interlocutors. (Note that even fully bilingual speakers may be more proficient in one or the other language dependent upon topic.) It is also not particularly fruitful to divide the potential speech community into four distinct categories, but rather to recognize the shifting nature of communicative competence. Note also that this continuum addresses only the issue of oral competence; we return to issues of literacy skills in section 4.1.

A more finely tuned scale is presented by SIL International and can be found in an appendix to *The Ethnologue* (Grimes 2000), under the heading "Second Language Proficiency Estimate of Vernacular Speakers." Within this survey is a ranking for first-language proficiency, with specific instructions to "estimate the percentage of first language speakers between ages 10 and 70 years at each of the following levels. Remember that women probably constitute 50% of the speakers. Please do not include members of the ethnic group who are not mother tongue speakers of this language" (Grimes 2000:850).[2] The proficiency ranking is as follows:

Level 0   Unable to function in the spoken language. Oral production is limited to occasional isolated words. Has no communicative ability.
Level 1   Able to satisfy minimum courtesy requirements and maintain very simple face-to-face conversations on familiar topics.
Level 2   Able to satisfy routine social demands and limited requirements in other domains.
Level 3   Able to speak the language with sufficient structural accuracy and vocabulary to participate effectively in most formal and informal conversations on practical, social, and occupational topics.
Level 4   Able to use the language fluently and accurately on all levels normally pertinent to needs. The individual's language usage and ability to function are fully successful.
Level 5   Speaking proficiency is functionally equivalent to that of a highly articulate well-educated native speaker and reflects the cultural standards of the country where the language is natively spoken.

[2] Barbara Grimes (2000:850) directs the reader to SIL Second Language Oral Proficiency Evaluation 1987 (*Notes on Language* 40a) for further information, including more detailed descriptions of the different proficiency levels and guidelines for testing. Joseph Grimes (1995) includes a chapter on SLOPE, with further references. He provides a more gradient system with intermediate rankings between levels, with 1–, 1, 1+, 2–, and so on.

We include this ranking here despite our own preferences for a simpler system for a number of reasons. It is a useful system because it provides more finely tuned information about speaker knowledge of the local language. Furthermore, this is the system used in *The Ethnologue*, which continues to provide the most comprehensive and reliable count of numbers of speakers of the world's languages. (We recognize that individual language surveys may have far more accurate counts for a specific language, but *The Ethnologue* is unique in bringing together speaker statistics on a global scale.) Thus it is important to be able to interpret the data in *The Ethnologue*, and helpful to compare one's own assessment. Of course, accurate proficiency testing is time-consuming and requires a level of experience with survey-taking that may not be available. Using a coarser scale for assessment, such as the one we suggest above, may be best for the initial stages of revitalization. It provides a snapshot of language proficiency that will suggest which models of revitalization are well suited to the local situation. A more thorough assessment might be undertaken later once the basic approach to revitalization has been implemented. The more sophisticated assessment could then be used as a benchmark for later analysis of the effectiveness of the revitalization efforts, and it could serve as a guide to any adjustments that have to be made to its original design.

Regardless of the particular assessment scale involved, the manner in which the information is collected is also important. Most language surveys rely on self-assessment, which is notoriously unreliable because speakers may not have an accurate idea of how well they speak the language. Moreover, because language is such an important part of identity, speakers may claim to know more or less of a particular language because that claim reinforces their sense of identity.[3] Ideally, then, a more objective measurement of language proficiency should be used, though it may not be feasible in many instances due to limitations on time, expertise and the materials necessary to carry out this sort of testing.

For linguists, anthropologists, missionaries, and humanitarian workers who have not spent a significant amount of time living and working in a community, the sense of levels of proficiency is often derived by one community member's personal evaluation of another's language abilities. Put simply, speaker X is seen as speaking "good" Navajo/Cherokee/

---

[3] An extreme version of this is found in censuses where individuals self-identify their ethnicity. In the former Soviet Union, for example, the census counts for various ethnic groups would vary from census to census depending on whether individuals preferred to ally themselves with, or distance themselves from, a given group due to social and/or political factors of the moment (Grenoble 2003b).

Evenki, etc., and speaker Y as speaking "less good" or "bad." One must be careful how to interpret these evaluations because they can be grounded in culturally specific notions of good/bad language use. In some cases they may stem from the high value a community places on oral skills, such that a "good" speaker is in fact a good storyteller, or one who knows many traditional texts, or who uses a wide range of phrases and turns of speech. In others it may signal language loss or interference from the contact language.

Examples of this kind of evaluation by community members are very common and can be found in even the earliest accounts from the field. Bloomfield (1927:436) points out that "the Menomini Indians of Wisconsin, a compact tribe of 1700 people, speak a language without dialectal differences and have no writing. Yet the Menomini will say that one person speaks well and another badly, that such-and-such a form of speech is incorrect and sounds bad, and another too much like a shaman's preaching and archaic ('the way the old, old people talked')." Bloomfield continues to explain that he, although clearly not a native speaker and not a community member, tends to share the value judgments of the Menomini speakers, and provides a ranking of some of the speakers. Similarly, in a case study of the Kaqchikel Maya of San Marcos La Laguna, Julia Becker Richards notes an overall high level of awareness about speaking styles and who is an accomplished speaker, with remarkable levels of agreement (Garzon et al. 1998:82–3). All who are considered to be accomplished speakers have achieved some stage of maturity (at the time of her field research, all were over 40) and have high rank within the community; as she points out, in a community "not marked by overt wealth and social differences, oratory skills figure as important markers of status and prestige" (1998:83).

Though speaker evaluations of each other may not provide the data needed to place people along a proficiency scale of the sort mentioned above, they play a very helpful role in language assessment and in indicating directions that revitalization should or should not take. They can signal what the community values in language and how such value judgments are assigned. Thus in the Menomini case, for example, a revitalization program would want to avoid teaching a form of speech which would be viewed by speakers as archaic (and therefore "bad").[4] In the San Marcos La Laguna

---

[4] By way of comparison with the situation which Bloomfield reported in 1927, it is useful to note that Grimes (2000) gives the following statistics for Menomini: 39 first-language speakers, 26 second-language speakers, 15 others aged 30 to 50, and an additional 50 people aged 20 and above who have learned Menomini to understand it. In the "others" category are those who have learned Menomini to teach it. The total ethnic population is 3,500; the language is ranked by Grimes as *nearly extinct*.

case, any work on language development would need to begin with the "ways of speaking" which the community already recognizes. In addition, the recognized accomplished speakers would be the logical body to turn to with questions involving language development issues, such as standardization, corpus development, compilation of dictionaries, and so on.

It is fitting to end this section with a reminder that there is a difference between *language ownership* and *language knowledge* (see Evans 2001 for an important discussion of this topic). Language ownership has to do with a relationship between language and social group membership, or what in many cases may be perceived as ethnic group membership. This same concept is translated into Western contexts in terms of one's heritage language, or one's "native" language, where "native" does not refer to fluency but to the language of one's ancestors. This connection is distinct from actual linguistic competence, so being a language speaker may not necessarily be equated by a community (or an individual) as granting one the right of language ownership. In many communities, the language "owners" are the ones who are perceived, or who perceive themselves, as having the right to determine the future of the language by virtue of their position in society. They possess authority to state what counts as the authentic or real variety of the language. The issue of who has control over language revitalization decisions is often a contentious matter, which hinges on language ownership, a notion that may not have clear boundaries in a given community or communities.

In situations of language attrition and endangerment, there may be only a handful of speakers, or even a single individual, who speaks the language fluently. While assessing proficiency can reveal this fact, it cannot reveal whether their knowledge of the language is sufficient to imbue them with the authority to make language-related decisions for a revitalization effort. Their overall validity as language representatives stems not only from their actual linguistic performance, but also from the ways they are perceived by community members. Language affiliation often has more to do with social group membership than linguistic competence *per se*.

1.3   Assessment of language variation

Though it is convenient to speak of a language as a clearly delineated object, the boundaries and characteristics of a language are not fixed. There is always some variation among speakers of the "same" language, and this fact becomes relevant to revitalization in that decisions have to be made about which variety (or varieties) people will be encouraged to speak. Therefore, planning a language revitalization project should involve an assessment of the variation one encounters in the use of a language (or used to encounter, in the cases where few fluent speakers remain).

By *variation* we mean differences in speech (e.g. pronunciation, lexicon, syntax) among different groups of speakers. These differences may be correlated with any number of variables, including age of speakers, sex, socioeconomic status, level of education, religion, or region of origin. In the present section we are exclusively concerned with variation in the local language, as opposed to variation among speakers who have adopted a language of wider communication. In those communities where only a few speakers remain, it may be inappropriate to address language variation in the same way as when the speaker base is much larger. There may, however, be significant speech differences among even individual speakers. Although such differences may simply be idiosyncratic, they may reflect variation patterns among what were formerly speaker groups. Regardless, it is important to ascertain which variants exist and how they are viewed by community members. In some cases there may be published linguistic descriptions available as a resource, but these always need to be supplemented with up-to-date information that is relevant to the particular location(s) where revitalization is be undertaken. Speakers are almost always aware of language variation, and of the different situations where one variant may be deemed preferable over another. For a number of obvious reasons it is important to determine how language variation affects communication and whether it limits or inhibits communication within the community between different social groups. Part of understanding variation in a speech community is understanding the various attitudes or feelings of community members toward these variants (see section 1.4).

In terms of regional variation, speakers may recognize different dialects and may have names for them. Ethnonyms can also provide clues to language variation. It is important to remember that language and identity are intimately linked and that variation within a language can serve as an indicator of how speakers view themselves and others. If ethnic lines are firmly drawn and groups view one another as separate entities, different linguistic variants may need to be developed as separate languages even if this is not linguistically warranted. Social considerations can outweigh purely linguistic ones. As we have repeatedly argued throughout this work, revitalization can only be successful when the community takes ownership in the revitalization work, so community perceptions are paramount.

Though very often a basic linguistic description or other linguistic documentation exists for a language being revitalized, rarely do these offer a good picture of the variation. Consequently, information on the variation must be collected; and one common way to do this is through a language survey (some guides to conducting surveys are Blair 1991; Grimes 1995; Loving 1977).[5]

Established language survey techniques are based on the premise that there is a fairly large body of speakers, or at least a body of speakers, who speak a number of different varieties, so they are often not designed with endangered languages in mind. In communities where the local language is endangered, however, the language situation is apt to be a sensitive matter and to require extra care on the part of the fieldworker. Moreover, basic survey techniques may need to be adapted as required by the local particulars.

In the initial stages of building a language revitalization program, in particular one that will involve teaching a language to semi-speakers or non-speakers, one must determine whether variation is limited enough that a single standard can be used or whether varieties are different enough that more than one will need to be developed. Lexical similarity can be used as a quick measure to determine whether to develop one or more varieties. As a general rule of thumb, low measures of lexical similarity (say, 70 percent or less for basic core vocabulary) are good indicators of low mutual intelligibility. For revitalization programs, the lower the measures of lexical similarity, the more different the varieties are, and the greater the chance that different varieties will need to be developed and taught. The converse, however, is not true, and high lexical similarity does not guarantee intelligibility (Grimes 1995:22). Therefore, *intelligibility testing* can be used in order to help answer whether any one single variety is suitable for serving as the basis of a standardized variety, or which (if any) of the varieties requires a separate description or orthography.

One basic method of testing intelligibility has speakers listen to a prerecorded text and answer questions about its content. Grimes (1995) outlines one way of carrying this out. A sample text is first recorded, and at least thirty questions about its content are then generated; the thirty-question minimum is aimed at texts of at least two minutes in duration. If this number of questions cannot be generated, it suggests that the text is overly simplistic for the testing purposes and a different text should be selected. Once a recording and questionnaire are ready, they should be tested among a control sample of at least ten people who are believed to speak the same variety as the original recording. Only questions which receive the same response from all subjects should be included in the actual

---

[5] Doing language survey work involves many of the same methodological and ethical issues that surround fieldwork more generally. Whether working as an activist in one's own local setting or being involved in revitalization work as an outsider, it is important to have some background understanding of these issues. A number of guides to fieldwork have been published to assist in this (Johnstone 2000; Milroy 1987; Newman and Ratliff 2001; Vaux and Cooper 1999).

test; this step should result in a minimum of ten questions. Certain texts are less suitable than others for testing purposes. In general, texts with well-known content and/or formulaic speech should be avoided. Translated texts are also not preferred. Personal narratives have been found to be ideal for a variety of reasons, in particular because, as people become involved in the telling of a personal experience, they become less self-aware of their speech (Labov 1972:354–5), which often produces the most natural-sounding speech.

The results from intelligibility testing provide only a partial answer to the question of whether two language varieties are close enough to be considered the same for purposes of revitalization. This is so because intelligibility is dependent not only on strictly linguistic factors but on social and contextual ones as well. One key factor is the speaker's motivation to understand the other variety. In asymmetrical social relationships, speakers of the less dominant or less prestigious social group tend to have a greater need to understand speakers of the more dominant or prestigious group than vice versa. Therefore, the intelligibility of their speech varieties operates only in one direction. A member of the less prestigious group may have little trouble understanding the language variety of the dominant group, but a dominant group member lacks comprehension of the less prestigious variety.[6]

Intelligibility testing is particularly useful where similar dialects and languages are in contact because the points of variation can be complex. It is important, therefore, to identify the language/dialect boundaries and centers. What is critical here is that the core is often not defined geographically but rather is a social construct; the "core" can be the high-prestige variety and the "periphery" made up of varieties of lower prestige. In general it is incumbent upon the speakers of peripheral varieties to understand the core variety.

Note that the testing optimally provides critical information about the limits of language variation as well as about social dynamics. All things being equal, if only one variety is to be advanced in a revitalization program, it should be the variety which the greatest number of speakers understand and is the easiest for speakers of other dialects or varieties to acquire. It should also be the variant with higher prestige. Not surprisingly, linguists weight linguistic factors heavily when evaluating the

---

[6] This is true not just for situations of language endangerment but is true for language settings generally. It can be said to be true across the boundaries of well-established languages as well. For example, in the Soviet era speakers of Estonian claim to understand Finnish very well, whereas the reverse was not true. This is in part due to the fact that Estonians relied on Finnish television and radio transmissions, but also due to the higher prestige of Finnish during the Soviet years.

simplest form of a language or an orthography to learn, and they show a strong bias toward favoring these features when advising which variety will serve as a standard. Speakers of a language, or those who are recognized to have ownership over language choices, often respond to social criteria, and may favor a variety which carries greater prestige, even though it is not, from a strict linguistic standpoint, that which is spoken by more people or is even more readily intelligible. As a further footnote, we should point out that we are treating each linguistic variety as if it were a distinct entity, where in fact one should take care to examine different linguistic variables. It is the cluster of variables which constitute a given variety or dialect, but there may be cases where a particular variable is favored from a different region, or from a different "cluster." In other words, the variety cannot be treated as a monolithic, determined set but should be viewed with some flexibility.

Because language revitalization sometimes begins in situations where there are very few speakers, variation among them needs to be taken into consideration in ways that might be unusual for languages with large speaker bases. In such cases it is important to interview each speaker carefully, and to elicit as much information about each one's background as possible. This may provide clues as to how to interpret the variation, whether it represents regional or social variation for when the language was spoken more widely, or whether it is simply the sort of individual variation that is always found in language use.

Assessment of variation is an important precursor to creating a revitalization program that can be sustained over the long term. Understanding the basis of language variation helps in making decisions about standardization that will be maximally beneficial to the largest number of people. It can also assist in avoiding conflict among different constituencies involved in revitalization. When points of linguistic variation are not recognized or, more accurately, are not reconciled, there is the potential for arguments about whose language is "correct" or "real." Where only a few speakers remain, this can all too easily become personalized.

A full-scale assessment of language variation can take many years, however, and we would again generally advise communities to determine how much time to invest in it, depending on the resources available and the overall vitality of the language. For language revitalization, time is always a critical factor.

1.4   Assessment of needs, goals, and attitudes

In addition to assessing language vitality and use in the community, it is very important to understand the range of different kinds of attitudes among members. These include not only the goals and motivations of the community in its revitalization program, but also fundamental questions about how the group, and individuals within the group, perceive themselves, their culture, and their language.

1.4.1   Assessing attitudes

The assessment of speaker attitudes[7] tends to be more complex than assessing the range and distribution of linguistic variation. There are at least two sets of beliefs in potential revitalization communities, both of which need to be analyzed. First is the attitudes toward the local language versus one or more languages of wider communication. Second is the attitudes toward different variants of the local language. It is important to assess both of these.

In the first instance, one needs to determine attitudes toward the local language, how these attitudes have affected language shift, and to what extent they are reversible. What is the relative prestige of the local language versus the language of wider communication? How does the community perceive speakers who know only the local language? How do they perceive bilingual speakers? How do they perceive community members who speak only the language of wider communication? In many cases, the language of wider communication is associated with economic advancement and higher social prestige. If so, what drives the positive attitudes in the community toward the local language? More to the point, why does the community want to revitalize it? The assessment is a critical part of what has been called "prior ideological clarification" (Dauenhauer and Dauenhauer 1998; Fishman 1991). Before beginning a revitalization program, a community needs to determine what it really feels about the language and why it wants to revitalize it, or to confront such questions as whether the desire to revitalize represents more of a nostalgia toward the past than a vision for the future.

Second, the community needs to examine attitudes toward different variants of the local language. We have seen that attitudes are relevant in the intelligibility of closely related linguistic variants and that, due to social stratification, intelligibility is generally asymmetric (section 1.3). A full assessment of attitudes toward variation is thus important for the same kinds of reasons that make an assessment of variation itself important. Are certain variables associated with different groups of people? If so, what is their relative prestige? Do issues of language ownership intersect with

---

[7] We do not address the thorny issue of defining "attitudes" or the boundary between beliefs and attitudes here; see Agheyisi and Fishman (1970) for a summary discussion of the literature. We presuppose that speaker attitudes exist and that they are relevant to language attrition and revitalization.

social standing, and with language variation? Does the community value some variants more than others? The purpose of making attitudes explicit is twofold. The analysis will lay the foundation for determining which variants should be developed and whether more than one separate standardized form is needed. Moreover, this study can draw out underlying attitudes toward the local language in general, and so help determine how to proceed with building a revitalization program. Just as linguistic variables can be correlated with different ages, sexes, socioeconomic groups, and so on, so too can attitudes toward these variables. It is therefore important to work with a representative cross-section of the (potential) speaker population, so as to sample attitudes of both men and women of different social groups, of differing levels of education, living in different regions, and so on. We underscore the need to survey the *potential* speaker population, as opposed to the *actual* speaker population. The potential population is the target population which intends to learn the language and be involved in its revitalization. Members of this group may have different levels of knowledge of the local language, ranging from none or very little to full fluency, representing all positions on the continuum outlined in section 1.4.3 of this chapter. The actual speaker population could be narrowly defined as only speakers with full native fluency, or more broadly defined to include semi-speakers.

Sociolinguistic tests designed for assessing language attitudes have been created by and large with vital language situations in mind. They are potentially powerful tools which can be used as "sensitive measures of the place of a given variable on a scale of social awareness" (Labov 2001:196). Although they are usually written for testing a body of speakers who speak the target language fluently, they are adaptable to language revitalization efforts without too much difficulty. In general, the more successful tests for attitudes do not explicitly ask questions about a speaker's own feelings toward a given variable or set of variables. The *self-report test* avoids overt surveying of attitudes but gets at them rather indirectly (Labov 1966, 2001:194; Trudgill 1974).[8] In this test, subjects are given a range of variants and are asked which one most closely matches their own pronunciation. Typically, speakers select those variants with high social prestige, regardless of their actual pronunciation, which is suggestive of the form of a local language that can be employed as a standard for teaching or developing an orthography. This test cannot be used to assess language variation itself, as the results do not show which speakers use which variants, but rather which variants they wish to be associated with.

---

[8] Labov (2001:193–223) provides an excellent discussion of how he has used the self-report test in his own research on American English.

Rather it assumes a knowledge of variation within a community to begin with or the test will not lend particularly useful information, and therefore is only suitable for languages with a relatively large number of fluent speakers.

As a second sort of measure, Bourhis et al. (1981) argue for the testing of a group's perceptions of its own vitality and the vitality of its language. Their survey consists of a series of questions aimed at eliciting these attitudes, plotted on a scale of seven intermediary stages between the two polar ends. (Representative questions are provided in section 9.3 with sample questionnaires.) Bourhis et al. argue that the subjective perception of vitality may be as significant as objective measures in terms of determining intergroup relations and behaviors. Because the relations that a local community has with others are a major factor in the ultimate success of any revitalization program, it is indeed helpful from the outset to understand the value a community holds for itself and its language. In many instances, raising this esteem by promoting pride in a language (or other aspects of the community's traditional culture) will need to play a significant role in revitalization. Subjective perceptions can be and have been intentionally manipulated by outside dominant groups who wish to minimize the local community's self-perceptions and esteem. World-wide many native communities have been proclaimed by outsiders as "primitive" or "backward," with the result that generations of speakers have been ashamed to speak the local language and reluctant to use it with their children. The resulting attitude in the community is that they view their own language and culture as inherently "bad" in some way, and the language/culture of the external, dominant group as "good" (Dauenhauer and Dauenhauer 1998; Zepeda and Hill 1991).

1.4.2   A reality check on surveys

In the past couple of sections, we have pointed to surveys as a useful way to discover information about language variation, language vitality, and attitudes about the language. Objective data on these matters are extremely useful when designing a revitalization program. Survey data are typically much more reliable than the intuitions of the designers themselves, who can easily mistake their own perceptions as being typical of the community as a whole. The problem is compounded if linguists, missionaries, or other outsiders, are deeply involved. While an outsider's perspective can be helpful in its own right, outsiders rarely have enough experience with the community using a local language to understand the complexities of perceptions about it. This is true even in cases with missionaries who have been living in a community for decades.

Surveys, however, introduce a new set of issues. We have, at several points, noted the most obvious. Surveys are difficult to construct well and time-consuming to implement, so much so that in some cases they may not be feasible for a community considering revitalization. There are other issues as well which are exacerbated because the surveys need to be conducted in a bilingual community. The language of the survey is itself problematic; conducting the survey in the language of wider communication may in fact be a necessity in cases of attrition, but this alone sends a message about the importance of that language. Conducting it in the local language may not be possible, if that language is not comprehensible to many of the people taking the survey. The relationship and linguistic ability of the surveyor is also an issue. It is usually preferable that the surveyor be a member of the community and, in the best cases, bilingual in the local language and a language of wider communication. It is important, however, to determine this person's status within the community, as that status can have a significant impact on how people react to the survey.

1.4.3   Goals and needs

Alongside the evaluation of resources and attitudes, a community considering revitalization should assess its goals for the endeavor. What is the long-term vision for revitalization? What would be considered a successful outcome for the effort? The explicit goals need not be static concepts but may develop and change through the assessment process itself, and continue changing as the revitalization program progresses. Even so, without clearly articulating what the point of a revitalization effort is meant to be, the appropriate approach for a particular community cannot be determined.

The way in which revitalization goals are formulated can vary widely from one instance to the next. Minimally, however, they should include a recognition of who is being targeted primarily in the revitalization process, the level of language proficiency that revitalization is meant to bring about, and the intended domains in which the local language will be used. It is often helpful to the process of determining goals to conceptualize them as falling somewhere along a relative scale of outcomes, such as the following:

1. Full fluency (spoken and written command) of all community members; full use of the local language in all domains.
2. Spoken command by all community members; full use of the local language in all (spoken) domains.
3. Full fluency (spoken and written command) for some community members; use of the local language in many domains.
4. Full fluency for some to most community members; use of the local language in limited domains.

5. Partial knowledge among some community members, with fluency on some topics; use of the local language limited to restricted domains (e.g. traditional culture, stories, songs, religion).
6. No functional fluency; use of language limited to set phrases, memorized texts.

Note, first of all, that this set of possibilities is not meant to be exhaustive; many other combinations certainly exist. Second, the definition of domains of use is very much dependent upon the community and its needs; the local situation may make it very unrealistic to think that a local language could be used in literally all domains. Therefore, the specific potential domains for local language use can only be determined on a case-by-case basis. Third, the scale provided above should not be taken to imply that the written command of a language is somehow "better" than the spoken command, though it is meant to capture the fact that achieving literacy in a local language will place additional burdens on revitalization efforts in terms of resources. As discussed in Chapter 5, most advocates of language revitalization see literacy as an integral part of the revitalization process, but it may be neither feasible nor desirable to implement literacy in all cases. Obviously, more fine-grained distinctions can be drawn between these different levels, but the point is to underscore the need to set goals that are realistic for a given situation. Those working to revitalize a language must determine what levels of fluency they believe can be achieved, who will use the language, and in which domains.

Once an understanding of the goals for revitalization has been achieved,[9] the course of action a community must take to achieve its goals become clearer. If, on the one hand, the goal is full-fledged fluency and literacy in the local language, to be achieved through a total-immersion-type school system, the first steps of revitalization might involve battling legal barriers to creating such a school and developing educational resources for use in the school. Such activities may, in turn, require enlisting outside assistance, making decisions about standardization, or engaging parents in discussions about why the immersion school is preferable to other educational options for their children. On the other hand, if the goal is to preserve the use of the local language in a particular domain (e.g. for ceremonial purposes), it may be preferable to devote energy and time into recording this aspect of language use as much as possible, e.g. making video and audio recordings of recognized expert users, as well as creating opportunities for teaching community members how the language works in this setting. Here the

---

[9] The goals for language revitalization, more often than not, need to be negotiated because individuals have different visions for the role they see the local language playing in their daily life and the life of their community.

focus would be impressing upon community members how vitally linked the local language is to the proper functioning of the ceremony.

Regardless of the specific goals, they are always set relative to the current circumstances surrounding people who use, or want to use, a language. How much are they willing or able to invest in the effort? What resources are available to them? What kinds of resistance might be met both internally and externally to the community? Perhaps more than any step in the process of goal-setting, matching one's deeply held hopes for a language with achievable outcomes requires a good balance of optimism and realism. Language revitalization requires an amount of idealism because the obstacles to success often seem insurmountable. Without people who are willing to promote a vision for the possibilities, revitalization efforts can quickly give into pessimism and grind to a halt. Without people who keep that vision in check with carefully laid out strategies, revitalization efforts can involve frenzied activity, yet be entirely ineffective. In short, communities must be honest in their assessment of the level of commitment to achieving their goals, and honest in assessing whether the goals are realistic, but they also need to be boldly visionary.

2   Potential problems and how to avoid them

Communities from even the most diverse cultures frequently encounter the same kinds of problems in language revitalization. Within the community itself, such problems can include a lack of sustained commitment to revitalization, unrealistic expectations on the part of community members, a lack of sense of responsibility for the project, differences of opinion about language ownership, and flagging motivation when obstacles are encountered. In addition to internal concerns, there is an array of external issues, including language and educational policies, and limited or even no access to resources. In this section we examine a number of strategies which can help minimize the potential of such difficulties.

2.1   Problems that occur internal to the community

A very common obstacle in language revitalization is a mismatch between the resources available for language revitalization, including also a consideration of community support as a resource, and the goals for a revitalization program. If this is the case, the goals should be reassessed and adjusted as needed. They can also be expanded or contracted as the program progresses, but regardless, it is important to start a program with realistic goals. Unrealistic goals can lead to demoralization and frustration and may even cause community members to abandon the program. Creating and maintaining morale are thus linked to realistic expectations of the community. Motivation can often be enhanced by contact with other groups working on revitalization, even when the languages are unrelated. There is still a common experience, in particular if the groups work within the same national context.

Building rewards into the program can also play an important role in maintaining motivation. These might take the form of field trips for students who are learning a language, or special recognition awards for outstanding teachers. They might involve a banquet hosted in honor of elders who have given of their time, or they might be a casual event for people involved in the revitalization efforts to come and unwind.

Disagreements in language ownership and authenticity can create unfortunate rifts in communities and destabilize revitalization efforts. It is critical to recognize and confront such issues early on and invest the necessary time to reach a resolution and resolve conflict. The larger the overall effort, the greater the capacity to survive contention over questions of language ownership, but even here infighting can greatly hamper success. Of course, a degree of disagreement and debate can be healthy. They often provoke innovation and creativity, yet when disagreements devolve into fights over control of resources, competing for allegiances and the like, revitalization efforts are not energized but enervated, and they can unravel quickly.

Therefore, effort should be made to avoid potential flash points which involve who "knows" the language, who is "qualified" to teach it, who has the "ownership" rights to the language. In some communities, there are clearly identifiable language "experts," often those of the older generation or those known for their verbal skills. Where there is agreement among the experts, such disagreements are generally avoided. But where there are differences of opinion as to what form is "correct" or who speaks "better," an early resolution, one often involving compromise, is called for. This is one area where a professional linguist can provide much-needed help. Linguists can help others understand what variation occurs and, assuming they hold some respect in the community, can help educate members about the nature of variation, and guide in the decisions about which variants to use.

A lack of trained teachers is a frequent difficulty for revitalization programs that involve formal schooling. Here a stepwise approach to teacher training is often advisable, by using qualified speakers in addition to trained teachers as much as possible. This generally means pairing elders with teachers, often as classroom assistants, until younger teachers can be trained to use the language. In programs that do not rely on formal education, fluent speakers usually fully take on the role of informal teacher or language master. Some communities may desire to bring in outside experts in the language, often trained linguists, to help with initial instruction and training. Others may prefer to avoid reliance on outsiders altogether. It is important to recognize this problem from the beginning of the revitalization effort and to build into the program a means for correcting it. Thus a critical component of the revitalization program must be the training of future teachers who are, in essence, language leaders. In many parts of the world these teachers must be at least bilingual in the national language and the local language in order to attain teacher certification and in order to teach the curriculum to students.

There is no sure-fire method for guaranteeing that a community will not encounter conflicts and internal disagreements as it implements a language revitalization program. The most reliable way to avoid the majority of disagreements is to provide ample time for consultation in the beginning of the program, and to be willing to readjust its methodologies, goals, or intents as the program progresses. In communities with strong leaders, it is very important to have their commitment to the program from the outset. This may entail investing more time in the early stages of a revitalization program, but other activities can also occur while the political groundwork is being laid. Local politics can be divisive, but used properly can be a powerful advocacy force for revitalization.

One final problem that commonly arises in language revitalization is planning for continuity in leadership over the long run. Many revitalization efforts, particularly for languages where the number of fluent speakers is small, get started because of the vision and energy of a single person, or of a small group of people. Their charisma and dedication drive the program forward and inspire others. However, reversing language shift in a community, i.e. successfully revitalizing a language, is a slow, arduous process, one that will outlast those who start it, as their life circumstances change, their health fails, or they become burned out. Without the development of a new group of leaders who can take over, the revitalization program is completely vulnerable to unpredictable turns in the lives of its founder(s).

2.2   *External barriers*

As discussed in Chapter 2, macro-variables play a significant role in language endangerment; they are frequently overlooked in discussions of revitalization but are of central concern. Among the most important are language policies, education policies, and financial resources. It is difficult to make any particular recommendations because the specifics of different governmental systems vary greatly, and the amount of leverage and potential influence local communities may have also vary considerably from country to country. In some regions local communities may have a relatively powerful voice, while in others they may be silenced. That said, we can make generalizations about the kinds of factors that feed into national-level policies, with insights into how they might in the abstract be influenced.

Spolsky (2004:133) proposes a theoretical model in which language policy in any nation-state is shaped by four interrelated factors that may at times be at odds with one another. These are: the actual sociolinguistic situation; a set of beliefs influenced by national or ethnic identity claims; the spread of English as a global language (English has become such a driving force in the linguistic marketplace that it cannot help but affect language policies at the national level); and emerging pressure for rights for linguistic minorities. Notably, where these factors translate into educational policies requiring study of a second language, a common choice here is English, as the most "useful" of an array of international access languages. Only rarely do educational policies pay any tribute to local languages; as in the Mohawk case, which competes with both French and English in Canada (Chapter 4, section 3). When policies do permit the teaching of a local language, it is typically understood to be subordinate to the teaching of a language of wider communication. Only communities which remain outside of the reach of a national education system (perhaps because they are very remote, or the nation in which they exist lacks sufficient funds to administer educational decisions for the country) will not be directly affected by educational policy at some point. Therefore, there is often a need to advocate for linguistic rights in the realm of education.

The notion of linguistic rights,[10] at least in principle, is not new, dating in Europe at least to a 1516 treaty between France and the Helvetic state which granted rights to monolingual German speakers in the Helvetic state; a series of treaties, similar in spirit, can be found in Europe in the seventeenth century (Varennes 1997, cited in Spolsky 2004:114). Interest in linguistic rights became more acutely defined over the course of the twentieth century; beginning around 1990, a number of steps were taken on an international level to move toward securing them. Implicit in these measures is the assumption that linguistic rights are part of a larger package of fundamental human rights, a stance which has been gaining ground in Europe and the United States over the last decade or so, and has been at the heart of some legislation that guarantees the right to use minority languages, at least in principle. The European Charter for Regional or Minority Languages is one such document, and it provides provisions for the support of local languages.

---

[10] For an overview of the history of linguistic rights, see Spolsky (2004:113–32).

Recognition of the status of "regional or minority" is not, however, automatic, and gaining such recognition can be an important step in a revitalization process, as witnessed in the case of Cornish (Chapter 2, sections 2.2.1 and 2.2.4). In some countries local groups can work for their linguistic rights without harsh repercussions, and may find strength in numbers by uniting with other local communities. Moreover, international groups such as the United Nations and UNESCO have made it part of their own charge to be advocates for linguistic rights.

Yet, although states may have the obligation to protect linguistic rights, it is the responsibility of individuals to use them. Spolsky (2004:130–1) argues that the State's obligation is restricted to making it possible to speak a language; analogous to the observation of religion, the act of actually speaking a local language, and moreover maintaining it, falls to the individual and to the community, i.e. the collective individual speakers.

History has shown negative national language policies to have an adverse effect on language vitality; in some countries they are a potentially insurmountable obstacle. Yet we have also seen the powerful impact of activism on the part of language communities in resisting and changing such policies (e.g. French speakers in Québec or Basque speakers in Spain). Smaller groups may find a stronger political voice if they band together, as have many Native American peoples in North America. It is also possible to appeal for extra-national help; language is increasingly seen as a human right (Chapter 5, section 3.1.3), and such international organizations as UNESCO have issued strong statements to that effect. We do recognize that in some communities such activism is not possible. In these cases, conflict often centers around the language of education and who has control of local schools. Communities may determine that they are better advised to institute models which are community-based and rely less on support for regional or national governments. A fundamental part of determining which revitalization model is appropriate is assessing what is possible, given the constraints (or lack thereof) placed on a community by governmental policies.

A related issue is the question of financial resources. In some regions, governments are required to provide support for local language education and development. On the opposite end of the spectrum, others have no such requirement and providing such resources runs against their own language policies.

3   Updating the lexicon

Endangered languages tend to be used in increasingly limited domains, and these tend to be more traditional settings, with the language of wider communication used for domains which require speech about newer aspects of society, government, technology, and so on. As a result, creating a language revitalization program frequently involves updating the lexicon of a local language to meet the demands of the domains in which it will be used. If the language is still spoken by a body of fluent speakers, and community planners assume it will continue to be used only within its current domains, there may be no need to update the lexicon, yet this is a rare situation.

It is not uncommon for groups which are revitalizing their language to create a committee to test out new words. Consider Chochenyo, a Costanoan language spoken in the United States. In order to revive the language, which has not been spoken in about sixty years, it was necessary to fill a number of lexical gaps, not only to allow use of the language in new domains, but also because some vocabulary is not attested in existing documentation, e.g. words for 'a hug' and 'to feed' (Blevins and Arellano 2004). Therefore, a committee of seven members was chosen to represent different lineages in the tribe. In consultation with linguists, they develop new words to make the lexicon more robust. Similarly, the Hawaiian revitalization program makes use of a Lexicon Committee (Wilson and Kamanā 2001:168–9), which oversees all new Hawaiian words and votes on their approval. Their duties include publication of an annual update of newly created words, or newly documented ones. Groups with some official standing in the community, like the Hawaiian Lexicon Committee, do more than help regulate and standardize building of the lexicon; their standing helps ensure that the community will accept and use their recommendations, thereby circumventing possible conflict.

There are a number of means for deliberately creating new vocabulary. Depending upon the language and the community, a program may adopt only one or two specific methods, or use all. These methods include:

Borrowing from a language of wider communication. This method is often not favorable with local communities which are deliberately trying to minimize the influence of the language of wider communication. There may, however, be certain areas of the lexicon where using borrowed words is a reasonable and practical solution. These would possibly include new technology, media and computing, and perhaps popular culture. It may be particularly appropriate to adopt globally used words for items like *telephone*, *computer*, and *CD*. Some might argue about the inevitability not only of cultural infiltration in such arenas, but also of the linguistic infiltration (or contamination) that comes with it, so borrowings are often a point of contention in revitalization efforts.

Borrowing from related languages. The possibility of borrowing words from related languages and adapting them to the phonemic and morphemic systems of the local language may be an attractive solution for many communities. This has the advantage of avoiding any sense of accommodation to a language of wider communication.

Creating new words using the resources of the local language. This can be done in a variety of ways: by calques; by using the lexemes of the local language to build new vocabulary; by reassigning meaning to terms which have gone out of use. Let us consider each of these separately.

One common method is to create new vocabulary through calques, or loan translations, by using the word in the source language as the basis for recreating that word in the target language, but with morphemes from the target language (e.g. one might take the structure of the English word *winterize*, the root *winter* plus a causative suffix, to create an equivalent by employing the root for 'winter' and the causative from the local language).

Alternatively, new words can be created by using the local language's own resources without making any attempt to model them on other, foreign words, but rather building them internally only. This has been a common practice in Chochenyo revitalization, for example (Blevins and Arellano 2004). Based on attested pairs of words such as *hinna* 'to breathe'/ *hinnan* 'a breath' and *muyye* 'to eat pinole'/*muyyen* 'pinole', the lexicon committee decided to create the word for 'hug' by adding the nominalizer –*n* to the attested verb *pekre* 'to hug', ending up with the form *pekren*. The process of creating new lexical items for a language need not assume a one-to-one mapping between words in a language of wider communication and the local language. For example, in Chochenyo, the Lexicon Committee decided on *Huyya Warep* (literally, 'brown hills') to signify the month of June (Blevins and Arellano 2004).

Last, existing words and phrases in a local language can be extended to mean new things, thereby filling a lexical gap. In Chochenyo, it was decided, for instance, that the word *wirak* 'feather' would also be used as the generic word for *bird*. Such shifts can be particularly useful when a word in the local language has fallen out of use because culture has shifted. The word can be reassigned a more modern meaning.

We can further illustrate these different processes and how they can be combined by returning to the example of Kaurna reclamation, introduced in Chapter 3, section 7, with examples taken from Amery (2000:122–30). Kaurna provides a particularly useful illustration of lexicon building because so much of the vocabulary needed to be constructed in order for any reclamation to be possible. The reclamation movement is in many ways part of a quest to establish identity, and so borrowings from English (the contact language) are avoided as much as possible. As a result, there are only approximately twenty words borrowed from English. Some borrowings come from other South Australian languages, a preferred source.

In these cases the loanwords are assimilated to the Kaurna phonemic system. Examples include Kaurna *watteparu* 'seal,' literally 'meat in the middle,' from Narungga *wadiparu* or Kaurna *ga* 'and,' from Pitjantjatjara *ka*, Yolngu Matha *ga*. A preferred method is to use Kaurna resources to construct new vocabulary, such as in creating new compounds. For example, rather than borrow the word for 'garfish' from Ngarrindjeri (*rippuri*), it was decided to coin a new word based on the appearance of the fish, i.e. Kaurna *ta towinna < *ta* 'mouth' + *towinna* 'long, stretched, extended.' Calques operate on a similar principle, translating the source word, morpheme by morpheme or lexeme by lexeme, into the target language: Kaurna *wilto yerlo* 'sea eagle' < *wilto* 'sea' + *yerlo* 'eagle.' Morphemes from related languages can serve here as well, as in Kaurna *marrawitte* 'octopus' < Narungga *mar:awitji* (<*marra* 'hand' + *witji* 'much'). In addition to these methods, new vocabulary has been created by looking internally into the language. Kaurna, for example, has a number of affixes which can creatively be used to form new words, e.g. –*butto* 'full' (*yertabutto* 'dirty,' literally 'full of earth'); –*tidli* 'having' (*yangarratidli* 'married,' literally 'wife having'); and so on. Such morphemes are regularly used in coining words in many languages; what is different here is their intentional use by speakers to fill in gaps in the language's vocabulary.

Although Kaurna resists English borrowings, one area of the lexicon where we find loanwords in many local languages is in counting, measurements, and other numerical concepts, including days of the week. These enter the vocabulary of the local language under the influence of the culture of the external group. As Amery (2000:143) points out, many Australian languages have minimal counting systems, with words only for 'one,' 'two,' 'three,' 'many,' and 'few,' and so one is likely to find English loans for numbers in native Australian languages. Even where the numerals exist, when the concepts shift radically, the cultural changes may be accompanied by loanwords. It may be desirable to promote different uses of the system of original terms as opposed to the system which has been borrowed. As one example, in Kobon, a language spoken in Papua New Guinea, there is an extensive native counting system, based on body parts, which coexists with borrowed terms for time concepts and numerals (Davies 1989:143–4). Days of the week are represented using either the (borrowed) Tok Pisin names, or the Kobon numerals (though the concept of a seven-day week is borrowed from the national culture, representing a major cultural shift for the Kobon). For traditional transactions, Kobon numerals and Kobon shell "currency" are used, but when trade occurs in a Western-style store, purchases are made in paper currency; the counting is done with Tok Pisin numerals (Davies 1989:120).

4   Creating a literacy program

There is general consensus that a written language and literacy are necessary components of the majority of revitalization programs. Although a few groups may opt to remain strictly oral, most will turn to literacy as one important tool in the revitalization process. This is a complicated issue, requiring an honest evaluation of the attitudes and needs of the community, the development of a place for local literacy, and the development of some sort of educational system to teach the language. This all requires the creation of written materials as well as the training of teachers. Often the creation of an orthography and written language is necessary. For all of this, communities may need to turn to some sort of outside support. This support may come in the form of linguistic expertise in the creation of the written language, or as pedagogical support in creating pedagogical materials and teacher training, or as financial support. We cannot overemphasize that external support personnel are that – support – and that the literacy program must be created by and for the community. The number of field reports which document the failure of literacy programs due to a lack of community involvement, or a disregard for community desires, is striking.

In this section we discuss each of the key points in detail. A number of detailed handbooks have been aimed at non-linguist fieldworkers with very practical information for developing and implementing literacy, such as Bhola (1994) for the UNESCO approach, and Gudschinsky (1973) or Waters (1998) for SIL. All three provide very accessible overviews to guide language planners and community members through the steps in establishing literacy programs.

4.1   Literacy assessment

From the outset, communities need to be self-reflective and examine the role of literacy within their community. As we have seen, community members may have any of a wide range of attitudes toward literacy, varying from a strong belief that local literacy is impossible or without value, to a firm commitment to developing local literacy. Thus, before even creating a literacy program, it is important to evaluate the range of attitudes toward literacy in the community. In addition, it is critical to evaluate the levels of literacy in the community. If any segment of the population is already literate, or semi-literate, in any language, this has a profound impact on attitudes toward literacy as a whole. We divide our discussion of assessment into two sections, centering around these two main issues – assessing attitudes and assessing literacy levels. For a sample literacy survey that asks questions about both, see Waters (1998:40–2).

Key questions need to be asked in the assessment process to attain some sense of the general attitudes toward literacy. This process can actually serve the dual function of not only determining what current attitudes are, but also initiating discussion and posing new possibilities. These include a discussion of the places of local literacy and literacy in the language of wider communication. Are there inherent differences? When and where would community members anticipate using local language literacy? Related to this, are there any particular cultural taboos with regard to writing oral stories, folk tales, traditions, or religious texts and ceremonies?

In framing literacy assessment, it is useful to invoke the notion of literacy as defined by such proponents of the New Literacy Studies as Street (1994), with recognition that literacy goes beyond the mechanical skills of reading and writing; it is culturally shaped and determined (see especially Chapter 5, section 2.3). This means that, in order for literacy to be successful, contexts for its use – in exclusion of a literacy in a language of wider communication – need to be created. Establishing domains and uses for local language literacy is a necessary concomitant to the foundation of literacy instruction. One of the obvious contexts is the local culture itself, yet some cultures have taboos concerning writing another person's words, recording religious texts, and so on, which will make this obvious domain, or parts of it, impossible. Equally important is the question of why the community is considering local language literacy and what they hope to achieve by implementing literacy. Literacy does not, in and of itself, revitalize a language.

A second but related issue is the assessment of existing literacy skills. Community members may be fully or semi-literate in one or more languages of wider communication, and/or may be literate to some degree in the local language. Therefore, it is important to determine which literacies already exist in the community and how they shape ideas about what local literacy should look like and do. To return to the case of Evenki villages in Siberia, children receive some rudimentary writing and reading skills in Evenki, are fully educated in Russian, and some study English as a "foreign" language (Chapter 4, section 1). Our strong sense (without a formal survey) is that they view Russian as the national language, necessary for daily life in the country; English as a global language, helpful for economic advancement and for connecting with US culture; and Evenki is the language used by reindeer herders. People frequently comment on the need to know Evenki if you are with the herds; the view is that one cannot herd in another language. But there is no perceived need for a written Evenki language, since writing is not needed to herd. Part of the failure of Evenki literacy is the failure to create domains for written Evenki (Grenoble and Whaley 2003).

This leads to the question of when, if ever, a local literacy is necessary. Grimes (1985) sees the decision as to whether to develop a written form of the local language and introduce literacy as based on an interplay of levels of comprehension and attitudes toward the two languages, assuming a model of a bilingual community with two competing languages, the local language and the language of wider communication. Using a metric which takes into account comprehension in the local language and in the language of wider communication, as well as attitudes toward both of these, she concludes that local literacy is not needed in those situations where comprehension in both languages is high and attitudes toward both languages are positive. In these cases, Grimes argues that literature in the language of wider communication is sufficient and can be used by all. That said, this is a rare scenario in language revitalization. A second and more frequent scenario is when the comprehension is high in both languages and attitudes positive toward the language of wider communication but negative toward the local language. Here Grimes also argues that it is unnecessary to develop a literature in the local language and cites the case of Swiss German.

A literature in the local language needs to be developed in several different scenarios. These include those cases where comprehension is good in the language of wider communication but attitudes toward it are negative, as those negative attitudes interfere with literacy acquisition in the language of wider communication. This is exemplified by the Eastern Tucanoan languages of the Vaupés region of Colombia and Brazil. Elsewhere, where there is inadequate comprehension in the language of wider communication but positive attitudes toward it (and negative attitudes toward the local language), "comprehension needs require literature in the first language, but a programme to promote the validity and use of the first language needs to be carried on" (Grimes 1985:175). This is a fairly common situation for local minority languages. If we focus on the needs of local languages, however, it is important to expand her conclusions. As we know, with endangered languages, attitudes toward the language of wider communication may be positive, negative, or mixed, but language shift occurs as the result of some kind of pressure (internal or external) to speak the language of wider communication instead of the local one. A central goal of revitalization is to offset that pressure; local literacy can be a powerful tool, as Grimes suggests, to promote and validate its use.

4.2   Creating a written language

There are two basic types of situations where creating a written language is necessary. The first are those where no written form of the local language has been established; and the second is where some written form has already been created but, for whatever reasons, it is not widely used in the community. Even in the first scenario, it is not the case that one can normally start with a clean slate. Most communities will have some awareness of literacy in the language of wider communication even if community members are not literate. Many groups will also at least be aware of English as a global language; this alone may increase the prestige value and/or the acceptability of a Roman-based alphabet.

The situation is quite different where some written variant (or variants) has already been established but is neither widely used or accepted. Here, of course, it is critical to understand the causes underlying the lack of success. Do they stem from some problems inherent to the written form itself, or from a failure to make literacy part of the community? Or some combination of both? If literacy has not found a place within the community, is this the result of local level factors (lack of commitment, prestige, resources, etc.) or the result of higher-level administrative decisions (ranging from lack of support to deliberate suppression)?

Once the contextual issues for a writing system have been identified, the work of designing orthography and determining the standard form of a language begins (discussed extensively in Chapters 5 and 6). More often than not it is useful to consult with those who have some expertise in linguistics or literacy, but always with the recognition that good choices about a writing system are as much socially driven as linguistically driven. Orthographies and standardization can become symbolic of divisions within or among communities.

4.3   Creating materials

In this section we consider the creation of pedagogical and reading materials. In order to teach the local language, pedagogical materials about the local language are needed. This may be clear in programs which have a literacy component, but those that do not will still require that the teachers have access to pedagogical materials to aid them in the instruction process, to help them clarify details of grammar, and so on. In total-immersion programs, a full range of materials needs to be created for each of the subjects taught in the school. This entails the creation not only of textbooks and workbooks for such topics as mathematics and science, but often the development of terminology for these disciplines as well. This in turn requires deliberate language planning for the creation and adoption of a technical lexicon recognized as valid by community members. Reading matter is also needed. Simply put, in order for literacy to have vitality – outside of the school system and outside of any focused revitalization program – local language users must have materials to read in their local language. Translations are an obvious and easy solution to this, but hardly an ideal one.

The decision to create a program under the rubric of functional literacy entails producing certain types of pedagogical materials. Although some functional literacy programs have required that all such materials be produced locally, in the community, this is not an attitude which UNESCO sees as practical (Bhola 1994:99). They see this as unreasonable expectation of grassroots workers who should, instead, be encouraged to understand the materials so as to be able to adapt them to meet local needs rather than producing them all from scratch.

As discussed in Chapter 5 (section 2.4), functional literacy consists of three components – literacy, functionality, and awareness – and the instruction of each of these requires specific materials (Bhola 1994:98–112). For the literacy component, printed materials of all kinds are needed. Functional literacy materials may differ from those of other types of literacy programs in that a key goal of this program is to incorporate the functional (i.e. economic) component directly into the teaching materials. In other words, the content of what is read should be about, or relevant to, economic and vocational development, at both a personal and a community level. This reflects a very concrete goal of teaching not only reading and writing but also skills that increase a worker's or farmer's productivity and/or generate sources of revenue. Thus a central goal of functional literacy is to provide learners with materials that integrate literacy and economic skills.

Awareness materials may be more demanding to create. This challenge stems from the very nature of awareness education, which is seen as necessarily addressing issues of freedom and justice. They are viewed as ongoing, "timeless" issues, although the specific implications of these concepts change daily for people, making it difficult to create lasting materials. Moreover, not all grassroots workers are in a position to handle discussions of these issues (Bhola 1994:100). Our own concerns here involve politicizing literacy programs and revitalization programs in regions where their very existence may be highly sensitive and suspect to governing political bodies. Accordingly, the UNESCO recommendations involve a very different set of materials (and teaching strategies) for the awareness component, such as theater and the use of media, puppet shows, sociodrama, and a focused use of printed matter and discussion sheets.

At the opposite end of the spectrum are programs which, for any number of reasons, have decided to forego literacy. Examples would include those groups working within the rubric of the Master-apprentice program (Chapter 3, section 6) or groups which have determined that they wish to maintain a strictly oral culture. At first it may seem that such programs will not need pedagogical materials, yet here too certain kinds of pedagogical materials may prove useful. Hinton et al. (2002), for example, include a set of sample drawings designed to elicit conversation. Note that Hinton et al. (2002) is actually a general training manual, written in English, aimed at all potential language learners and masters, regardless of the target language. This is a striking example of a published manual, provided in a language of wider communication, as a particularly creative means for reaching a broad range of potential users where no one language has what would be considered a critical mass of speakers or potential speakers to create a local literacy. Not all material development necessarily involves the local language.

5   Teacher training

Teacher training is a critical aspect of language revitalization and cannot be taken for granted. In fact, the lack of adequate teaching training has been cited as the primary cause for failure in the teaching of endangered languages (Hinton 2001c:349; and see section 2.1 above). The reasons for this are relatively clear. Many endangered languages are spoken primarily by an elderly generation which is not likely to have formal training in teaching at all, let alone in teaching their local language. Those community members who do have formal training in education tend not to know the language well. Therefore, it is a matter of some difficulty to find people who are good teachers, are able to serve in that capacity, *and* speak the local language.

  One common solution is to begin by pairing native speakers with trained teachers. In communities where only the elderly have maintained a fluent command of the language, this can be very difficult, as the speakers may not have the energy needed to work with children in schools (Jacobs 1998), but where it is possible the results have been good. The burden of finding qualified teachers who speak a local language is most pressing for revitalization that depends on formal education, but even in other cases there is a need to foster language exchange between the most expert speakers and others. In the Master-apprentice program, for example, this is done by creating opportunities to train both the master and the apprentice together, in large part by teaching them to rely on their own knowledge of the language when they are interacting.

  Strategies for teacher development must play a role in the design of language revitalization programs. In this there must be a willingness to bow to practical considerations. In the development of Hawaiian immersion schools, for example, semi-fluent teachers have been used extensively by necessity. This has had the consequence of creating a form of Hawaiian which is distinct from that spoken by older fluent speakers and from the Hawaiian still spoken by the Niʻihau community. But the use of Hawaiian, at least in school settings, continues to grow, and a language that had a clear trajectory towards extinction may just remain vibrant after all.

6   The role of technology

Emerging technologies, especially on the internet, are seen as highly beneficial to language revitalization. Without a doubt, they can recharge and enhance language revitalization programs, and they offer a way for communities to make themselves better known in a regional, national, or international context. Current technology can also offer relatively inexpensive ways of developing language materials; it can be used to document language materials more efficiently than in the past, to create online dictionaries and other reference tools. The use of multimedia in instructional programs can be an effective way to enliven language classes (at least where such use does not come into conflict with traditional culture). In perhaps the most optimistic view of the role of technology, some see it as a way to create or expand the speech community and the situations where the language is used. As Buszard-Welcher (2001:343) puts it, "As new technologies develop and more people access and use the Web to do more things, the importance of the Web in *creating and maintaining community* can only grow" (emphasis ours).

Recently, a number of large-scale programs have been developed for documenting and archiving language data, such as the Rosetta Project and E-MELD. In addition, software has been developed to facilitate documentation and description, and a number of programs are currently available for creating large databases. Such projects and software are potentially very useful for communities that want to create dictionaries or records of oral histories, traditional stories, folklore, and so on. Recent advances in technology also make collaboration with experts easier. More importantly for many communities, new technologies make it possible for them to connect with other local communities, and share innovations, setbacks, and overall aspirations. This is useful simply for the exchange of information that can take place, but also because a key motivator in revitalization can be the sense that they are not "going it alone." Email, improved telecommunication, and the internet all help foster the building of bridges between different ethnolinguistic groups.

While the internet and computer technology may be the most appealing kind of technology, many communities do not have easy access to technological resources. In some cases they have easier access to other media, such as radio, television, and newspapers. Programs which propose a heavy reliance on technology can only be used in certain parts of the world. Both access to information technology (IT) and financial resources for technology are heavily concentrated in particular regions; the United States alone account for roughly 46 percent of the world's IT market, and the G7 countries altogether (Canada, France, Germany, Italy, Japan, United Kingdom, United States) make up about 88 percent of the total (Burn and Loch 2001; Grenoble 2003a). In regions where IT infrastructure does not exist, relying on new technologies may hurt revitalization more than it assists. For example, developing CDs for language instruction commits a language revitalization effort to providing people computer access and insuring that they can make use of it. Given the nature of computer technology, this also commits them to regularly upgrading software and hardware. It assumes some degree of local technical expertise. Such commitments are expensive, and unless local financial resources are also available the language revitalization effort will need to include a higher level of securing financial resources. Thus, while use of the internet and new technologies are often described as *inexpensive* ways for dispersed members of speech communities to communicate with one another or to make language materials available, this is not exactly right. And again, computer-based solutions to language revitalization are practical only for a minority of the world's local languages. At present only 10 percent of the world's population makes up the "cyberworld," 80 percent rely on analog communications; the remaining 10 percent have no mass communications whatsoever (Hodge 2001).

Internet access is growing rapidly, however, and such figures quickly become dated, but local communities in many parts of the world are still a long way from having internet access and the technology to take advantage of it. In 2001, the United Kingdom Government Department for International Development commissioned a study of the costs of internet access in a handful of developing countries (Cambodia, India, Nepal, South Africa, Zambia); note that these are all multilingual countries with many endangered languages. The report[11] concludes that, while many of the costs of providing internet access to these countries are not particularly high by OECD standards, even these relatively low costs are far out of reach for most potential users. In addition, a number of fundamental problems, such as high long-distance call charges, poor quality of technology, which can result in repeat calls and slow downloads, and the basic

---

[11] A full copy of the report is available at http://www.itu.int/asean2001/documents/pdf/Document-16.pdf.

lack of (fixed) lines in at least Cambodia and Nepal, for example, has impeded internet development there. The lack of telecommunication infrastructure is cited as one of the causes holding back large regions of the world, including portions of China, Latin America, and Africa.

7   The role of the outsider

The role of the outsider in establishing and assisting a language revitalization program has received a fair amount of attention in both academic and local community circles (Dorian 1993; Gerdts 1998; Grinevald 1998; Kipp 2000; Ladefoged 1992; Newman 2003, to name a few), though nothing near consensus has been reached on what kind of involvement is appropriate or desirable. One finds the full range of attitudes, everything from the notion that language revitalization should be a professional or ethical priority for linguists or missionaries, to the notion that they should stay away. For example, Darrell Kipp, co-founder of the Blackfeet immersion school (Piegan Institute Cut-Bank Language Immersion School) specifically advises communities *not* to work with linguists (Kipp 2000:4): "Don't hire linguists. They can speak the language, but the kids won't, and in bilingual education, they still can't. Nothing against linguists, they can talk the language, but they don't *act* like us. They are not us; they are recorders." The lack of consensus on the role of the outsider is due to highly varied personal experiences, particular understandings of the job of professional academics, and very different views on missionary activity and projects for economic development. We suspect that this kind of disagreement is in some way inevitable because of the very nature of language revitalization. As we have argued repeatedly, successful programs depend heavily upon community involvement and ownership; any dependence on someone outside the community subverts community ownership to some degree, yet at the same time an outsider may be a catalyst for change, may provide needed expertise, or provide access to resources. There is, accordingly, an inherent tension.

Currently, it is most common to find missionary-linguists or academics somehow involved as "experts" in revitalization. As programs are initiated and developed, it is important for communities to determine the precise roles that are appropriate for such people (as well as for the missionaries and academics to determine how they fit into the picture). What should they be doing? What should they not do? At what point do the they bow out? Is their continuing interest in a project beneficial? What follow-up might be needed?

Our focus here is specifically on people entering into a program from the outside. Linguists, educators, activists, or literacy experts who come from within a community (as most in Hawaiian revitalization have) may be focal points for questions about who has authority to make language decisions, but that dynamic is very different from when an individual comes into a community for professional, religious, and/or humanitarian reasons. In a sense they work for the community, but in another sense they want something from that community (data, religious conversion, or social change of some sort). The dynamic becomes even more complicated when they are not called in for a specific purpose by a local community (such as being hired to write language materials, or asked to come in to build a church), but rather have taken the initiative to be in a community.

7.1   The academic

The relationships between the professional academic (typically a linguist or an anthropologist) and community members have the potential to be truly symbiotic, with both sides benefiting in immeasurable ways, but this is predicated on the academic approaching the community with respect and letting decisions be made by the appropriate individuals in the community. The ideal role of the academic is one of consultant and facilitator, as determined by the community and its needs. The success of this relationship also relies on the community's understanding that the academic has professional obligations which can limit the amount of time available for revitalization work and that she is expected to generate scholarly work on the basis of time spent in the community.

The relationship between the academic and the community can be initiated in several ways. A researcher may have been working in the community for some time and be known to community members, who may come to the conclusion that they are interested in revitalizing their language. Alternatively, a researcher may enter the community for the first time, perhaps specifically because the language is threatened, with a desire to document it (or some other aspect of the culture). The work of the academic linguist or anthropologist – even the mere presence of one – may send signals to the community about the need to be active to prevent the language from disappearing. As field linguists and anthropologists know, it is rare to be working on the documentation and description of a potentially endangered language without confronting the issue of revitalization.

Communities may also initiate contact with academics to seek their guidance and assistance. For example, when they first set out to establish a revitalization program, the Mohawk community at Kahnawà:ke approached the linguist Marianne Mithun to consult with her about the linguistic structure of the language. Although there were still fluent speakers of Mohawk at this point, the community recognized the need for professional consultation to construct grammars, dictionaries, and other reference and pedagogical materials. This decision was presumably informed by two aspects of their situation. First, language transmission in its natural form had ceased; parents were no longer teaching the language to their children. This meant that the current parent generation and their children were not first-language speakers. Second, the community made the decision to implement a formal educational program which required the kinds of materials they worked with Mithun to create. This collaboration was successful in large part because of the mutual respect of both parties, and because it was initiated by the community (see Chapter 4, section 3 for a fuller description of this revitalization effort).

The need for linguistic expertise is apparent to community members in language reclamation projects in particular, as it is often unclear how to even begin without consultation. A recent example is provided by the Muwekma Ohlone Tribe, which approached Juliette Blevins for her advice on revitalizing their tribal language, Chochenyo, which had formerly been spoken in the San Francisco Bay Area (Blevins and Arellano 2004). The Muwekma Ohlone Tribe established a special language committee in September 2002; and the committee essentially began the revitalization work in January 2003. The language committee oversees the revitalization work, making all decisions not only about how the work itself will proceed but also about which linguistic forms will be adopted. The members of the committee are the first set of language learners whose task, ultimately, is to become language teachers as well.

At the time of the first report of their work one year later, they had made impressive, in fact inspiring, progress. A large amount of linguistic work needed to be done to reconstruct the language so that it could be learned and taught. There were no speakers and no speech recordings, although there were some recordings of songs. These songs, however, did not have many actual words and so give few clues as to actual pronunciation. The expertise of a professional linguist, in this case Juliette Blevins, was needed to reconstruct pronunciation on the basis of the available written materials with comparisons to other Costanoan languages. This is the kind of work which would be simply impossible for community members without extensive formal training in Costanoan languages and historical phonology.

In addition, a lexicon needed to be in part retrieved and in part constructed. Existing documentation of Chochenyo is scanty, consisting primarily of the notes of J. P. Harrington but also mission documents and some field notes. All in all, these materials lend a lexical base of some 1,500–2,000 words and roots, which falls below what is needed for basic conversation. A large number of new words needed to be created. The basic methodology for creating new words follows the guidelines provided in section 4, with a strong preference for the use of existing Chochenyo roots and word-formation processes to be used whenever possible. Our focus here is the positive interaction between the linguists on the project and the language committee: the linguists present options to the committee, which makes the decisions about which to use. In citing the factors which have led to successful revitalization, Blevins and Arellano (2004) include, first and foremost, the hard work and dedication of the members of the language committee and the entire community, along with regular consultation with linguists.

Though it would be a simple matter to point to a large number of cases where interactions have not been as productive, it is important to underscore that there are also many instances where the mutually beneficial nature of the interaction has been clearly seen by those involved. Amery, for example, reports:

As a non-Indigenous researcher my interests have coincided with the directions in which the Kaurna community was already moving. Members of the Kaurna community have inspired my research. In turn, my research has acted as a catalyst for the development of programs in the education sector and stimulates interest in the language within the community. Both feed off each other in a mutually beneficial relationship, though the initial impetus came from the community. (Amery 2000:11)

Finally, there are encouraging developments where local communities or groups of communities are making explicit statements about the interaction of academics with communities involved in language revitalization or culture reclamation. As one example, the Assembly of Alaska Native Educators includes among its published *Guidelines for Strengthening Indigenous Languages*[12] specific recommendations for linguists, along with those aimed at native elders, parents, education agencies, and so on. The guidelines for linguists consist of seven different points, which focus on the use of linguistic expertise to further the goals of the community. They advocate that linguists use their specialized training to work with the community to collect and analyze data, to help prepare materials, including the development of computer software and fonts, and to assist in the conservation and preservation of language materials. Their efforts should be "of direct benefit to indigenous people in their heritage language efforts."

---

[12] These are available at http://www.ankn.uaf.edu/standards/Language.html.

7.2   The missionary-linguist

Historically the missionary-linguist has been an instrumental figure in the documentation, description, and literary development of lesser-studied languages. Many missionary-linguists leave the familiarity of their home and their social network to go spend many years (often decades) in local communities, learning the local language and local customs and beliefs. The motivation to do so is deeply held convictions about the universality of the truths of their faith, and about the need for others to hear these truths. This underlying motivation all but guarantees a tension between ideals. On the one hand, the very reason the missionary is there is to change an aspect of the culture, most typically religious beliefs. On the other hand, language revitalization is often geared toward preserving traditional cultural domains, and traditional religious practices are commonly targeted.

As was noted in Chapter 5, missionaries have been instrumental in developing literacy around the world. There is, in fact, a high correlation between writing systems and religions, as religion often brings with it literacy, and can replace the local literacy with its own system. Obvious examples include the spread of Islam and the Arabic alphabet replacing other systems in Persian and Malay, or the spread of Christianity and the Roman alphabet taking over the writing of Old Norse and the languages of the Philippines (Ferguson 1982:95). This connection is to be expected. By and large the missionaries are committed to bringing their religion to a people and, whether through a sense of expediency and/or sensitivity, opt to do so through the local language. In terms of expediency, common-sense reasoning suggests that the mission's religious message will most quickly be delivered and accepted in the language with which the targeted population is most comfortable and in which it is most fluent. As we have seen, literacy brings numerous advantages with it, particularly in a globalized world. To that end, missionaries have produced not only biblical and religious material, but also descriptive grammars, lexicons, primers, and textbooks. They have established schools and in most cases taught in them. Some religions (in particular, Buddhism and Christianity) strongly encourage the translation of their texts into local languages, and so again the missionary may be simultaneously working to be an agent of culture change and playing an important role in language documentation and other forms of language preservation (such is the case presently with SIL). Again, there is an inherent tension here.

Not surprisingly, then, one finds mixed reports and differing attitudes among community members and outsiders about the appropriateness of a missionary-linguist's involvement in a community. It often seems that for every report of sincere efforts to assist communities in all different kinds of ways, there is a report of relationships that have gone bad and torn communities apart. It is all to easy to demonize the missionary-linguist, who can readily become the scapegoat for problems facing local cultures today. That said, we should be careful not to romanticize the relationship. As Ferguson (1987:233) points out in his discussion of Diyari, "we must not overlook that the missionary – in spite of his interest in the culture and his identification with the people, often in opposition to government officials and other fellow countrymen – was uncompromisingly opposed to many aspects of the traditional religion."

The basic rules and principles which we have outlined for (academic) linguists apply to missionary-linguists as well. We suspect that both groups would agree that the good of the community is their central concern, but there is often disagreement as to how to define that "good." We are firmly committed to any group's right to self-determination. There is a fundamental requirement to respect the community, its needs, desires, and aspirations. Community members, in turn, have the right to expect an honest account of why the missionaries are there, as well as what their goals are.

8   Evaluation and long-term prognosis

We consider evaluation to be an integral part of the revitalization process. Many revitalization programs will need to shift their goals, strategies and approaches as they develop in time. How is the success of a program evaluated? What is the long-term prognosis for a given language community? What does the prognosis depend upon? Evaluation should be an on-going activity, occurring with adequate frequency to insure that the community is achieving its goals, or adapting its goals or strategies as necessary. Frankness in this process is critical. As Hinton (2001a:17) says (italics original):

Honesty is crucial, because we want so badly for our efforts to succeed that it is not always easy to stand back and see if what we are doing is really working. It is important to look critically at the program and see what it is that it is actually accomplishing and what problems it has. Are the learners really learning the language as well as they could? Are the materials being developed really useful? How can the program improve? Should some directions be abandoned? Should new directions be taken? What is the next goal? Good ongoing programs, no matter how successful they are, never stop asking these questions.

Evaluation of a literacy program in formerly oral cultures requires special attention inasmuch as the introduction of literacy is a profound cultural change. The extent to which this change has been accepted and incorporated into daily life is a key factor in the long-term viability of a revitalization program. The creation and acceptance of literacy is a multi-stage process and should be evaluated as such. The very first step is awareness; in order for a group to contemplate local literacy, it must first consider it as an option. (Given the dominance of literacy in the language of wider communication, this is not so obvious to oral communities.) Only when the community has reached some conclusions about the possibility of local literacy can they accept it. Thus acceptance will be followed by proficiency and usage, in this order. Usage will come only after people are sufficiently literate to use the written language (Williams 1981).

9   Sample survey questions

The preceding sections have introduced a range of issues, many of which are best assessed in a particular community through surveys. Not all contexts are conducive to elaborate surveys, and the urgency for revitalization may preclude the necessary investment of time. Even in cases where formal survey work will not be undertaken, it is useful to keep in mind the core questions that surveys are designed to answer. To that end, we provide an overview of the kinds of questions that appear on different surveys: numbers of speakers, fluency, and levels of bi- or multilingualism (section 9.1); language variation (section 9.2); speaker attitudes (section 9.3); and literacy (section 9.4). Finally, we have proposed considering a survey after implementation of a literacy program, as part of the evaluation process (section 9.5).

Readers in need of more thorough guides to surveys would benefit from consulting the following: Grimes (2000:847–51) for the SIL basic survey template, which includes survey questions aimed at speaker statistics, multilingualism, second-language proficiency, and typological characteristics of the surveyed language; Waters (1998:40–5) for information specific to literacy surveys; Grimes (1995) for a basic handbook on conducting language surveys, with many references for more focused reading; Agheyisi and Fishman (1970) and Giles et al. (1987) for language attitude surveys; Robinson (1994) for various aspects of local language literacy and its place in the community; and Bourhis et al. (1981) for a sample survey for assessing attitudes toward language and ethnicity in Melbourne. These are all useful handbooks for constructing a range of surveys; again, any questionnaire needs to be tailored to the local specifics.

9.1   Language vitality

1. What is the approximate size of the speaker population? How many speak the language as a first language? As a second language? How

many speakers are monolingual? Bilingual? Multilingual? What are the numbers of speakers at different levels of fluency?

2. What is the age of the speaker population? (How many speakers of each generation?) How does age correlate with fluency?

3. How many speakers use the local language as their primary means of communication in all domains? In some but not all domains? At work? At home? In the school? Are there domains where only the local language is used? Where the local language is not used at all?

9.2   *Variation*

1. What kinds of regional variation exist? What are the names and numbers of dialects? How are dialects determined and named? How are they geographically distributed? How many speakers of each dialect? Is there any socioeconomic correlation with regional variation?

2. What is the size of the speaker base for each dialect? Are there speakers who use more than one dialect?

3. What kinds of register variation can be determined? Is the local language used in multiple domains and multiple registers, or does it occur in only limited domains? What is the relationship between different domains and dialects? In other words, which varieties are used for religious purposes, political purposes, education, and so on?

4. What are the attitudes toward different variants? Do the dialects vary in terms of prestige? What are the socioeconomic factors which underlie use of a given variety? More specifically, what are the attitudes toward the speakers of different dialects?

5. How well can speakers of one dialect understand another dialect? Assess degrees of intelligibility between dialects: not intelligible; intelligible only with difficulty; not sufficient to understand complex and abstract discourse in the other dialect; possibly sufficient to understand complex and abstract discourse; definitely sufficient to understand complex and abstract discourse.

9.3   *Attitudes*

As discussed in section 1.4, we see a need to assess both community perceptions about language use and language vitality, as well as independently measuring actual numbers of speakers, proficiency levels, and so on. The questions in this section are geared toward perception and attitudes, but many of them could also be used in a survey designed to assess the reality (e.g. which languages are taught in the schools, and so on). It is not uncommon to find a mismatch between perceptions of language vitality and actuality, for example.

The questions provided here are taken primarily from Bourhis et al. (1981); many are not as relevant for relatively isolated communities but rather are aimed at larger villages or even cities, in particular where speakers of a local language and a language of wider communication reside in the same location. That said, they can be adapted for other situations and can be useful in providing information about how a local group perceives itself and its relationship to other groups.

1. *Language perceptions*: How highly regarded is the local language? How is the language of wider communication regarded? How are they regarded internationally? How much are the languages used in the local government? In local administration? In such places as the post office, stores, library? How much is the local language used in the national government? Which languages are taught in the schools? Which languages are used in mass media? In business institutions? In churches and other places of worship?

2. *Group identity perceptions*: How often do speakers of the local language (and their descendants) marry only within their group? Immigrate to the region (village, town, etc.)? Emigrate from the region? How wealthy are they? How highly regarded are they? How much control do speakers of local languages (and their descendants) have over economic and business matters in the community? Are speakers of the local language proud of their cultural history and achievements? How much contact is there between representatives of the local language/culture and others? How frequently is the local language used in places of religion, religious worship, and ceremonies? In the language of wider communication? How *strong* and *active* are representatives of the local language/culture in the community? How strong and active do you think they will be in twenty or thirty years?

9.4   Basic literacy survey

The following provides some indication of the kinds of questions to be asked in a basic literacy survey. Note that, in any evaluation of literacy, it is important to distinguish reading from writing skills and use.

1. *Assess the use of literacy in the community*: How many people are literate and at what levels (high, medium, low, preliterate)? Does literacy in the community involve passive literacy (reading) or active literacy (reading and writing)? How many people in each household or family unit can read and write? In what domains is literacy used?

2. *Consider the relationship of literacy to sex*: Are both men and women literate? Do literacy levels vary with sex and with generation? Can men and women (boys and girls) both study in the same classes? Teach one another? Can older women read and write?
3. *Assess the status of written languages in the community*: What is the state of written development in the local language and any other languages spoken in the community? If written languages have been established, do they use the same or different orthographic systems? Is there a need for different orthographies for different languages? For different varieties of the local language? Are the varieties or dialects sufficiently distinguished from one another that more than one written form is needed? (Note that "distinguished" may encompass not just linguistic differences, but social/attitudinal ones as well.)
4. *Assess the range of attitudes toward literacy found in the community*: Distinguish between attitudes toward local language literacy and attitudes toward literacy in the language of wider communication.
5. *Assess literacy outcomes*:
   a. How many people in the community use their literacy skills? When and what do they read? Write? How often are they seen reading and writing?
   b. What language (or languages) is used for writing? For reading? What are the attitudes toward reading and writing in the local language? What attitudes do people have toward literacy in these different languages? Do the different literacies serve different purposes? Which purposes do they serve?
   c. Do people buy printed matter (books, magazines, newspapers)? Do they have the money to buy printed materials? Are such materials available?

9.5   Program evaluation

1. *Acceptance*: What percentage of the population writes in the local language? When and where do they read and write in the local language? What percentage have purchased literature in the local language?
2. *Proficiency*: What levels of proficiency are found in reading? In writing? How do proficiency levels correlate with age? With sex? With socio-economic status? What percentage of the total population reads well? Writes well?
3. *Usage*: Consider the informal and formal uses of both reading and writing in the local language.
   Formal usage of reading. Consider the formal settings in the community, such as the school, workplace, administrative offices, church or other

religious places. How much time do people read in the local language in these formal settings? Take into account the age and sex of the readers. The school is often the first (and frequently the only) formal setting for reading in the local language, so one ultimate question is whether literacy has found a domain beyond that of formal schooling.

Informal usage of reading. The practice of reading the local language in informal settings is a measure of the success of a literacy program. This variable is the percentage of the population who spend time reading weekly in informal settings (i.e. outside school and church).

Formal usage of writing. What documents and texts are generated by community members? Is the local language used for the writing of public announcements, local laws, newspapers, works of fiction, oral histories? Who does the writing?

Informal usage of writing. What language is used for informal notes, shopping lists, email messages, letters, and so on? What language is used for writing texts designed to be read only by the writer (diaries, memos to oneself, etc.)?

10   Checklist of procedures

In conclusion to this chapter we present a checklist of the steps involved in setting up a revitalization program as discussed here. Again we emphasize that not all steps are relevant in all programs, and each one must be assessed against the backdrop of the local community and its goals. This checklist is presented roughly in chronological order, but it should also be understood that in most programs one or more steps may be undertaken simultaneously. The steps are similar in spirit to those advocated by Fishman (1991) for reversing language shift, but differ in the level of detail: Fishman provides a long-term series of actions, whereas the procedures here are designed for only the early stages of reversing language shift.

1. *Vitality assessment*
   a. determine the number of speakers, relative age, and generational distribution
   b. determine the numbers and levels of speaking abilities, levels of fluency, and monolingualism or bi- or multilingualism
2. *Variation assessment*
   a. delineate the group or community boundaries
   b. determine the relevant dimensions of variation within the sampling universe, considering (in particular) sex, age, ethnicity, socioeconomic class, and domain of language use

3. *Assess community resources*
   a. assess human resources, which includes speakers (assessed in step 1) plus potential revitalization workers, numbers of trained teachers, etc.
   b. determine financial resources, including those held locally, regionally, federally
   c. determine access to other kinds of resources: access to media, levels of input to education/schools
4. *Determine community goals*
   a. what kinds of revitalization programs are possible and/or desirable?
   b. establish realistic goals and reasonable time frames within which to meet them. What does the community hope to achieve in the immediate future? In five years? In ten years?
5. *Consider potential obstacles and strategies for overcoming them*
   a. evaluate language and education policies to determine if the community's goals are realizable. Consider taking the necessary steps to change hostile policies where appropriate.
   b. reconsider revitalization goals in face of resources. Are the goals realistic and reasonable? If not, goals should be modified at this point.
6. *Literacy*
   a. assess attitudes toward literacy in the community; negative attitudes may mean either beginning with a program to educate community members about the benefits of literacy, or abandoning plans to institute literacy
   b. begin establishing potential domains for literacy; these may affect the way the written language is developed (c, d) and the kinds of written materials developed (g)
   c. determine the writing system
   d. establish a standardized norm for the language
   e. pilot-test the orthography and the standardized norm with a representative sample of community members, being sure to include community leaders and bilingual speakers, in particular those who are literate in a language of wider communication, as well as speakers who are not literate, if there are any
   f. adjust the written language
   g. begin creating reading materials and reference/pedagogical materials, such as dictionaries, primers, textbooks
   h. create reading materials for more proficient readers
   i. establish broader reading materials, including newspapers or columns in newspapers, journals, and so on
   (Simultaneously to undertaking many of these steps, other – public – uses of the written language can be instated, such as street signs, shop

signs, and so on. Such measures require relatively few resources and time and can have tremendous symbolic value.)

7. *Preparation for formal education*
   a. teacher training; depending on the nature of the program, this may be targeted at training language teachers or at training speakers to teach other subjects in the local language. Consider the use of teacher aides in the classroom.
   b. creation of pedagogical materials including textbooks in all target subjects (for immersion programs)
   c. implement introductory pilot programs to test materials and pedagogy

8. *Evaluation and assessment of the program*
   a. evaluate aspects of the program as appropriate
   b. modifications of the program based on the evaluation

We recommend building in an evaluation period at the onset of the program and basing it on the premise that one result may be a readjustment of goals and/or strategies.

This checklist consists of a brief and approximate set of procedures for the early stages of establishing a revitalization program. It will need to be modified to suit each individual community and is intended here as a basic guideline.

Appendix: Online resources

I. Reference materials

Code of Ethics of the American Anthropological Association
http://www.aaanet.org/committees/ethics/ethcode.htm

Guidelines for Strengthening Indigenous Languages
http://www.ankn.uaf.edu/standards/Language.html

Universal Declaration of Linguistic Rights
http://www.egt.ie/udhr/udlr-en.html

Teaching Indigenous Languages
http://jan.ucc.nau.edu/percent7Ejar/TIL.html

Native Languages Revitalization Resource Directory
The Indigenous Language Institute
http://www.indigenous-language.org/resources/directory/

Language vitality and endangerment
http://portal.unesco.org/culture/en/ev.php@
URL_ID = 9105&URL_DO = DO_TOPIC& URL_SECTION = 201.html

II. Examples of specific revitalization projects

Hawaiian
http://www.ahapunanaleo.org/

Māori
http://www.rakaumanga.school.nz/

Mohawk
http://www.schoolnet.ca/ aboriginal/survive/index-e.html

Comanche
http://www.skylands.net/ users/tdeer/clcpc/index.htm

III. Sources of support

First Peoples' Cultural Foundation
http://www.fpcf.bc.ca/

Foundation for Endangered Languages
http://www.ogmios.org/home.htm

Endangered Languages Fund
http://www.ling.yale.edu:16080/~elf/

Volkswagen-stiftung
http://www.volkswagen-stiftung.de/foerderung/foerderinitiativen/
merkblaetter/merkdoku_e.html

Hans Rausing Endangered Languages Project at SOAS, University of London
http://www.hrelp.org/

References

Adegbija, Efurosibina. 1993. The graphicization of small-group language: A case study of Oko. *International Journal of the Sociology of Language* 102:153–73.

Agheyisi, Rebecca and Joshua A. Fishman. 1970. Language attitude studies: A brief survey of methodological approaches. *Anthropological Linguistics* 12/5:137–57.

Agnihotri, R. K. 1994. Campaign-based literacy programmes: The case of the Ambedkar Nagar experiment in Delhi. In David Barton, ed., 47–56.

Alloni-Fainberg, Yafa. 1974. Official Hebrew terms for parts of the car: A study of knowledge, usage and attitudes. In Joshua A. Fishman, ed., *Advances in language planning*, 493–517. The Hague: Mouton.

Alpatov, V. M. 1997. *150 iazykov i politika: 1917–1997*. Moscow: IV RAN.

Amery, Rob. 2000. *Warrabarna Kaurna! Reclaiming an Australian language*. Lisse: Swets & Zeitlinger.

Amonoo, Reginald F. 1989. *Language and nationhood: Reflections on language situations with particular reference to Ghana*. Accra: Ghana Academy of Arts and Sciences.

Annamalai, E. 1991. Satan and Saraswati: The double face of English in India. *South Asian Languages Review* 1/1:33–43.

Annual Reports of the Kurdish Human Rights Project. 2002. http://www.khrp.org/country/syria.htm.

Ansre, Gilbert. 1974. Language standardization in sub-saharan Africa. In Joshua A. Fishman, ed., *Advances in language planning*, 369–89. The Hague: Mouton.

Arasteh, Reza. 1962. *Education and social awakening in Iran*. Leiden: E.J. Brill.

Asher, James. 2000. *Learning another language through actions*. 6th edition. Los Gatos, CA: Sky Oaks Productions.

Asumana, Charles. 2004. As Liberian language studies continue at Lott Carey: Elementary students exhibit academic skills in Vai. 16 July 2004. allAfrica.com http://allafrica.com/stories/200407160103.html.

Baker, Philip. 1997. Developing ways of writing vernaculars: Problems and solutions in a historical perspective. In Andree Tabouret-Keller, Robert LePage, Penelope Gardner-Chloros, and Gabrielle Varro, eds., 93–141. Oxford and New York: Clarendon.

Barton, David. 1994a. *Literacy: An introduction to the ecology of written language*. Oxford: Blackwell.

ed. 1994b. *Sustaining local literacies*. Clevedon, UK: Multilingual Matters.

Batibo, Herman. 1998. The fate of the Khosean languages of Botswana. In Matthias Brenzinger, ed., 267–84.

Beauvais, Jeannine and Philip Deer. 1976. *Kahnawake feasibility study of local control of education*. Commissioned by the Kahnawake Combined Schools.

Benham, Maeneette K. P. and Ronald Heck. 1998. *Cultural and educational policy in Hawaiʻi*. Mahwah, NJ: Lawrence Erlbaum Associates.

Benton, Richard A. 1981. *The flight of the Amokura: Oceanic language and formal education in the South Pacific*. Wellington: New Zealand Council for Educational Research.

  1986. Schools as agents for language revival in Ireland and New Zealand. In Bernard Spolsky, ed., *Language and education in multilingual settings*, 53–76. Clevedon, UK: Multilingual Matters.

  1991. Tomorrow's schools and the revitalization of Māori: Stimulus or tranquilizer? In Ofelia Garcia, ed., *Bilingual educations: Focusschrift in honor of Joshua A. Fishman on the occasion of his 65th birthday*, 135–47. Amsterdam: John Benjamins.

Bhola, H. S. 1984. *Campaigning for literacy. Eight national experiences of the twentieth century, with a memorandum to decision-makers*. Paris: UNESCO.

  1994. *A sourcebook for literacy work: Perspective from the grassroots*. Paris: UNESCO.

Biggs, Bruce. 1968. The Māori language past and present. In Eric Schwimmer, ed., *The Māori people in the nineteen sixties*, 65–84. Auckland: Blackwood and Janet Paul.

Bird, Steven. 1999. Strategies for representing tone in African writing systems. *Written Language and Literacy* 2/1:1–44.

  2000. Orthography and identity in Cameroon. *Notes on Literacy* 26/1–2:3–34.

Blair, Frank. 1991. *Survey on a shoestring*. Dallas, TX: Summer Institute of Linguistics.

Blanchard, David. 2003. *Seven generations: A history of the Kanienkehaka*. http://www.schoolnet.ca/aboriginal/7gen/index-e.html. Accessed November 2003.

Blench, Roger. 1998. The status of the languages in central Nigeria. In Matthias Brenzinger, ed., 187–205.

Blevins, Juliette and Monica V. Arellano. 2004. Chochenyo language revitalization: A first report. Paper presented at the Annual Meeting of the LSA, Boston, January 2004.

Bloomfield, Leonard. 1927. Literate and illiterate speech. *American Speech* 2:432–9.

Boerger, Brenda H. 1996. When C, Q, R, X, and Z are vowels: An informal report on Natqgu orthography. *Notes on Literacy* 22/4:39–44.

Bottasso, Juan. 1983. Missions among the Shuar. *Cultural Survival Quarterly* 7/3:20–3.

Bourhis, Richard Yvon, Howard Giles, and Doreen Rosenthal. 1981. Notes on the construction of a "subjective vitality questionnaire" for ethnolinguistic groups. *Journal of Multilingual and Multicultural Development* 2/2:145–55.

Bradley, David and Maya Bradley, eds. 2002. *Language endangerment and language maintenance*. London: Routledge Curzon.

Brennan, Gillian. 2001. Language and nationality: The role of policy towards Celtic languages in the consolidation of Tudor power. *Nations and Nationalism* 7/3:317–38.

Brenzinger, Matthias, ed. 1992. *Language death: Factual and theoretical explorations with special reference to East Africa.* Berlin and New York: Mouton de Gruyter.

ed. 1998. *Endangered languages in Africa.* Köln: Rüdiger Köppe Verlag.

Brenzinger, Matthias, Bernd Heine, and Gabriel Sommer. 1991. Language death in Africa. In Robert H. Robins and Eugenius M. Uhlenbeck, eds., 19–44.

Bromley, H. Myron. 1961. The phonology of Lower Grand Valley Dani: A comparative structural study of skewed phonetic patterns. *Verhandelingen van het Koninklijk instituut voor taal-, land- en volkenkunde* 34. 'S-Gravenhage: Martinus Nijhoff.

Bulatova, N. Ja. 1992. *Evedy turen. Uchebnik dlia 2 klassa.* St. Petersburg: Prosveshchenie.

Bulatova, N. Ja., A. T. Lapuko, and L. G. Osipova. 1989. *Evenkiiski iazyk. Uchebnik i kniga dlia chteniia dlia 5-go klassa.* (*Evenki language. Textbook and reader for the 5th grade.*) Leningrad: Prosveshchenie.

Bulatova, N. Ja., N. B. Vakhtin, and D. M. Nasilov. 1997. Iazyki malochislennykh narodov severa. In D. M. Nasilov, ed., *Malochislennye narody Severa, Sibiri, i Dal'nego vostoka,* 6–27. St. Petersburg: ILI RAN.

Burn, Janice M., and Karen D. Loch. 2001. The societal impact of the world wide web – key challenges for the 21st century. *Information Resources Management Journal* 14/4:4–14.

Buszard-Welcher, Laura. 2001. Can the web help save my language? In Leanne Hinton and Ken Hale, eds., 331–45.

Cahill, Mike. 2001. Avoiding tone marks: A remnant of English education? *Notes on Literacy* 27/1:13–22.

Calvet, Louis-Jean. 1998. *Language wars and linguistic politics.* Oxford: Oxford University Press.

Camitta, Miriam. 1993. Vernacular writing: Varieties of literacy among Philadelphia high school students. In Brian V. Street, ed., 304–14.

Campbell, Lyle and Martha C. Muntzel. 1989. The structural consequences of language death. In Nancy Dorian, ed., 181–96.

Canger, Una. 1994. A book in an unwritten language. *Acta Linguistica Hafniensia* 27/1:79–89.

Chomsky, Noam. 1970. Phonology and reading. In Harry Levin and Joanna P. Williams, eds., *Basic studies on reading,* 3–18. New York: Basic Books.

Cook-Gumperz, Jenny, ed. 1986. *The social construction of literacy.* Cambridge: Cambridge University Press.

Cooper, Robert, ed. 1982. *Language spread.* Bloomington: Indiana University Press.

Corris, Miriam, Christopher Manning, Susan Poetsch, and Jane Simpson. 2002. Dictionaries and endangered languages. In David Bradley and Myra Bradley, eds., 329–47.

Coulmas, Florian. 1999. Development of orthographies. In Daniel A. Wagner, Richard L. Venezky, and Brian V. Street, eds., *Literacy: An international handbook*, 137–42. Boulder, CO: Westview Press.

Crawford, James. 2000. *At war with diversity: US language policy in an age of anxiety*. Clevedon, UK: Multilingual Matters.

Crofts, Marjorie. 1976. Must tone always be written in a tonal language? *Technical Papers for the Bible Translator* 21/1:212–15.

Crystal, David. 1997. *English as a global language*. Cambridge: Cambridge University Press.

2000. *Language death*. Cambridge: Cambridge University Press.

Dalby, David. 1968. The indigenous scripts of West Africa and Surinam: Their inspiration and design. *African Language Studies* 9:156–97.

Dauenhauer, Nora Marks and Richard Dauenhauer. 1998. Technical, emotional, and ideological issues in reversing language shift: examples from Southeast Alaska. In Lenore A. Grenoble and Lindsay J. Whaley, eds., 57–98.

Davies, John. 1989. *Kobon*. London: Routledge.

Davies, Norman. 2000. *The Isles. A history*. London: Macmillan.

Davis, Shelton and William Partridge. 1994. Promoting the development of indigenous people in Latin America. *Finance and Development* 31:38–9.

Dawson, Barbara Jean. 1989. Orthography decisions. *Notes on Literacy* 57:1–13.

Deering, Nora and Helga Harries Delisle. 1995. *Mohawk. A teaching grammar*. Revised edition. Kanien'kéha: Kanien'kéha Cultural Center.

Dixon, R. M. W. 1991. The endangered languages of Australia, Indonesia and Oceania. In Robert H. Robins and Eugenius M. Uhlenbeck, eds., 229–55.

Dorian, Nancy C., ed. 1989. *Investigating obsolescence: Studies in language contraction and death*. Cambridge: Cambridge University Press.

1993. A response to Ladefoged's other view of endangered languages. *Language* 69/3:575–9.

1998. Western language ideologies and small-language prospects. In Lenore A. Grenoble and Lindsay J. Whaley, eds., 3–21.

Druviete, Ina. 1997. Linguistic human rights in the Baltic States. *International Journal of the Sociology of Language* 127:161–85.

Durkacz, Victor Edward. 1983. *The decline of the Celtic languages*. Edinburgh: John Donald Publishers Ltd.

Dyer, Caroline and Archana Choksi. 2001. Literacy, schooling and development. In Brian Street, ed., 27–39.

European Charter for Regional and Minority Languages of the Council of Europe. http://conventions.coe.int/Treaty/Commun/QueVoulezVous.asp?NT = 148& CM = 8&DF = 05%2F11%2F02&CL = ENG.

Evans, Nicholas. 2001. The last speaker is dead – long live the last speaker! In Paul Newman and Martha Ratliff, eds., 250–81.

Evans-Pritchard, E. E. 1956. *Nuer religion*. Oxford: Oxford University Press.

Fellman, Jack. 1973. *The revival of a classical tongue: Eliezer Ben Yehuda and the modern Hebrew language*. The Hague: Mouton.

Ferguson, Charles A. 1982. Religious factors in language spread. In Robert L. Cooper, ed., 95–106.

1987. Literacy in a hunting-gathering society: The case of the Diyari. *Journal of Anthropological Research* 43/3:223–37.

Finnegan, Ruth. 1988. *Literacy and orality: Studies in the technology of communication.* Oxford: Blackwell.

Fishman, Joshua A. 1991. *Reversing language shift: theoretical and empirical foundations of assistance to threatened languages.* Bristol, PA: Multilingual Matters Ltd.

ed. 1999. *Handbook of language and ethnic identity.* Oxford: Oxford University Press.

ed. 2001. *Can threatened languages be saved?* Clevedon, UK: Multilingual Matters.

Forsyth, James. 1992. *A history of the peoples of Siberia.* Cambridge: Cambridge University Press.

Freire, Paulo and Donaldo Macedo. 1987. *Literacy: reading the word and the world.* South Hadley, MA: Bergin & Garvey Publishers.

Fuchs, Lawrence H. 1961. Hawai'i pono: A social history. New York: Harcourt, Brace & World, Inc.

Garzon, Susan, R. McKenna Brown, Julia Becker Richards, and Wuqu'Ajpub'. 1998. *The life of our language. Kaqchikel Maya maintenance, shift, and revitalization.* Austin: University of Texas Press.

Gee, James Paul. 2000. *Social linguistics and literacies: Ideology in discourses.* 2nd edition. London: Falmer Press.

Gendall, Richard. 1991a. *The pronunciation of Cornish.* Menheniot: Teere ha Tavaz.

1991b. *A students' grammar of Modern Cornish.* Menheniot: Cornish Language Council.

George, Ken. 1986. *The pronunciation and spelling of Revised Cornish.* Saltesh: Cornish Language Board.

Gerdts, Donna B. 1998. The linguist in language revitalization programmes. In Nicholas Ostler, ed., What role for the specialist?, Proceedings of the Foundation for Endangered Languages Conference II, Edinburgh, Scotland, September 1998, 13–22. Bath, England: Foundation for Endangered Languages.

Gharib, G. S. 1966. Training teachers for rural elementary schools in Iran. Unpublished M.A. Thesis, American University of Beirut, Lebanon.

Giles, Howard, M. Hewstone, E. B. Ryan and P. Johnson. 1987. Research on language attitudes. In Ulrich Ammon, Norbert Dittmar, and Klaus J. Mattheier, eds., *Sociolinguistics: An international handbook of the science of language and society,* 585–97. Berlin: Walter de Gruyter.

Goody, Jack. 1968. *Literacy in traditional societies.* Cambridge: Cambridge University Press.

1977. *The domestication of the savage mind.* Cambridge: Cambridge University Press.

1987. *The interface between the written and the oral.* Cambridge: Cambridge University Press.

2000. *The power of the written word.* Washington, DC and London: Smithsonian Institution Press.

Goody, Jack and I. P. Watt. 1963. The consequences of literacy. *Comparative Studies in History and Society* 5:304–45.

Gordon, Raymond G. 1986. Some psycholinguistic considerations in practical orthography design. *Notes on Literacy* Special Issue 1:66–84.

Gralow, Frances L. 1981. Some sociolinguistic considerations in orthography design. *Notes on Literacy* 33:8–14.

Grenoble, Lenore A. 2003a. Globalization: who is left behind? In Johann Vielberth and Guido Drexel. eds., *Linguistic cultural identity and international communication*, 93–109. Saarbrücken: AQ-Verlag.

2003b. *Language policy in the Soviet Union.* Dordrecht: Kluwer.

Grenoble, Lenore A. and Lindsay J. Whaley, eds. 1998a. *Endangered languages: Current issues and future prospects.* Cambridge: Cambridge University Press.

1998b. Toward a typology of language endangerment. In Lenore A. Grenoble and Lindsay J. Whaley, eds., 22–54.

1999. Language policy and the loss of Tungusic languages. *Language and Communication* 19/4: 373–86.

2002. What does Yaghan have to do with digital technology? *Linguistic Discovery* 1/2. http://journals.dartmouth.edu/webobjbin/WebObjects/Journals.woa/1/xmlpage/ 1/article/101.

2003. Evaluating the impact of literacy: The case of Evenki. In Johanna Destefano, Neil Jacobs, Brian Joseph, and Ilse Lehiste, eds., *When languages collide: Perspectives on language conflict, language competition, and language coexistence*, 109–21. Columbus: Ohio State University Press.

Grimes, Barbara F. 1985. Comprehension and language attitudes in relation to relation to language choice for literature and education in pre-literate societies. *Journal of Multilingual and Multicultural Development* 6/2:165–81.

ed. 2000. *The Ethnologue.* 14th edition. Dallas, TX: Summer Institute of Linguistics.

Grimes, Joseph E. 1995. *Language survey reference guide.* Dallas, TX: Summer Institute of Linguistics.

Grinevald, Colette. 1998. Language endangerment in South America: A programmatic approach. In Lenore A. Grenoble and Lindsay J. Whaley, eds., 124–59.

Gudschinsky, Sarah C. 1973. Notes on neutralization and orthography. *Notes on Literacy* 14:21–3.

Hale, Ken. 1998. On endangered languages and the importance of linguistic diversity. In Lenore A. Grenoble and Lindsay J. Whaley, eds., 192–216.

Hampton, Roberta S. 1989. Using insights from the naïve literate as a tool in the linguist's bag. *Notes on Literacy* 57:41–6.

Harawira, K. T. 1997. *Beginner's Māori.* New York: Hippocrene.

Harner, Michael. 1972/1984. *The Jivaro: People of the sacred waterfalls.* University of California Press.

Harris, Stephen. 1977. Milingimbi Aboriginal learning contexts. Unpublished Ph.D. dissertation, University of New Mexico.

Haruna, Andrew. 2003. An endangered language. The Gùrdùŋ language of the southern Baruchi area, Nigeria. In Mark Janse and Sijmen Tol, eds., 189–213.

Heath, Shirley Brice. 1983. *Ways with words: Language, life and work in communities and classrooms.* Cambridge: Cambridge University Press.

Heckathorn, John. 1987. Can Hawaiian survive? *Honolulu Magazine* 21:48–51, 81–4.

Henne, Marilyn. 1985. Why mother-tongue literacy failed to take root among the Maya Quiché: A study in the sociology of language in a field program of the Summer Institute of Linguistics, 1955–1982, Guatemala, Central America. Unpublished thesis, University of Texas, Arlington.

1991. Orthographies, language planning and politics: Reflections of an SIL literacy muse. *Notes on Literacy* 65/1:1–18.

Hinton, Leanne. 1997. Survival of endangered languages: The California Master-apprentice program. *International Journal of the Sociology of Language* 123:177–91.

2001a. Language revitalization: An oveview. In Leanne Hinton and Ken Hale, eds., 3–18.

2001b. The Master-apprentice language learning program. In Hinton and Hale, eds., 217–26.

2001c. Training people to teach their language. In Leanne Hinton and Ken Hale, ed., 349–50.

Hinton, Leanne and Ken Hale, eds. 2001. *The green book of language revitalization in practice*. San Diego: Academic Press.

Hinton, Leanne, Matt Vera, and Nancy Steele. 2002. *How to keep your language alive*. Berkeley, CA: Heyday Books.

Hitt, Jack. 2004. Say no more. *New York Times*. 29 February 2004. http:// www.swaraj.org/shikshantar/languageextinction.htm.

Hockett, Charles F. 1955. *A manual of phonology*. Bloomington: Indiana University Publications in Anthropology and Linguistics. Memoir 11.

Hodge, G. 2001. Information policy: From the local to the global. *American Society for Information Science* 27/4:9–14.

Hofman, John E. 1977. Language attitudes in Rhodesia. In Joshua A. Fishman, Robert L. Cooper, and Andrew W. Conard, eds., *The spread of English: The sociology of English as an additional language*, 277–301. Rowley, MA: Newbury.

Hollenbach, Barbara E. 1978. Choosing a tone orthography for Copala Trique. *Notes on Literacy* 24:52–61.

Hoover, Michael L. 1992. The revival of the Mohawk language in Kahnawake. *Canadian Journal of Native Studies* 12/2: 269–87.

Hornberger, Nancy. 1988. *Bilingual education and language maintenance. A Southern Peruvian Quechua case*. Dordrecht: Foris.

1995. Five vowels or three? Linguistics and politics in Quechua language planning in Peru. In James W. Tollefson, ed., *Power and inequality in language education*, 187–205. Cambridge: Cambridge University Press.

ed. 1997. *Indigenous literacies in the Americas: Language planning from the bottom up*. Berlin: Mouton de Gruyter.

Huebner, Thom. 1986. Vernacular literacy, English as a language of wider communication, and language shift in American Samoa. *Journal of Multilingual and Multicultural Development* 7/5:393–411.

Jacobs, Annette. 1998. A chronology of Mohawk language instruction at Kahnawà:ke. In Lenore A. Grenoble and Lindsay J. Whaley, eds., 117–23.

Janse, Mark and Sijmen Tol, eds. 2003. *Language death and language maintenance. Theoretical, practical and descriptive approaches*. Amsterdam: John Benjamins.

Jenner, Henry. 1904. *A handbook of the Cornish language*. London: David Nutt.

Jocks, Christopher. 1998. Living words and cartoon translations: Longhouse "texts" and the limitations of English. In Lenore A. Grenoble and Lindsay J. Whaley, eds., 217–33.

Johnstone, Barbara. 2000. *Qualitative methods in sociolinguistics*. Oxford: Oxford University Press.

Kamanā, Kauanoe. 1990. Punana Leo: Leading education for a new generation of Hawaiian speakers. In Stephen Canham, ed., *Literature and Hawaii's children. Spirit, land and storytelling: The heritage of childhood*, 171–80. Honolulu: University of Hawai'i.

Karetu, Timoti S. 1994. Māori language rights in New Zealand. In Tove Skutnabb-Kangas and Robert Phillipson, eds., *Linguistic human rights: Overcoming linguistic discrimination*, 208–18. Berlin: Mouton de Gruyter.

Keptuke, Galina. 1991. *Dvunogii da poperechnoglazyi chernogolovyi chelovek – Evenk i ego zemlia dulin buga*. Yakutsk: Rozovaia chaika.

Kibrik, A. E. 1991. The problem of endangered languages in the USSR. In Robert H. Robins and Eugenius M. Uhlenbeck, eds., 257–73.

King, Jeanette. 2001. Te Kōhanga Reo: Māori language revitalization. In Leanne Hinton and Ken Hale, eds., 119–28.

King, Robert D. 1998. *Nehru and the language politics of India*. Delhi: Oxford University Press.

  2001. The potency of script: Hindi and Urdu. *International Journal of the Sociology of Language* 150:43–59.

Kinkade, M. Dale. 1991. The decline of native languages in Canada. In Robert H. Robins and Eugenius M. Uhlenbeck, eds., 157–76.

Kipp, Darrell R. 2000. Encouragement, guidance, insights and lessons learned for native language activists developing their own tribal language programs. Browning, MT: Piegan Institute. Also available at http://www.grottofoundation.org/download_fset.html.

Klein, Harriet E. Manelis and Louisa R. Stark, eds. 1985. *South American Indian languages, retrospect and prospect*. Austin: University of Texas Press.

Klima, Edward S. 1972. How alphabets might reflect language. In James F. Kavanagh and Ignatius G. Mattingly, eds., *Language by ear and by eye: The relationship between speech and reading*, 57–80. Cambridge, MA: MIT Press.

Koelle, S. W. 1854. *Outlines of a grammar of the Vei language*. London: Church Missionary House. Reprinted Farnborough, England: Gregg International Publishers, 1968.

Koffi, Ettien N. 1994. The representation of tones in the orthography. *Notes on Literacy* 20/3:51–9.

Kolesnikova, V. D. 1989. *Evenkiisko-russkii slovar'*. 2nd edition. Leningrad: Prosveshchenie.

Krauss, Michael. 1992. The world's languages in crisis. *Language* 68/1:4–10.

  1997. The indigenous languages of the North: A report on their present state. Northern minority languages: Problems of survival. *Senri Ethnological Studies* 44:1–34.

Kreindler, Isabelle T., ed. 1985. *Sociolinguistic perspectives on Soviet national languages. Their past, present and future*. Berlin: Mouton de Gruyter.

Kutscher, Eduard Yechezkel. 1982. *A history of the Hebrew language*. Jerusalem: Magnus Press.

Kymlicka, Will. 1995. *The rights of minority cultures*. Oxford: Oxford University Press.

Labov, William. 1966. *The social stratification of English in New York City*. Washington, DC: Center for Applied Linguistics.

   1972. *Language in the inner city*. Philadelphia: University of Pennsylvania Press.

   2001. *Principles of linguistic change. Social factors*. Oxford: Blackwell.

Ladefoged, Peter. 1992. Another view of endangered languages. *Language* 68/4:809–11.

Lazore, Dorothy Karihwenhawe. 1993. *The Mohawk language standardisation project*. Conference report, 9–10 August 1993. Translated and edited by Annette Kaia'titahkhe Jacobs, Nancy Kahawinonkie Thompson, and Minnie Kaia:khons Leaf. http://www.edu.gov.on.ca/eng/training/literacy/mohawk/mohawk.html.

Levine, Kenneth. 1982. Functional literacy: Fond illusions and false economies. *Harvard Educational Review* 52:249–66.

   1986. *The social context of literacy*. London: Routledge & Kegan Paul.

Levy-Bruhl, Lucien. 1926/1966. *How natives think*. Translation of *La mentalité primitive*. New York: Washington Square Press.

Lewis, E. Glyn. 1973. *Multilingualism in the Soviet Union. Aspects of language policy and its implementation*. The Hague: Mouton.

Linn, Andrew R. and Nicola McLelland, eds. 2002. *Standardization. Studies from the Germanic languages*. Amsterdam: John Benjamins.

Lo Bianco, Joseph and Mari Rhydwen. 2001. Is the extinction of Australia's indigenous languages inevitable? In Joshua Fishman, ed., 391–422.

Loving, Richard, ed. 1977. *Language variation and survey techniques*. Workpapers in Papua New Guinea Languages, vol. 21.

McConnell, Grant D. and B. P. Mahapatra. 1990. The written languages of India. *Proceedings of the Indo Canadian Round Table*, New Delhi, India, 7–8 March 1988. Publication B 174. CS: Laval University, Québec. International Center for Research on Bilingualism.

Macdonald, Theodore. 1986. Shuar children: Bilingual-bicultural education. *Cultural Survival Quarterly* 10/4.18–20.

McKay, Graham R. 1982. Attitudes of Kunibidji speakers to literacy. *International Journal of the Sociology of Language* 36:105–14.

   1983. Lexicography and Ndjebbana (Kunibidji) bilingual education program. In Peter K. Austin, ed., *Papers in Australian linguistics no. 15: Australian Aboriginal lexicography*, 19–30. Pacific linguistics A-66. Canberra: Department of Linguistics.

Mackerras, Colin. 1994. *China's minorities: Integration and modernization in the twentieth century*. Oxford: Oxford University Press.

Maffi, Luisa. 2001. Introduction: On the interdependence of biological and cultural diversity. In Luisa Maffi, ed., *On biocultural diversity: Linking language, knowledge and the environment*, 1–50. Washington: Smithsonian Institution.

Magner, Thomas F. 2001. Digraphia in the territories of the Croats and Serbs. *International Journal of the Sociology of Language* 150:11–26.

Maksimova, A. I. 1995. *Dukuriva alamavun. Posobie dlia I klassa.* Yakutsk: Bichik.

Maybin, Janet, ed. 1994. *Language and literacy in social practice.* Clevedon, UK: Multilingual Matters.

Milroy, Lesley. 1987. *Observing and analysing natural language: A critical account of sociolinguistic method.* Oxford: Blackwell.

Morgan, Clare. 2003. Cornish is to be promoted. *Geolinguistics* 29:273–4.

Moynihan, Daniel Patrick, 1993. *Pandemonium: Ethnicity in international politics.* New York: Oxford University Press.

Mugele, Robert L. 1978. The pedagogical implications of undersymbolization in orthography. *Notes on Literacy* 24:22–5.

Mühlhäusler, Peter. 1990. "Reducing" Pacific languages to writing. In John E. Joseph and Talbot J. Taylor, eds., *Ideologies of language,* 189–205. London: Routledge.

   1996. *Linguistic ecology: Language change and linguistic imperialism in the Pacific region.* London: Routledge.

Mullarney, Maire. 1987. *The departure of Latin. Language problems and language planning* 11/3:356–60.

Munro, Pamela, and Lopez, F. H. 2003. Can there be a Valley Zapotec Orthography? Paper presented at the annual meeting of the Society for the Study of the Indigenous Languages of America (SSILA), January 2003, Boston.

Myers-Scotton, Carol. 1993. *Duelling languages. Grammatical structure in code-switching.* Oxford: Clarendon Press.

Myreeva, A. N. 1993. Iazykovaia situatsiia i perspektivy razvitiia iazyka evenkov Iakutii. In M. M. Xatylaev, X. I. Dutkin and T. P. Rodionov, eds., *Malochislennye narody severa Iakutii: Sostoianie, problemy,* 71–4. Iakutsk: Iakutskii Naunchnyi Tsentr SO RAN.

Nahir, Moshe. 1984. Language planning goals: A classification. *Language problems and language planning* 8/3: 294–327.

Nance, R. Morton. 1929. *Cornish for all – A guide to Unified Cornish.* 3rd edition 1958. Penzance: Saundry for Federation of Old Cornwall Societies.

National Indian Brotherhood/Assembly of First Nations. 1972. *Feasibility Study on Indian control of Indian education.* Policy paper presented to the Minister of Indian Affairs and Northern Development. Ottawa: Assembly of First Nations.

Neroznak, V. P., ed. 1994. *Krasnaia kniga iazykov narodov Rossii.* Moscow: Academiia.

Nettle, Daniel and Suzanne Romaine. 2000. *Vanishing voices: The extinction of the world's languages.* Oxford: Oxford University Press.

Newman, Paul. 2003. The endangered languages issue as a hopeless cause. In Mark Janse and Sijmen Tol, eds., 1–13.

Newman, Paul and Martha Ratliff, eds. 2001. *Linguistic fieldwork.* Cambridge: Cambridge University Press.

Obeng, Samuel Gyasi and Efurosibina Adegbija. 1999. Sub-saharan Africa. In Joshua F. Fishman, ed., 353–68.

Oegir, Nikolai. 1987. *Ile upkattuk engesitmer.* Krasnoyarsk: Krasnoe knizhnoe izdatel'stvo.

Olson, David. 1977. From utterance to text: The bias of language in speech and writing. *Harvard Education Review* 47/3:257–81.

1994a. Literacy and the making of the Western mind. In Ludo Verhoeven, ed., 135–50.

1994b. *The world on paper: The conception and cognitive implications of writing and reading.* Cambridge: Cambridge University Press.

Olson, David, Nancy Torrance, and Angela Hildyard. 1985. *Literacy, language, and learning.* Cambridge: Cambridge University Press.

Ong, Walter. 1982. *Orality and literacy: The technologizing of the word.* London: Methuen.

1996. *The natural world of the Māori.* 2nd edition. Auckland, David Bateman.

Orbell, Margaret. 1995. *The illustrated encyclopedia of Māori myth and legend.* Christchurch: Canterbury University Press.

Paulston, Christina Bratt, Pow Chee Chen, and Mary C. Connerty. 1993. Language regenesis: A conceptual overview of language revival, revitalization and reversal. *Journal of Multilingual and Multicultural Development.* 14/4:275–86.

Phillipson, Robert. 1992. *Linguistic imperialism.* Oxford: Oxford University Press.

Pike, Kenneth L. 1948. *Tone languages – a technique for determining the number and type of pitch contrasts in a language, with studies in tonemic substitution and fusion.* University of Michigan publications. Linguistics, 4. Ann Arbor: University of Michigan Press.

Posner, Rebecca and Kenneth H. Rogers. 1993. Bilingualism and language contact in Rhaeto-Romance. In Rebecca Posner and John N. Green, eds., *Trends in Romance linguistics and philology*, Vol. 5, *Bilingualism and linguistic conflict in Romance*, 231–52. Berlin: Mouton de Gruyter.

Powlison, Paul. 1968. Bases for formulating an efficient orthography. *The Bible Translator* 19:74–91.

Proeve, E. H. and H. F. W. Proeve. 1952. *A work of love and sacrifice: The story of the mission among the Dieri tribe at Cooper's creek.* Tanuda, Australia: Auricht's Printing Office.

Reinecke, John E. 1969. *Language and dialect in Hawai'i: A sociolinguistic history to 1935.* Honolulu: University of Hawai'i Press.

Rice, Keren D. 1995. Developing orthographies: The Athapaskan languages of the Northwest Territories, Canada. In I. Taylor and D. R. Olson, eds., *Scripts and literacy*, 77–94. The Netherlands: Kluwer.

Robbins, Frank. E. 1992. Standardization of unwritten vernaculars. In Shin Ja J. Hwang and William R. Merrifield, eds., *Language in context: Essays for Robert E. Longacre*, 605–16. Dallas, TX: Summer Institute of Linguistics.

Robins, Robert H. and Eugenius M. Uhlenbeck, eds. 1991. *Endangered languages.* Oxford: Berg Publishers.

Robinson, Clinton D. W. 1994. Local languages for local literacies? Debating a cultural dilemma. In David Barton, ed., 69–74.

Rogers, Henry. 1995. Optimal orthographies. In Insup Taylor and David R. Olson, eds., *Scripts and literacy*, 31–43. Dordrecht: Kluwer.

Romaine, Suzanne. 1991. The status of Tok Pisin in Papua New Guinea: The colonial predicament. In Ulrich Ammon and Marlis Hellinger, eds., *Status change of languages*, 229–53. Berlin: Mouton de Gruyter.

1994. *Language in society. An introduction to sociolinguistics*. Oxford: Oxford University Press.

Rubenstein, Steven Lee. 1995. The politics of Shuar shamanism. Unpublished Ph.D. dissertation, University of Columbia.

Salazar, Ernesto. 1977. *An Indian federation in lowland Ecuador*. Document 28. Copenhagen: International Work Group for Indigenous Affairs.

Sampson, Geoffrey. 1985. *Writing systems*. Stanford: Stanford University Press.

Sasse, Hans-Jürgen. 1992. Language decay and contact-induced change: similarities and differences. In Matthias Brenzinger, ed., 59–80.

Saulson, Scott B. 1979. *Institutionalized language planning: Documents and analysis of the revival of Hebrew*. The Hague: Mouton.

Schäppi, Peter. 1974. Die rechtliche Stellung des Rätoromanischen im Bund und in Kanton Graubünden. In Theo Kunz, ed., *Rätoromanisch – Gegenwart und Zunkunft einer gefährdeten Sprache*, 75–98. Aarau: Sauerländer.

Schiffman, Harold F. 1998. Standardization or restandardization: The case for "standard" spoken Tamil. *Language in Society* 27:359–85.

Schmidt, Ronald. 2000. *Language policy and identity politics in the United States*. Philadelphia, PA: Temple University Press.

Schmitt, Robert C. 1968. *Demographic statistics of Hawai'i 1778–1965*. Honolulu: University of Hawai'i Press.

Scribner, Sylvia and Michael Cole. 1981. *The psychology of literacy*. Cambridge, MA: Harvard University Press.

1988. Unpackaging literacy. In E. R. Kintgen, Barry M. Knoll, and Mike Rose, eds., *Perspectives on literacy*, 57–70. Carbondale: Southern Illinois University.

Shield, Lesley E. 1984. Unified Cornish – Fiction or fact? An examination of the death and resurrection of the Cornish language. *Journal of Multilingual and Multicultural Development* 5/3–4:329–37.

Simons, Gary F. 1994. Principles of multidialectical orthography design. *Notes on Literacy* 20/2:13–34.

Singh, Udaya Narayana. 2001. Multiscriptality in South Asia. *International Journal of the Sociology of Language* 150:61–74.

Skutnabb-Kangas, Tove. 1994. Linguistic human rights in education. *Language Policy in the Baltic States. Conference Papers*, 173–91. Riga: Gara pupa.

2000. *Linguistic genocide in education – or worldwide diversity and human rights?* Mahwah, NJ: Lawrence Erlbaum.

Slezkine, Yuri. 1994. *Arctic mirrors: Russia and the small peoples of the North*. Ithaca: Cornell University Press.

Snider, Keith L. 1992. "Grammatical tone" and orthography. *Notes on Literacy* 18/4:25–30.

Spolsky, Bernard. 2003. Reassessing Māori regeneration. *Language in Society* 32:553–78.

2004. *Language policy*. Cambridge: Cambridge University Press.

Spolsky, Bernard and Patricia Irvine. 1982. Sociolinguistic aspects of the acceptance of literacy in the vernacular. In Florence Barkin, Elizabeth A. Brandt, and Jacob

Ornstein-Galicia, eds., *Bilingualism and language contact: Spanish, English and Native American languages*, 73–9. New York: Teachers College Press.

Spolsky, Bernard, G. Engelbrecht, and L. Ortiz. 1983. Religious, political and educational factors in the development of biliteracy in the kingdom of Tonga. *Journal of Multilingual and Multicultural Development* 4:459–69.

Stary, Giovanni. 2003. Sibe: An endangered language. In Mark Janse and Sijmen Tol, eds., 81–8.

Steenwijk, Hans. 2003. Resian as a minority language. In Mark Janse and Sijmen Tol, eds., 215–26.

Street, Brian. 1984. *Literacy in theory and practice*. Cambridge: Cambridge University Press.

Street, Brian, ed. 1993. *Cross-cultural approaches to literacy*. Cambridge: Cambridge University Press.

1994. What is meant by local literacies? In David Barton, ed., 9–14.

1995. *Social literacies: Critical approaches to literacy development, ethnography, and education.* New York: Longman.

ed. 2001. *Literacy and development: Ethnographic perspectives*. London, New York: Routledge.

Stubbs, Michael. 1986. *Educational linguistics*. Oxford: Blackwell.

Tabouret-Keller, Andree, Robert Le Page, Penelope Gardner-Chloros, and Gabrielle Varro, eds. 1997. *Vernacular literacy: A re-evaluation*. Oxford and New York: Clarendon.

Teichelmann, C. G. 1857. Dictionary of the Adelaide dialect. Manuscript. No. 59, Bleek's Catalogue of Sir George Grey's Library dealing with Australian languages. South African Public Library.

Teichelmann, C. G. and Schürmann, C. W. 1840. *Outlines of a grammar, vocabulary, and phraseology of the Aboriginal language of South Australia, spoken by the natives in and for some distance around Adelaide.* Adelaide. Published by the authors at the native location. Facsimile edition 1962. Adelaide: Libraries Board of South Australia. Facsimile edition 1982. Adelaide: Tjintu Books.

Trudgill, Peter. 1974. *The social differentiation of English in Norwich*. Cambridge: Cambridge University Press.

UNESCO. 2003. *Language vitality and endangerment*. http://portal.unesco.org/culture/en/ev.php-URL_ID = 9105&URL_DO = DO_TOPIC&URL_SECTION = 201.html.

Unseth, Peter. 1980. The consideration of non-Roman orthographies in literacy programs. *Notes on Literacy* 29:16–21.

Unseth, Peter and Carol Unseth. 1991. Analyzing ambiguities in orthographies. *Notes on Literacy* 65:35–52.

Vakhtin, N. B. 2001. *Iazyki narodov Severa v XX veke. Ocherki iazykovogo sdviga.* St. Petersburg: Dmitrii Bulanin.

Varennes, Fernand de. 1997. *To speak or not to speak: The rights of persons belonging to linguistic minorities*. Working paper: UN Subcommittee on the rights of minorities.

Vaux, Bert and Justin Cooper. 1999. *Introduction to linguistic field methods*. Munich: Lincom.

Verhoeven, Ludo, ed. 1994. *Functional literacy: Theoretical issues and educational implications.* Amsterdam, The Netherlands: John Benjamins.

Wakelin, Martyn F. 1975. *Language and history in Cornwall.* Leicester: Leicester University Press.

Walker, Roland W. 1988. Toward a model for predicting the acceptance of vernacular literacy by minority-language groups. *Notes on Literacy* 54:18–45.

Warner, Sam L. No'eau. 1999a. Hawaiian language regenesis: Planning for intergenerational use of Hawaiian beyond the school. In Thom Huebner and Kathryn A. Davis, eds., *Sociopolitical perspectives on language policy and planning in the USA*, 313–32. Philadelphia: John Benjamins.

1999b. Kuleana: The right, responsibility, and authority of indigenous peoples to speak and make decisions for themselves in language and cultural revitalization. *Anthropology and Education Quarterly* 30/1: 68–93.

2001. The movement to revitalize Hawaiian language and culture. In Leanne Hinton and Ken Hale, eds., 133–44.

Warschauer, Mark and Keola Donaghy. 1997. Leoki: A powerful voice of Hawaiian language revitalization. *Computer Assisted Language Learning* 10/4:349–62. http://www.gse.uci.edu/markw/leoki.html.

Watahomigie, Lucille J. and Teresa L. McCarty. 1997. Literacy for what? Hualapai literacy and language maintenance. In Nancy Hornberger, ed., 95–113.

Waters, Glenys. 1998. *Local literacies: Theory and practice.* Dallas, TX: Summer Institute of Linguistics.

Whaley, Lindsay. 2003. The future of native languages. *Futures* 35:961–73.

Whaley, Lindsay J., Lenore A. Grenoble, and Fengxiang Li. 1999. Revisiting Tungusic classification from the bottom up: A comparison of Evenki and Oroqen. *Language* 75/2:286–321.

Whitney, Scott. 1999. Ka'ōhiakūika'a'ā Ho'ōla 'Ōlelo Hawai'i: Saving Hawaiian. *Honolulu Magazine*, July:1–5.

Wiesemann, Ursula. 1989. Orthography matters. *Notes on Literacy* 57:14–21.

Williams, J. 1977. *Learning to write, or writing to learn.* London: National Foundation for Educational Research.

Williams, Kenneth. 1981. Motivational factors affecting Chuj literacy. *Notes on Literacy* 36:14–19.

Williams, Nicholas. 2000. *English–Cornish dictionary.* Redruth: Agan Tavas.

Wilson, William H. 1998. Ika 'Olelo Hawai'i ke Ola, "Life is found in the Hawaiian language." *International Journal of the Sociology of Language* 132:123–38.

1999. The sociopolitical context of establishing Hawaiian-medium education. In Stephen May, ed., *Indigenous community-based education*, 95–108. Clevedon, UK: Multilingual Matters.

Wilson, William H. and Kauanoe Kamanā. 2001. Mai loko mai o ka 'i'ini: Proceeding from a dream. The 'Aha Pūnana Leo connection to Hawaiian language revitalization. In Leanne Hinton and Ken Hale, eds., 147–76.

Wong, Laiana. 1999. Authenticity and the revitalization of Hawaiian. *Anthropology and Education Quarterly* 30/1:94–115.

Wurm, Stephen A. 1998. Methods of language maintenance and revival, with selected cases of language endangerment in the world. In Kazuto Matsumura, ed. *Studies in endangered languages*, 191–211. Papers from the

International Symposium on Endangered Languages, Tokyo, 18–20 November 1995. Tokyo: Hituzi Syobo.

2002. Strategies for language maintenance and revival. In David Bradley and Maya Bradley, eds., 11–23.

Zepeda, Ofelia and Jane H. Hill. 1991. The conditions of Native American languages in the United States. In Robert H. Robins and Eugenius M. Uhlenbeck, eds., 135–55.

Zimt, Petr. 1974. Digraphia: the case of Hausa. *Linguistics* 124:57–69.

Index of languages

Information is provided in the following format: Language (genetic affiliation; primary region). In some cases, in addition to the primary region, we also list a region where the language is spoken, as discussed in preceding chapters. Information is drawn from a variety of sources, including Grimes (2000) and those references cited in the text. We do not identify the region for international access languages.

Afrikaans (Indo-European; South Africa) 29
Altai (Turkic; Russia) 71, 72
Arabic (Semitic) 23, 27, 42–3, 106, 107

Basque (isolate; Spain) 180
Belorussian (Indo-European; Belarus) 40
Bengali (Indo-European; Bangladesh) 144
Bora (Macro-Carib; Peru) 147
Buriat (Mongolic; Russia) 30, 36, 71, 75, 77

Chechen (North Caucasian; Russia) 146
Cherokee (Iroquoian; USA) 139
Chinese *see* Mandarin
Chiapanec (Oto-Manguean; Mexico) 19
Chipewyan (Na-Dene; Canada) 24
Chochenyo (Penutian; USA) 181
Choctaw (Muskogean; USA) 51
Chuj (Mayan; Guatemala) 124
Chukchi (Chukotko-Kamchatkan; Russia) 31, 36
Chuukese (Austronesian; Micronesia) 32
Coreguaje (Tucanoan; Colombia, Mexico) 138, 146
Cornish (Indo-European; United Kingdom) 45–8
Cree (Algonquian; Canada) 7, 12
Croatian (Indo-European; Croatia) 42, 144

Dani (Trans-New Guinea; Irian Jaya) 152
Diyari (Pama-Nyungan; Australia) 128, 197
Djuka (English-based creole; Suriname) 139
Dogrib (Na-Dene; Canada) 24
Dolgan (Turkic; Russia) 30–1, 72
Dschang (Niger-Congo; Cameroon) 150

Edo (Niger-Congo; Nigeria) 37
Efik (Niger-Congo; Nigeria) 37
English (Indo-European) 12, 23, 24, 27, 29, 30, 32, 36, 37, 39–41, 42, 45–6, 54, 78, 95, 96, 107, 115, 131, 172, 179, 187
Estonian (Finno-Ugric; Estonia) 25, 29, 169
Even (Tungusic; Russia) 29, 38
Evenki (Tungusic; Russia) 30–2, 36, 38, 42, 72–7, 78, 185
Éwé (Niger-Congo; Ghana, Togo) 132

Fijian (Austronesian; Fiji) 155
Finnish (Finno-Ugric; Finland) 169
French (Indo-European; France) 12, 24, 27, 87, 132, 179, 180
Friulian (Indo-European; Italy) 39
Fulfulde (Niger-Congo; Cameroon) 37

German (Indo-European; Germany) 128, 131, 179, 186
Gola (Niger-Congo; Liberia) 107
Gujarati (Indo-European; India) 144
Gùrdùṇ (Afro-Asiatic; Nigeria) 43
Gurumukhi (Indo-European; India) 144
Gwich (Na-Dene; Canada) 24

Hausa (Afro-Asiatic; Nigeria) 37, 43
Hawaiian (Austronesian; USA) 24, 32, 60, 94–101, 121, 146, 161, 183, 190
Hebrew (Semitic; Israel) 63–4, 65, 115
Hindi (Indo-European; India) 144, 153
Hualapai (Hokan; USA) 127

Idoma (Niger-Congo; Nigeria) 37
Igbo (Niger-Congo; Nigeria) 37

General index

Printed in the United States
103568LV00002B/76/A